Fitting Rocks:
Lithic Refitting Examined

Edited by

Utsav Schurmans
Marc De Bie

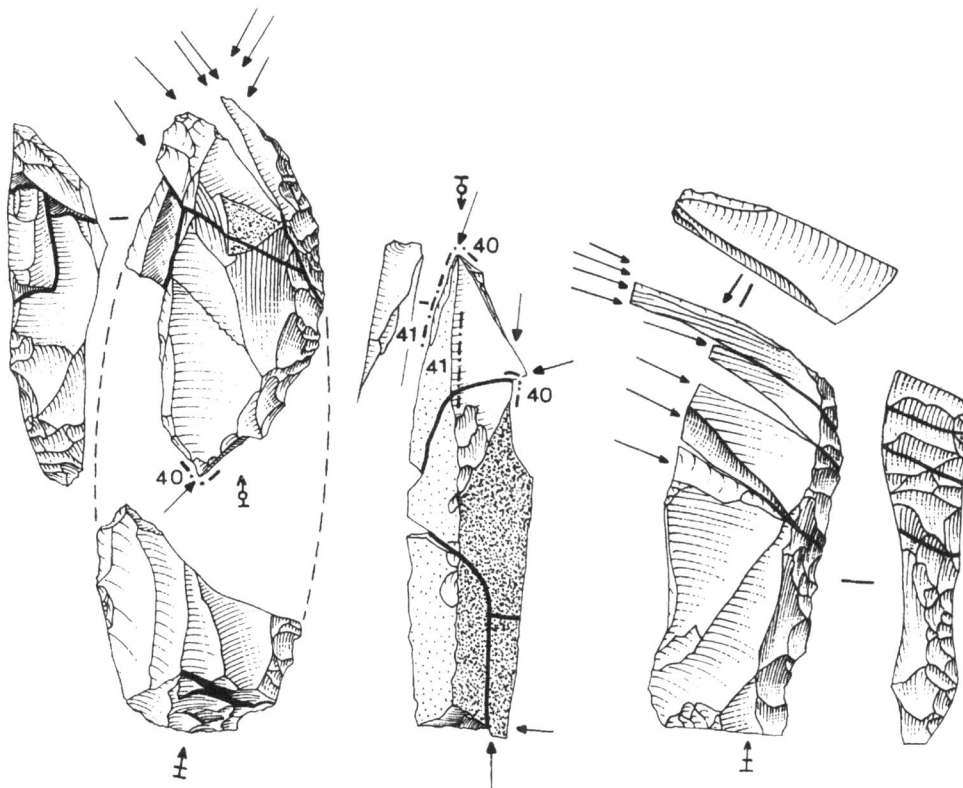

BAR International Series 1596
2007

Published in 2016 by
BAR Publishing, Oxford

BAR International Series 1596

Fitting Rocks: Lithic Refitting Examined

ISBN 978 1 4073 0012 2

BAR Publishing is the trading name of British Archaeological Reports (Oxford) Ltd.
British Archaeological Reports was first incorporated in 1974 to publish the BAR
Series, International and British. In 1992 Hadrian Books Ltd became part of the BAR
group. This volume was originally published by Archaeopress in conjunction with
British Archaeological Reports (Oxford) Ltd / Hadrian Books Ltd, the Series principal
publisher, in 2007. This present volume is published by BAR Publishing, 2016.

Printed in England

BAR
PUBLISHING

BAR titles are available from:

BAR Publishing
122 Banbury Rd, Oxford, OX2 7BP, UK
EMAIL   info@barpublishing.com
PHONE   +44 (0)1865 310431
FAX   +44 (0)1865 316916
www.barpublishing.com

TABLE OF CONTENTS / TABLE DES MATIÈRES

FITTING ROCKS. LITHIC REFITTING EXAMINED

Edited by Utsav SCHURMANS and Marc DE BIE

INTRODUCTION

Utsav SCHURMANS and Marc DE BIE

The contributions in this book mainly resulted from the symposium, "*Fitting Rocks, the big Puzzle Revisited,*" held in 2001 at the XIVth U.I.S.P.P. conference in Liège, Belgium. Unfortunately not all participants to the symposium were able to contribute to the current volume. The symposium brought together a wide variety of researchers who use refitting in one way or another to answer archaeological questions. The aim was to cover both geographical space and a variety of time periods. Some of the variety represented in the symposium could not be represented in this volume, but nevertheless we feel that what is left constitutes an interesting diversity of approaches to the use of lithic refitting in archaeological research.

Lithic refitting has been around for well over a century now. While the mechanics of conjoining artifacts have remained unchanged, despite some recent attempts to automate at least part of the process, the questions that have been addressed with refitting data changed dramatically over time and probably will continue to do so in the future.

This volume reflects both well-established uses of refitting as well as some novel approaches. In the first chapter Schurmans argues that refitting is standard practice in the Europe while it is not in the Americas. This difference he argues can be explained both by philosophical differences about the way research should be conducted as well as fundamental differences in the archaeological record itself.

De Bie provides an overview of what he has learned from his refitting experience working with the material from Rekem, Belgium. He argues that we should strive to fit refitting into a larger research program. The evidence gained from refitting only can become meaningful within a research context that brings together multiple lines of evidence including microwear evidence, attribute analysis, geomorphological evidence, etc.

Drawing on his refitting experience at the site of Pincevent, Bodu shares his thoughts on the limits and the benefits of the method. His contribution is somewhat provocative as he chose to highlight limits over benefits. The benefits he feels are well-known and need no further elaboration.

Ashton takes a look at Lower Paleolithic refitting research in the British Isles. He concludes that refitting has contributed little to our understanding of biface manufacture, but has contributed to our perceptions of core and flake working. He also highlights certain questions to which refitting research might contribute in the future.

In his contribution on the upper paleolithic of the cave of Lapa do Anecrial in the Portuguese Estramadura, Almeida and colleagues were able to refit a large portion of the artifacts recovered. This feat is fairly rare for a cave site and allows us to get a better understanding of the use of space in this setting.

Analyzing the site of Abric Romaní in Spain, Vaquero, Chacón and Rando speak to the definition of spatial units, the organization of campsites, and relationships between artifacts and space. They also make the compelling point that very few spatial studies of middle paleolithic sites have been done.

Philip Van Peer considers the contribution of refitting to a definition of the levallois concept – which he argues should be a simple one. Further, he argues that we can recognize individuals in the archaeological record using refitting. This leads him to reconsider the individual's role as a source of patterned variation in the paleolithic past. Both the contributions by Van Peer and Hiscock are replete with attempts to get at past dynamic processes. However, the way in which this is done and the conclusions drawn from it differ quite a bit theoretically.

Hiscock is interested in mapping the reduction process across the landscape – from the quarry to sites further removed from the original sources of the raw material. Hiscock suggests that the use of quantitative measures will allow us to more powerfully exploit the potential of refitting.

While the research papers presented in the volume cover sometimes very different ground, certain observations are made repeatedly. One of these is the old realization that the final state of a core or tool does not necessarily provide a good picture of an entire reduction. In fact, often the final products have little technological resemblance to what came before. While this observation is not new, it certainly is worth repeating as many studies try to extract meaning from cores about entire reduction processes.

A second point is that refitting is well suited to demonstrate the dynamic processes underlying the static archaeological record. This is the case both on a spatial level, linking particular concentrations of archaeological material, and on a technological one, showing how a block of raw material was reduced to produce blanks.

It is easy to point out the, in many ways, obvious advantages of refitting, but there are also serious costs involved. In order to refit one needs continuous access to the material, significant space, and sufficient time. Given these constraints it is not surprising that archeologists typically refit collections curated in their respective institutions. Particularly now that it is increasingly rare that foreign researchers are able to export excavated material for any time period outside of the country of origin, the possibility of refitting is severely limited. On the other hand, for those of us in this particular situation it does ensure, that if refitting is attempted, we carefully consider why we want to engage in refitting prior to actually doing it.

Refitting should not always be done. As mentioned there are significant costs in terms of person-hours and space required for the procedure. Some collections are better suited for refitting than others, for example, those from sites with a high diversity of raw materials or limited size and chronological extent of the occupation. Conversely, extremely large collections with limited raw material diversity can be a nightmare to refit. At some sites the limited area excavated or type of recording procedures also prevent the effective investigation of some questions that might be addressed using refitting. For example, if we are interested in Neanderthal use of intrasite space a significant portion of that space both needs to be excavated and have yielded conjoinable materials.

The interpretation of refit evidence typically starts from a physical fit between two objects. Archaeologists, with good reason, have been much more reluctant to interpret the absence of connections. We believe that more can and should be done with the absence of refits, but to get there we must report refit success as well as the approximate time spent in the effort. The latter tends to be lacking in the description of refit results.

We hope that the contributions in this volume will bring new ideas to researchers with refitting experience and perhaps entice others to consider adding the method to the set of methods they employ in interpreting archaeological assemblages. Refitting is a powerful method that has allowed us to draw connections and it will continue to help us puzzling together our past.

For completeness' sake we reproduce both the symposium abstract and the original abstracts of the presenters here.

SYMPOSIUM ABSTRACT

Since the "Big Puzzle" and other conferences in the late eighties, and early nineties there have been no international symposia or conferences devoted to the subject of lithic refitting. Nevertheless, the methodology of conjoining lithic artifacts remains widely used. This is in part a result of the valuable taphonomic information and the rich interpretative potential in terms of human behavior, both technologically and spatially, that refits provide.

Unfortunately the methodology and more importantly its interpretation have become somewhat "standard procedure" during the last decade. In this light it seems healthy that those engaged in refitting programs come together to share their insights, warn new converts to caveats, and keep long time proponents on their methodological and theoretical toes.

Drawing from new projects and ongoing refitting programs this symposium hopes to bring together those working on the refitting of stone artifacts in its many dimensions. The aim is to advance both the methodological and theoretical aspects of many puzzling hours into a coherent set of ideas and suggestions that reflect the current stage of this part of our methodological toolkit. Further it is our explicit aim to bring together researchers working on refitting outside the "Old World" and Stone Age periods.

INDIVIDUAL ABSTRACTS

Francisco ALMEIDA

REFITTING AT LAPA DO ANECRIAL: STUDYING TECHNOLOGY AND MICRO SCALE SPATIAL PATTERNING THROUGH LITHIC RECONSTRUCTIONS.

Lapa do Anecrial is a cave site located in central Portuguese Estremadura. Three field seasons already completed have provided a stratigraphic sequence spanning the transition from the Gravettian to the Solutrean in Central Portugal. In layer 2 (Terminal Gravettian), the more extensively excavated, excellent post-depositional conditions have preserved several clusters of lithic artifacts and fauna, representing activities taking place around a hearth. The refitting studies, already concluded, reaffirm the excellent post-depositional preservation of the site: more than 51% (92% by weight) of the lithic assemblage was refitted, making possible an almost complete view of the reduction sequences and strategies used.

This paper presents the various advantages of the application of refitting to the Lapa do Anecrial layer 2 assemblage: both for lithic technology and spatial analysis. The main technological characteristics of the studied assemblage will be described. The reconstructions show how a carinated thick-nosed bladelet production strategy was often associated (in the same block) with traditional prismatic bladelet technology. Such association, which results in high core to cobble ratios, was detected not only for flint, but also for quartz, a raw material usually considered as having inferior knapping qualities.

The combination of the lithic reconstructions with the tri-dimensional spatial patterning of the artifacts makes possible a first attempt to interpret the micro-scale spatial organization of the short-term occupation of Lapa do Anecrial, during Terminal Gravettian times.

Nick ASHTON

REFITTING AND THE BRITISH LOWER
PALAEOLITHIC: A CRITICAL REVIEW

Refitting is a well established but time-consuming and costly method of analysis, and in the context of the British Lower Palaeolithic has been criticised for telling us little about behaviour or cognition. This paper reviews the British evidence and the role refitting has played in enhancing our understanding of taphonomy, technology and behaviour. It is argued: that for taphonomy it is a basic and essential tool of analysis for assessing the integrity of assemblages; that for furthering our understanding of technology, its real potential has sometimes not been realised; and that for insights into behaviour, its real value lies in the recognition of repeated patterns of movement. Despite the costs it must remain an important tool for understanding fine-grained behavioural signatures.

Douglas BAMFORTH and **Mark BECKER**

REFITTING AND SPATIAL STRUCTURE AT THE
ALLEN SITE

This paper discusses patterns of lithic refits and artifact and feature distributions at the Allen site, a stratified Paleoindian camp in Nebraska. Low refit frequencies within and between horizontally discrete artifact concentrations suggest that these concentrations are aggregates deposited as dumps during camp cleanup. The similar locations of such concentrations throughout 2000 years of site occupation, and the lack of evidence in the refits for vertical movement of artifacts, suggest that old dumps were magnets for new ones. Variation in refit patterns and in the relation between artifact and hearth

frequencies in different levels suggests a long-term trend towards more temporary, and perhaps less frequent, site use that parallels trends in other aspects of the site assemblage.

Pierre BODU

DU BON USAGE DES REMONTAGES EN
PRÉHISTOIRE? (INTÉRÊTS ET LIMITES) LE CAS
DU GISEMENT MAGDALÉNIEN DE PINCEVENT.

Depuis près de 40 ans, le gisement magdalénien de Pincevent fait l'objet de fouilles scrupuleuses et développées tant au plan diachronique qu'au plan synchronique.

Claudine Karlin en 1964 lors de l'étude de l'habitation n°1 avait lancé « la mode » et systématisé ce qui devait devenir une véritable méthode d'étude des séries lithiques. Un peu moins de 40 ans plus tard et 4500 m2 fouillés plus loin, nous avons pu appliquer cette méthode au plus vaste sol d'occupation magdalénien du gisement de Pincevent, le niveau IV20. Les premiers résultats de cette réflexion avaient été présentés dans les actes du symposium : « The Big Puzzle » en 1990. Dans le cadre d'une thèse soutenue en 1994, il nous a été donné de documenter plus encore les comportements techniques mais aussi économiques et spatiaux d'un groupe de magdaléniens. En réalisant un taux de remontages de plus de 90% sur le matériel lithique provenant d'une zone du niveau IV20, nous avons en effet pu sérieusement traiter des modalités techniques et économiques du débitage, inscrire l'outillage au sein de son système de production mais également discuter de l'organisation spatiale des activités concernant la taille du silex et l'utilisation des produits obtenus. Quelques inférences sur la composition du groupe ont également pu être avancées s'inspirant des travaux de Nicole Pigeot menés à Etiolles ou de ceux de Sylvie développés à Pincevent.

A travers quelques exemples pris dans cette étude particulière, nous discuterons ici de l'intérêt de la méthode des remontages mais également de ses limites fusse t'elle appliquée à hauteur de 90 % d'une industrie lithique.

Marc DE BIE

BENEFITING BY REFITTING AT LATE
PALAEOLITHIC REKEM (BELGIUM)

The procedure of refitting is most benefited from when fully embedded in an integrated research program. Refitting can then help to entangle a wide variety of research topics also touched upon with other approaches (petrography, attribute analysis, usewear, etc.). The late Palaeolithic site of Rekem serves as a case study in this respect. The lithic material from this large camp site offered excellent refitting potential (some 2500 artefacts conjoined so far), permitting a detailed study of reduction strategies and spatial distributions. With regard to lithic technology, the refitting data provided better insights into both flint reducing methods and knapping styles as well as into the processes of tool manufacture, use, maintenance and discard. Derived from these data, the method also informed on social aspects (skills of the artisans) and economic features (the material 'output' of the various sequences and its role in further activities). On a spatial scale the results of refitting could be used to measure the degree of vertical dispersal and to assess the disturbance on the site by natural post-depositional processes. Most importantly, however, the mapping of refits supplied important insight into the horizontal patterning of human activities both in and between the various loci of the site. At Rekem, such patterning shows the relationship between manufacturing process and artefact discard and elucidates the transport patterns of various kinds of artefacts and tool types.

Anne DELAGNES

L'APPORT DES REMONTAGES DANS L'APPROCHE DE LA COMPLEXITÉ TECHNIQUE ET ÉCONOMIQUE DES CHAÎNES OPÉRATOIRES DU PALÉOLITHIQUE MOYEN.

La complexité des chaînes opératoires de production lithique au Paléolithique moyen est un phénomène que l'on perçoit depuis un certain nombre d'années au travers de pratiques telles que le débitage sur éclats. Grâce à l'exploitation de l'information dynamique apportée par l'étude d'ensembles remontés, on est désormais en mesure de cerner les mécanismes et la logique technique d'une telle complexité. Dans les deux gisements qui sont pris en exemple ici (Le Pucheuil et Etoutteville, Haute-Normandie, France), les remontages dévoilent l'existence de chaînes opératoires longues et ramifiées, avec plusieurs objectifs techniques clairement hiérarchisés. La chaîne opératoire principale fait appel dans les deux sites aux principes du débitage Levallois, sur lequel repose l'essentiel de l'investissement technique. Les chaînes opératoires secondaires sont réalisées à partir des sous-produits de la chaîne opératoire Levallois. A partir d'un même bloc de silex, 2 voire 3 principes de débitage ont été indépendamment mis en œuvre, pour autant de types de produits obtenus. Le débitage Levallois, généralement considéré comme très dispendieux en matière première, serait-il au contraire dans certains contextes l'un des champions toutes catégories de l'économie de la matière première?

Berit Valentin ERIKSEN

SICKLE MANUFACTURE IN BRONZE AGE DENMARK – PUZZLING FLINTS FROM BJERRE.

This contribution presents the results of an ongoing research project aiming at a contextual "chaîne opératoire" analysis of Early Bronze Age flint sickle production technology. The lithic inventories examined belongs to a cluster of seven settlement sites from Bjerre, situated in the flint-rich region of Thy, Northern Jutland. The analyses presented involve a reconstruction of core reduction sequences (through refitting) as well as technological studies (through attribute analyses) aiming at a dynamic reconstruction of primary production sequences. The following discussion will assert the "chaîne opératoire", complexity and completeness of assemblages, technological skills, and degree of specialization in tool production (pressure flaked artifacts versus simple retouched tools) as well as the resulting sociocultural and behavioral implications for our interpretation of Early Bronze Age lithic technology.

Peter HISCOCK

AUSTRALIAN POINT AND CORE REDUCTION: A REFITTING CASE STUDY

Refitting of knapping floors in Queensland Australia is used to analyze the production technology employed during the mid-late Holocene. Examination of refits at quarries is the basis of a study not only of the general sequence of reduction but also the solutions that knappers apply to solve problems they encounter. A series of refitted knapping floors at increasing distances from quarries reveals the progressive modification of bifacial points and cores as material is transported through the landscape. Some general principles are explicated.

Lykke JOHANSEN

THE HAMBURGIAN SITE AT OLDEHOLTWOLDE (NL): THE MULTIFACETED OUTPUT OF REFITTING

Refitting analysis of flint artefacts resulted in insights concerning a multitude of aspects. Its most rewarding contribution is the creation of dynamic pictures, e.g. showing movements of flint implements from production centres to activity areas. In total, 850 flint artefacts are involved in 179 refitgroups (containing up to about 100 artefacts). The Hamburgian *chaîne opératoire* for blade production could be reconstructed; the *en éperon* technique is not part of it. Because of differences in knapping skill, revealed by larger refitgroups, three flintknappers were identified: a master knapper (probably an adult man), an advanced pupil (probably an older boy) and a totally unskilled knapper (probably a young boy). Only a minority (about a quarter) of the tools were manufactured at the site. The many imported tools include all the points and most of the scrapers. Especially notched tools and 'Zinken' were made, used and discarded on the site. The final occupation phase saw the production of many tools and blades that were taken away from the site. By combining refitting results with ring and sector analysis, it can be shown that the occupants probably rotated around the outdoors hearth, in response to changes in wind direction.

Utsav SCHURMANS, Peter MCCARTNEY, Muyong Soo BAE, and Anshuman RAZDAN

TOWARDS AUTOMATED LITHIC REFITTING: DREAM OR REALITY?

The multidisciplinary "Partnership for Research in Stereo Modeling" (PRISM) at Arizona State University conducts research on various topics in 3D modeling. One of the pilot projects involves an attempt to (partially) automate the lithic refitting process. Lithic refitting has proven to be a tremendous tool for prehistorians to reconstruct lithic technology, study taphonomy, and investigate spatial patterning. The drawback to lithic refitting, as one of many lines of evidence drawn upon to study the prehistoric past, is the enormous time investment it requires. Furthermore, due to understandable limitations in the access to lithic collections imposed by the various antiquities departments throughout the world, lithic refitting is often left out of the research agenda altogether. These problems point to a need for automated lithic refitting.

We have scanned the products of an experimental lithic collection to serve as test data for creating a refitting program. The results of these tests and prospects for future development will be presented in this paper. Although numerous difficulties remain, we are optimistic that as 3D scanning technologies improve and research within computer "puzzling" applications advances, the initial difficulties in the development of automated lithic refitting will be overcome.

Philip VAN PEER

THE CONTRIBUTION OF REFITTING TO THE UNDERSTANDING OF THE LEVALLOIS REDUCTION STRATEGY

At the Middle Palaeolithic workshop site of Taramsa-1 in Upper Egypt, a number of dense lithic scatters were found in primary context. Raw material volumes exploited from nearby Nilotic gravels were reduced here

according to the Levallois strategy. For one of the scatters, dated around 65 ky, all the reduction sequences present were completely refitted.

Analysis of the temporal patterns present in these reductions shows a clear clustering of patterns. The latter are interpreted as implementations of individual design patterns by specialist-chertknappers. Spatial distribution patterns seem to support that interpretation. The paper concludes with a discussion of some wider implications of these results in terms of the nature of Middle Palaeolithic lithic reduction systems and behaviourial complexity.

Manuel VAQUERO

THE INTERPRETIVE POTENTIAL OF LITHIC REFITS IN A MIDDLE PALEOLITHIC SITE: THE ABRIC ROMANÍ (CAPELLADES, SPAIN).

The Abric Romaní (Romaní rockshelters) has provided a thick stratigraphic sequence including several Middle Paleolithic archaeological levels dated between 40 and 70 ka BP. These levels have been exposed over large surfaces and are characterized by a high temporal resolution. Moreover, many structures, including hearths, have been documented. This allows spatial analysis to be developed. Refitting of lithic artifacts forms a substantial part of this analysis. The refits obtained at a series of levels excavated in recent years and dated between 45 and 52 ka BP have provided some interesting results especially concerning three main issues: a) the definition of spatial units, especially in hearth-related assemblages; b) the organization of campsites and the connection between activity areas; and c) the temporal relationships between the artifacts and spatial units.

REFITTING IN THE OLD AND NEW WORLDS

Utsav A. Schurmans

Abstract

In this chapter the history of refitting is reviewed and a comparison made between the use of refitting in two journals from France and two from the United States. From these comparisons it is clear that refitting is much less ubiquitous in the United States than it is in France. Further, it is argued that differences in the use of refitting between France and the United States are a reflection of differences in theoretical orientation as well as differences in the archaeological record itself. In France, and Europe more generally, blank production technologies dominate the archaeological record whereas in the United States and the Americas more generally, coretool technologies characterize many prehistoric periods. These differences have an impact on the 'refitability' of the assemblages. Finally, a plea is made to more carefully consider what we can learn from European and American approaches to refitting in order to better understand our respective archaeological records.

Résumé

Cet article a pour objet l'historique de la méthode d'analyse qu'est le remontage. Dans le cadre de ce travail, nous avons comparé la manière dont le remontage est utilisé en industrie lithique par les chercheurs français d'un côté et par les chercheurs américains de l'autre, en partant de la lecture de plusieurs publications. Grâce à ces comparaisons, il apparaît clairement que le remontage est beaucoup moins généralisé aux Etats-Unis qu'en France. De plus, il est possible d'argumenter que l'utilisation différentielle du remontage est le reflet d'orientations théoriques distincte et le reflet de différences des données archéologiques lui-même. En France, et d'une manière générale en Europe, les technologies de production des supports sont dominant alors qu'aux Etats-Unis, et globalement aux Amériques, les technologies de l'outil-matrice sont caractéristiques de plusieurs périodes préhistoriques. Ces différences dans le materiel archéologique ont un impact considérable sur la possibilité de remonter ces assemblages. Un plaidoyer est réalisé pour une plus grande ouverture face aux éléments que l'on peut apprendre par les diverses approches européennes et américaines, en matière de remontages, afin de mieux comprendre les résultats de nos analyses respectives.

INTRODUCTION

Lithic refitting has been used off and on in archaeology since the end of the 19th Century. However, it has become "a standard method of scientific research" (Cziesla 1990: 11) only much more recently. This chapter asks: has refitting really become standard practice or are there differences in the use of refitting between Old and New World archaeologists? Is refitting unified in both the kinds of refits that are searched for and the questions that refitting research could answer? The answers to these questions are negative. Unraveling lithic refitting, then, both in time and place, is what this paper sets out to do. In particular, the focus is on the uses of refits in France and the United States of America as French and American refitting are good polar representations of what really amounts to a continuum in the practice and application of lithic refitting research.

This chapter is divided into three main components: background, journal review, and discussion. In the first basic background information essential to an understanding of refitting studies is provided. This background consists of first, a description of the basic types of refits and second, an overview of the uses to which refits have been put. A broad historical overview of lithic refitting based on review articles and the general literature follows.

In the second part of the chapter, the journal review, theoretical frameworks of prehistoric archaeology in France and in the U.S. are outlined. These frameworks are then used to try to understand the use of refitting in each of four journals respectively, the *Bulletin de la Société Préhistorique Française (BSPF)*, *Gallia Préhistoire (GP)*, *American Antiquity (AA)*, and the *Plains Anthropologist (PA)*. Each is examined for the period from 1960 to the present[1]. The aim is to document the prevalence of refitting throughout the period covered, and examine the kind of questions that have been addressed using refits.

The third part of the paper is a discussion of the patterns observed in the journal review. Further, differences and

---

[1] While the BSPF has been published since 1904, GP since 1958, and American Antiquity since 1935, I only looked extensively at the period from 1960 to 2002 to make the selection comparable to that of the Plains Anthropologist. This approach is further justified given that refitting does not become prevalent anywhere until after 1960.

similarities between the French and U.S. national archaeologies with respect to the study of refitting are briefly examined and possible explanations for their existence suggested. Examining these differences is particularly important given the increasing international cooperation among archaeologists and the resulting potential clash of theoretical frameworks associated with such endeavors (see e.g. Clark 1993; Clark 1997; Dibble and Debénath 1991).

REFITTING IN PERSPECTIVE

Refitting – putting back pieces in their 'original' position – can be done on a number of different types of archaeological material. We have all witnessed the result of ceramic refitting in museums, but more than for purposes of display, ceramic refitting can yield a number of analytically useful results (see e.g. Cahen and van Berg 1979; Lindauer 1992; Mills et al. 1992; Sullivan 1989). Along with ceramics, bone can also be refit, both its fragments (Marean and Kim 1998) as well as entire carcasses (Todd and Frison 1992; Enloe and David 1992; Poplin 1976). This paper is limited to yet a different type of refitting, lithic refitting, or the reassembly of lithic artifacts, ultimately to the nodule of raw material selected by prehistoric people for flintknapping.

First a description of the types of refits that can be made is given. While these distinctions are to a certain extent arbitrary there is a definite utility in them both for interpretive purposes as well as for our more immediate goal, a better understanding of the history and development of refitting. Next, the uses of refitting are discussed; what kind of questions can be addressed using the method of refitting? Using knowledge about types of refits and questions asked, a broad history of the use of refitting in archaeology is constructed.

Types of refits (after Cziesla 1990)

The first and most elementary type of refit is a *break refit* (see Figure 1). A *break refit* consists of simply fitting either intentionally or accidentally broken artifacts (from both tools and blanks) together. A second type of refit is a *production sequence refit* (see Figure 2). Production sequence refits essentially fit different blanks and/or a blank and a core together. Such fits allow us to get an insight into the technology used in the manufacture of blanks. The third kind of refit is a '*modification or resharpening refit*' (see Figure 3). Resharpening refits fit artifacts that created or maintained a tool such as burin spalls or retouch flakes with that tool[2]. Sometimes the

distinction between these different categories can become blurred. For example this is the case in technologies where the 'core' becomes the 'tool' (e.g. in the production of arrowheads or bifaces). At what point does the 'blank production' stop and the 'retouching' begin, or is there even any 'blank production' going on?[3] It is important to keep in mind that these are heuristic devices

Figure 1 *Refitted double burin from St. Marcel, Upper Paleolithic. (Adopted from Allain 1952: 219, Fig. 3)*

---

[2] Notice that I do not follow Tixier 1980: 51-52, who distinguishes between *break refits* and *production refits* by subsuming the third category (*resharpening refits*) under breaks – that it is important to make such a

distinction will become clear in subsequent parts of this chapter.
[3] This question is important to discuss, particularly in the New World where these kinds of technologies are so prevalent. However, in the end I would suggest that the distinction does not matter all that much. After all, both could be going on at the same time (resharpening/ modification and blank production).

to help us better understand the past, not some sort of archaeological or emic 'reality' stamped onto artifacts.

Questions addressed using refitting

The archaeological questions that have been addressed using refits (see table 1) can be divided into two main categories, post-depositional (or taphonomic) questions and behavioral questions (see e.g. Tixier 1980; Cahen 1987; Cziesla 1990; Hofman 1992; Larson and Ingbar 1992). The behavioral component itself can be subdivided into two different categories: technology, and spatial organization. The former can be further divided into technological questions about the production of blanks, and the resharpening or modification of tools. I will briefly address each in turn. Although these different categories are interrelated, they are conceptual tools aiding in the better understanding of the components.

Table 1: Questions addressed with refitting

1. Post depositional/taphonomic
2. Behavioral
   a. Technology
      i. Blank production
      ii. Tool resharpening and/or modification
   b. Spatial Organization

Post-deposition/taphonomic questions

The possibility of refitting to address the post depositional histories of sites is among the most important aspects of refitting. However, this fundamental aspect of archaeological investigation often has been ignored or treated too lightly. Assuming their sites are, if not entirely *in situ*, very close to undisturbed, researchers are tempted to pass over post-depositional questions and jump into behavioral interpretations The best-known examples of what refitting can add to a taphonomic assessment of a site are in the refitting of vertically dispersed artifacts (see e.g. Cahen and Moeyersons 1977; Villa 1982; 1983). This is particularly telling when artifacts recovered from different 'layers' are put together (see Figure 4). Along with speaking to vertical connections, on a horizontal plan, refits can also hold important clues about the post depositional history of a site. Is there a dominant orientation of refit lines? If so, are there other signs that might point to disturbance, such as size sorting? As in any investigation, it is key that the results from refitting are combined with other lines of evidence to build a robust interpretation (see e.g. De Bie and Caspar 2000a and b; Dibble et al. 1997)[4]. Put

---

[4] The problem when not using multiple lines of evidence is that any refit pattern might be a clue to either a post depositional interpretation or a behavioral one.

differently, vertical and horizontal refitting can hint at the presence of post-depositional disturbance.

Refitting can also help answer subsequent questions regarding the nature of the archaeological site. Two examples will suffice. First, implicit in a taphonomical investigation is the assumption that refits show contemporaneity. As Bordes was quick to point out (Bordes 1980a,b; see also Larson and Ingbar 1992), there

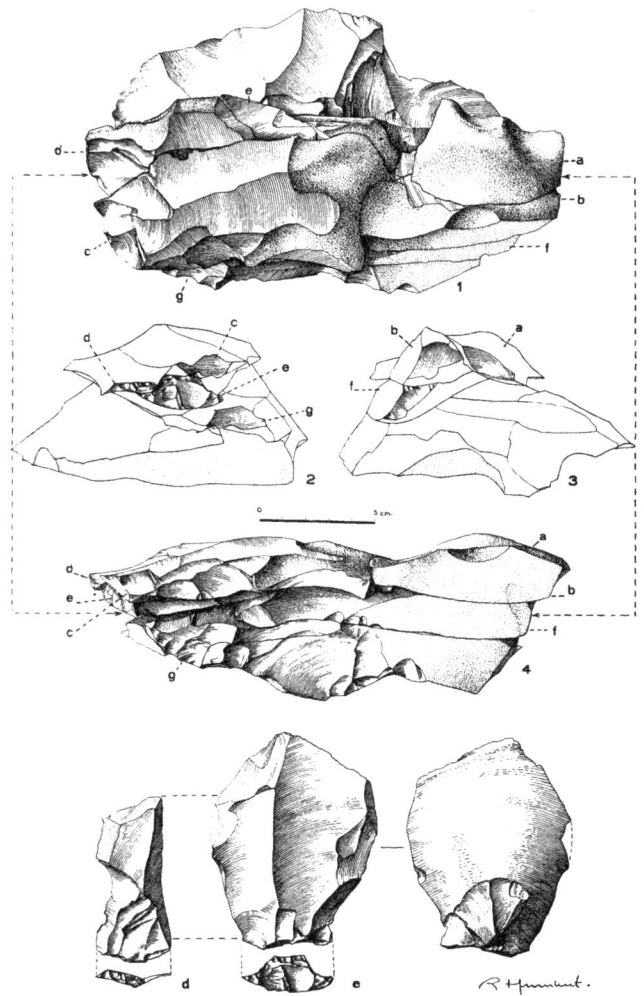

Figure 2 *Refitted nodule reduced using a Levallois technology from Briqueterie Peuleboeuf, Arras, Middle Paleolithic. The scale in the image represents 5 cm. (Adopted from Kelley 1954: 165, Fig. 10)*

are some important problems with this assumption. However, refitting itself can help answer questions of contemporaneity. One might ask, when dealing with a vertical dispersal of the artifacts, can unidirectional refit lines be observed? If so, it is likely that a core from an

---

Distinguishing between the two becomes very difficult when relying only on refitting evidence.

9

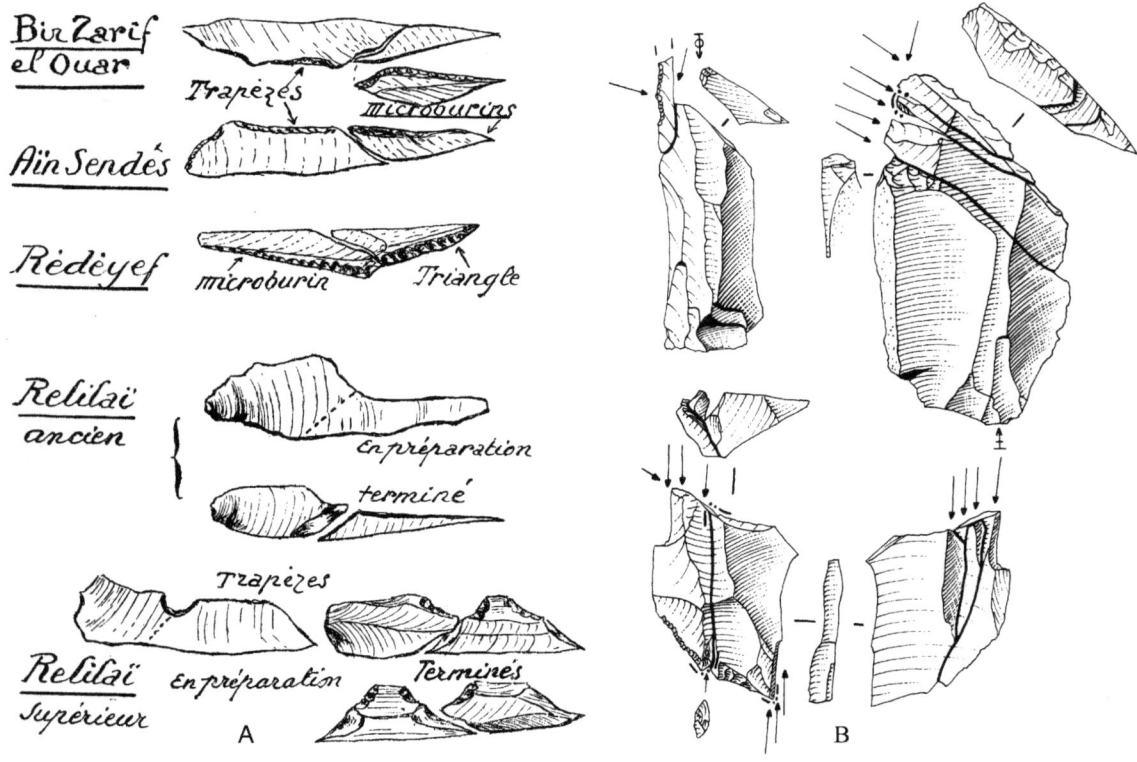

Figure 3 - A *Refitted microburins with their tools, Capsian. (Adopted from Vignard 1934: 459)*
B *Refitted burins and their burin spalls, Rekem, Epi-Paleolithic. (Adopted from De Bie and Caspar 2000b: 88, 92, 96, Pls. 82, 85, 90)*

older occupation was later reused. Second, fully excluding the possibility that a site consists of a palimpsest (multiple occupations represented in a single archaeological deposit) is virtually impossible. Again, refits can give at least some clues. For example, at the site of Rekem it seems unlikely that at least some of the scatters are not contemporaneous as refits go from one concentration to the next and back again. Here the use of multiple lines of evidence is crucial. If there are no artifacts present that are considered diagnostic of a different time period then it seems acceptable to assume that if re-occupation took place, it was the same or some closely related group of hunter-gatherers. It should be clear that the taphonomic histories of archaeological sites are typically far from straightforward and as such require a close and critical examination. After considering the taphonomic history of a site we can engage with questions more directly tied to our interests, the behavioral patterns of prehistoric groups.

Behavioral questions

Archaeologists are indeed mostly interested in making behavioral inferences from the archaeological record. The most straightforward information to be gained from refits, most specifically production sequence refits, is technological. How was a volume of raw material

exploited? How were particular preparations made for the extraction of numerous uni- or bi-directional blades from a core? These are questions that can be addressed successfully using refitting. Some archaeologists (*les technologues*) have argued that technological sequences can be reconstructed without recourse to refitting (see Tixier 1980: 50). However, I would agree with Volkman and others who have questioned such statements (Volkman 1983; Van Peer 1992; Dibble 1995). Volkman expresses doubt that "*one can infer method of production from final* [core] *morphology*" (Volkman 1983: 187),

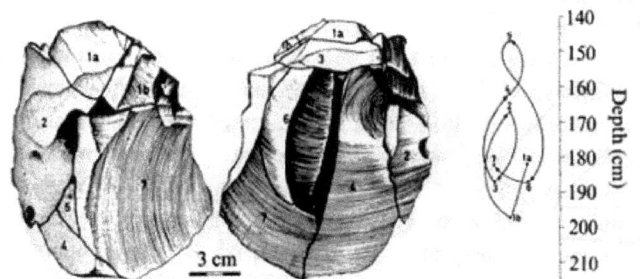

Figure 4 *Refitting of artifacts from different depths. Notice how the technological sequence does not match up with the stratigraphic position of the artifacts. (Adopted from Cahen and Moeyersons 1977: 813, Fig. 1a and b)*

based on the observation that technologies can and do change during the reduction process of blocks of raw material. Indeed, this observation has been made many times over by people engaged in refitting research (see contributions in this volume).

On a technological level we might also gain better insight into what Binford (1979) has called curated and expedient technologies, or as I prefer more or less formal technologies. More formal technologies are geared towards standardization of blanks and/or tools whereas less formal technologies are more ad hoc reductions of raw material. Larson and Ingbar argued in 1992 (152) that refitting studies are biased towards expedient technologies. Refitting of more curated or formal technologies is perhaps more difficult as more pieces are expected to be missing. However, as some examples point out, this potential problem has not stopped refitters from refitting formal technologies (see e.g. Cahen 1987: 8, Fig. 1.6; Eloy 1951: 29, Fig 2; Volkman 1983: 143, Fig. 6-5, for a few examples of highly formal/curated technologies). As far as expedient tools go, Larson and Ingbar are right by virtue of the theoretical definition of expedience they offer (expedient tools being tools made, used, resharpened, and discarded at the same site). However, information can be gained about curated tools using refitting as well. Namely, the absence of refits constitutes information as well – an approach that has unfortunately been underused in archaeology. An example of a commendable attempt at getting at this can be found in Morrow 1996 where he defines 'ghosts' and 'orphans'. The former designate artifacts (tools) that are missing from a refitted set, the latter tools that cannot be fitted to any other flakes.

In using 'ghosts' and 'orphans' Morrow attempts to get at another interesting behavioral aspect, that of group mobility. His assumption is that when the number of ghosts and orphans are high, the time at which the group is staying at that site is shorter than the use life of these artifacts indicating highly mobile groups. This then is one way to get at a particular type of spatial organization, that at the inter-site level. Extremely rare, some refits have even given direct insights into such inter-site connections, giving us glimpses of organization at the landscape level (see e.g. Singer 1984; Schaller-Åhrberg 1990; Close 1996). Typically, however, we are limited to the examination of the intra-site spatial organization. Examples of such research are plentiful (see e.g. the study of Pincevent, Meer II, and Rekem, bibliography for each of these can be found in table 3).

At some sites refitting studies have been particularly successful at demonstrating the spatial organization of specialized activity areas and their relation to other areas of the site. At both Meer II and Rekem this has been done in particular with the refitting of tool modification/rejuvenation and/or resharpening refits.

Such fits not only give an insight into the spatial organization of the site, but also the process of tool modification itself (e.g. De Bie and Caspar 1997; 2000a, b; Van Noten et al. 1978). Studies on tool modification or more specifically resharpening are common in the US as well (e.g. Frison 1968, 1970; Boldurian et al. 1987).[5]

HISTORY OF REFITTING

Refitting has a long, but not quite continuous history. The first documented uses of refits in archaeology date to the last decades of the 19th Century (see e.g. Spurrell 1880; de Mortillet 1881; Cels and Depauw 1885; de Munck 1893; Smith 1894). The question at the forefront of paleolithic research at the time was the association between human made stone artifacts and extinct animal species (Spurrell 1880; Van Riper 1993). It is in this very same context that the refitting activity of Spurrell is to be seen. Indeed, the tacit assumption of the fact that these artifacts refit is that they are from an undisturbed context and as such belong together with the bones with which they were found. As can be seen in Figure 5, the use of

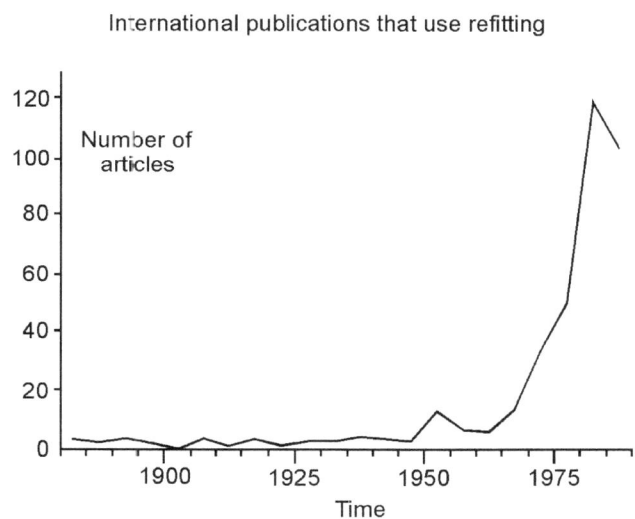

Figure 5 *Diagram of international publications that include refitting from 1880 to 1988. The last bar represents 4 instead of 5 years, n=282. (Adapted from Arts and Cziesla 1990: 652, Fig. 2)*

---

[5] A somewhat different use of refitting is found in combination with experimental studies. Questions asked in experimental studies span the various questions asked in archaeological studies using refitting, but most often involve some technological aspect (see e.g. Gryba 1987; Texier 1984). Particularly the combination of refitting studies and experimental studies can be informative. Experimental studies can provide a reference framework against which refitting results can be compared. Unfortunately such actualistic middle range studies have been done all too infrequently.

refitting is not continuous through time. More specifically, the use of refits often is insubstantial with regard to answering specific questions; rather refits are typically used for illustrative purposes (gluing a broken piece, see Figure 6). The refits shown in figure 6 could speak to the technology of blade production in the Belgian Neolithic, but the author does not address this in his article. This use of refitting is quite common and probably accounts for the majority of most early refits. However, contrary to Cziesla (1990: 11), refits were not regarded mere curiosities or "by-products." For example Allain (1952: 220) writes "*cette reconstitution d'un outil*

Another interesting aspect has to do with the kinds of refits that have been done through time. Undoubtedly the first 'accidental' refits were break refits. These were seldom used to address questions about the material, and as such did not make it into refitting bibliographies. Those that do make it often incorporate production sequence refits allowing the researchers to speak to technological issues (e.g. Comment 1909; Hamal-Nandrin and Servais 1929; Louis 1935; Eloy 1951; Kelley 1954). Since spatial recording was not an issue at the time, addressing taphonomic questions or questions about spatial organization the way we would today

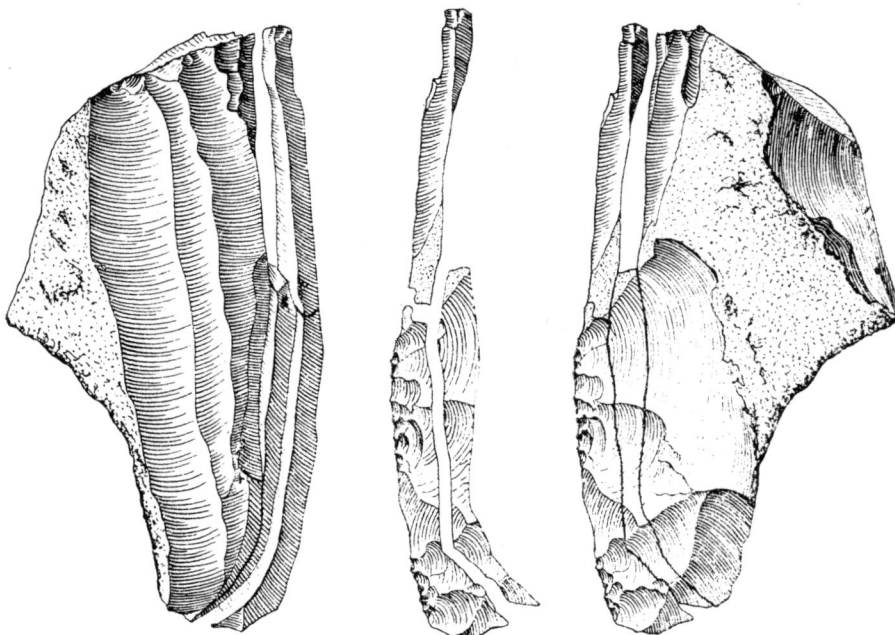

Figure 6 *Break refit of a blade, together with another broken blade fitted onto a core. Both blades show evidence of a crested blade preparation of the core. (Adapted from Eloy 1957: 465, Fig. 3)*

de silex avec des fragments épars dans les couches n'est pas une réussite isolée," rather, they tried and succeeded to refit several tools and relate the results to an attempt to better understand the technology of tool making at the site in question. All researchers who tried to systematically refit, as can be expected, did use the results with particular questions in mind. Among the more prevalent refitters of the first half of the 20th Century were several researchers from Liège (Eloy 1951, 1952; Louis 1935; Hamal-Nandrin and Servais 1929) continuing a tradition of refitting, mostly of Neolithic material (Cels and Depauw 1885; de Munck 1893). From these early publications it becomes clear that refits were primarily accidental finds that were later actively pursued to more successfully answer the questions they raised. In other words, the refits came before questions were asked that could be addressed with refitting. This is largely true for most uses of refitting until late in the 20th Century.

remained unused. However, the presence of refits did speak to the integrity of an assemblage (see e.g. Spurrell 1880) as it still does today. The most difficult type of refit, modification or resharpening refits, make it into the literature only much later[6] (see e.g. Frison 1968, 1970; Leroi-Gourhan and Brézillon 1966; Van Noten et al. 1978; Hinout 1985).

Until the 1970s refitting remains a method in the margins. However, in the early seventies this pattern begins to change. Important in this regard are undoubtedly the monumental work on Pincevent (Leroi-Gourhan and Brézillon 1966, 1972), Rheindahlen (Bosinski 1966), and somewhat later Meer II (Van Noten et al. 1978). With this work came articles that spoke directly to the advantages of refitting (Cahen 1976; Cahen et al. 1979;

---

[6] For a notable exception to the late adoption of modification refits see Vignard 1934.

Cahen and Keeley 1980; Tixier 1980). These articles were generally well received by the profession[7] (see replies to Cahen et al. 1979; Hofman 1981). From the 1980s on there is a veritable explosion in the use of refitting. Many articles on lithic analysis include refitting, and the profession, at least in the Old World, regards refitting as standard practice for any comprehensive site analysis involving lithic artifacts (De Bie personal communication 2000). However, in the New World this is not the case. For example, in a recent handbook on lithic analysis by a New World archaeologist, Andrefsky (1998), *Lithics: Macroscopic Approaches to Analysis*, refitting cannot be found in the index or glossary, and the topic does not have a section devoted to it. Odell (2004) on the other hand does include refitting in his recent overview of stone tool research. Interestingly Andrefsky is not involved in Old World research, while Odell is.

The first refits in the United States date to the same general period as early investigations including refits in Europe (see table 2). Since those early investigations little refitting work was done in the United States until the 1960 when George Frison regularly used the method at the sites he excavated. In Europe the method although used intermittently does seem to be used more often than in the United States. When we consider sites that are well known for refitting components, most are found in the Old World, and more specifically in Europe (table 3).

Table 2: Refitting Firsts (table adopted and modified from Cziesla 1990)

England: 1880 (Spurrell)
France: 1881 (de Mortillet)
Belgium: 1885 (Cels and Depauw)
Egypt: 1892 (Petrie)
Germany: 1897 (Müller)
Denmark: 1918 (Johansen; Rasmussen)
United States: 1897 (Philips)

Three trends seem to emerge from this historical overview. First, break fits are most important early on, next production sequence refits gain importance, and finally, modification refits are more actively pursued. This is not to say that current refitters focus only on modification refits, rather they focus on all fits, but more and more active attempts are made to include modification refits in the total ensemble of refits at a site. This can be related to the ease of each of the types of refit. As mentioned, break refits tend to be the most easily found, production sequence refits less easily, and modification refits are not easy at all.

---

[7] A notable exception is an exchange between Bordes and Cahen concerning the issue of contemporaneity (Bordes 1980a, b and Cahen 1980a, b).

Table 3: Some sites with refitting components

Pincevent (Leroi-Gourhan and Brézillon 1966, 1972; Bodu et al. 1990) (Upper Paleolithic)
Etiolles (Pigeot et al. 1976; Pigeot 1987) (Upper Paleolithic)
Terra Amata (Villa 1982, 1983) (Lower Paleolithic)
Gönnersdorf (Bosinski 1979; Franken 1983; Veil 1983) (Upper Paleolithic)
Rheindahlen (Bosinski 1966; Thieme 1983, 1990) (LP/MP)
Meer II (Van Noten et al. 1978) (Epi-paleolithic)
Rekem (De Bie and Caspar 2000) (Epi-paleolithic)
Boxgrove (Roberts and Parfitt 1999; Bergman et al. 1990) (Lower Paleolithic)
Boker Tachtit (Volkman 1983) (Middle and Upper Paleolithic)
Casper Site (Frison (ed) 1974) (Paleoindian)

Second, there is a trend in the kind of questions that are being asked. Technological questions, more specifically those addressing blank production, have been a priority on the agenda of refitters. In fact, I would argue that particularly in France that is still true today. However, over time more and more different kinds of questions are increasingly being addressed. The first of those seems to be that of the spatial organization of sites strongly tied to an assumption of contemporaneity. Still later taphonomic concerns were addressed, although it must be said that this potential of refitting still seems to be largely underused.

Third, I would argue that there is a trend in which the use of refitting is driven by the 'accidental' finding of fits for most of the history of refitting. It is only after the series of articles commending the use of refitting that one could argue that there is an increasing search for refits in an attempt to answer particular questions about the archaeological material, rather than questions following the finding of fits. At the same time, the methodology of refitting is considered more or less standard practice in the Old World and resulting from that there is perhaps a bit of automatism involved in setting out to look for refits, rather than setting out to answer particular questions. This as argued below probably has to do with the differences in the theoretical orientation between the New and Old World, in which the New World is more question/theory driven whereas research in continental European is often driven by methodology (see e.g. Audouze and Leroi-Gourhan 1981).

JOURNAL REVIEW

To get a detailed view on the differences, if any, between the use of refitting in the Old and New World, I reviewed four journals. These are the *Bulletin de la Société*

Préhistorique Française (BSPF), Gallia Préhistoire (GP), American Antiquity (AA), and the *Plains Anthropologist.* It is important when trying to understand these journals to view them within their paradigmatic framework – clearly research does not exist in a vacuum. To this effect I will outline a brief sketch of the relevant theoretical paradigms[8] in both France and the U.S. For a general outline of the theoretical framework in France I rely primarily on publications by Sackett (1991), and one by Audouze and Leroi-Gourhan (1981). I rely on an article by Binford and Sabloff (1982) for an outline of the paradigms in the U.S. as well as a textbook by Sharer and Ashmore (1993).

The French paradigms

In France two major paradigms are relevant for the period from 1960 to the present. The first of these is what Sackett (1991: 132) calls the "Bordesian Era." Its most important figures are François Bordes and Denise de Sonneville-Bordes. Armed with a tool type-list and a quantitative approach to characterizing lithic tool-type assemblage variability, Bordes effectively took down some of the previously held assumptions about the past, including one which tried to see strict evolutionary developments in the prehistoric past. The Bordes' uncoupled natural sequences from cultural ones, argued for the co-existence of different cultural groups and discarded a narrow emphasis on a limited number of *fossils directeurs* in the recognition of assemblages. F. Bordes' main approach to archaeology was through stratigraphic excavations, particularly in the Dordogne region of France. As such a heavy emphasis, as before, was invested in the documentation of the sequence of assemblage types (facies). I would argue that the Bordian era starts somewhere in the 1950s and continues more or less until F. Bordes' death in the early 1980s.

The second period, what Sackett (1991) calls the "Contemporary Era," builds momentum in the preceding period and is centered on André Leroi-Gourhan. Its gradual, but increasing, importance seems to really break through around the early eighties. The main concern seems to be general discontent with the way prehistoric archaeology was done in France. At the time many French archaeologists lamented "une sorte de 'déshumanisation' de la pièrre taillée" (Tixier 1980: 5). The goals of the new paradigm are characterized by ethnological excavations, the reconstruction of chaîne opératoires, the investigation of lithic economies – in short, the reconstruction of prehistoric behavior, not just

---

[8] I use 'paradigm' in the Kuhnian sense although I realize that Kuhn (1962) argued that the social sciences are not characterized by paradigms as he described them for the natural sciences. Still I think, as do other archaeologists, that the word has some use for describing theoretical schools in archaeology.

prehistoric chronology. As typical for France, the changes are not theory per se, but rather methodology driven. An important aspect of this new paradigm, particularly in light of this chapter, is the importance of refitting in it. An exchange that illustrates these divergent views particularly well is the one between Bordes and Cahen on the subject of lithic refitting in the BSPF (Bordes 1980a, b and Cahen 1980a, b). Therefore we would expect an increase in the amount of refitting papers in the BSPF and GP from the time the new paradigm gains momentum in France. The importance of refitting for the new French paradigm is reflected in both the spatial potential of refitting, as well as the technological aspects. However, it should be said that much technological work is done without refitting, following Tixier (1980) with the use of so-called "schémas diacritiques." Such schemes reconstruct technological sequences by analyzing the direction of removals seen on cores in particular and other flakes to a lesser extent. Theoretical paradigms in the U.S. have some parallels to some of the developments in France, although a dominant concern with prehistoric behavior and process occurs somewhat earlier in time.

The American paradigms

In the U.S. there are three main paradigms to take into consideration. The first is the so-called 'culture history' paradigm. The major concern in this paradigm is the reconstruction of culture histories in both time and space. In that sense it is very similar to the 'Bordian Era' in French prehistory. The 'culture history' paradigm runs until the 1960s at which time it is slowly but surely supplanted by a second paradigm. That paradigm calls itself the 'New Archaeology' and was/is advocated primarily by Binford in the U.S. With this new paradigm there was a dramatic shift away from an unrelenting focus on history and with it chronology. In its place came an emphasis on prehistoric behavior and process. This entailed an increased interest in spatial organization (Binford 1978) and a revival of the reduction sequence approach Holmes had argued for at the end of the 19th Century (Holmes 1894; 1897). In the articles promoting this shift no explicit mention was made of lithic refitting, however we would expect this method to be picked up given its seemingly good fit with the aims of the 'New' or 'Processual' archaeology.

A third and final paradigm shift is less relevant for prehistoric archaeology as the majority of prehistorians are still 'processualists.' This paradigm has been gaining momentum since the 1980s. It is typically called 'postprocessual archaeology.' Although it is certainly not as unified as the name would make one suspect, there are some trends that can be generalized. One is the emphasis on the active role of the individual; another, increasing attempts to analyze the ideological frameworks in the past; and finally, an attempt to discover the emic perspective (Sharer and Ashmore 1993). Here too refitting can play a role as it might be argued by some that refitting provides a glimpse into the mind of the prehistoric flintknapper. Based on these paradigms a shift towards increasing use of refitting would be expected with the onset of processual archaeology at the late 1960s and the beginning of the 1970s.

French journals

All articles were reviewed beginning in 1960 until the present[9]. Several elements were counted such as the number of articles in each volume[10], those dealing with lithic analysis, and those with a refitting component. More specifically, the kind of questions addressed was recorded for each paper that had a refitting component. These include four different categories: unsubstantial refitting component[11], technological analysis, spatial organization, and taphonomy. It should be noted that I was extremely lenient in classifying an article as containing a refitting component. When an article addressed different questions using refitting, its value was divided among the various relevant categories. For example, an article using refitting with a technological and a spatial component received a score of 0.5 for each.

The pattern that can be observed for the BSPF (Figure 7) and GP (Figure 8) coincides nicely with the pattern in Figure 5. In the BSPF during the 1960s there is only one article that includes a substantial refitting component. In the 1970s there is an increase in the articles that have an insubstantial refitting component, but still only one article that touches on a substantial refitting element. This pattern first begins to change in the 1980s, and continues on its increasing trend throughout the 1990s.

In the GP the importance of refitting rises earlier than it does in the BSPF. Among the articles is the seminal one from Leroi-Gourhan and Brézillion on Pincevent (1966). Further, the percentages of articles that include a substantive refitting component are much larger in the GP than they are in the BSPF. This pattern is best explained by the 'site report-like' nature of articles in the GP, which tend to cover more of the research efforts engaged in than do BSPF articles. Further, Leroi-Gourhan and later Brézillion were directors of *Gallia Préhistoire* undoubtedly helping to promote the type of research they were more favorable towards.

[9] Raw data can be obtained from the author.
[10] Some articles were fairly long others really short (1-2 pages). However, if they were labeled as articles, they were counted as such regardless of length. Reports, notes, book reviews and/or recent discoveries were not counted.
[11] The articles counted under this heading did not really address any refitting question, but had either an illustration of a refitted artifact, typically a break refit or a single refit line on a map that was not addressed specifically in the text as being significant.

Bulletin de la Société Préhistorique Française

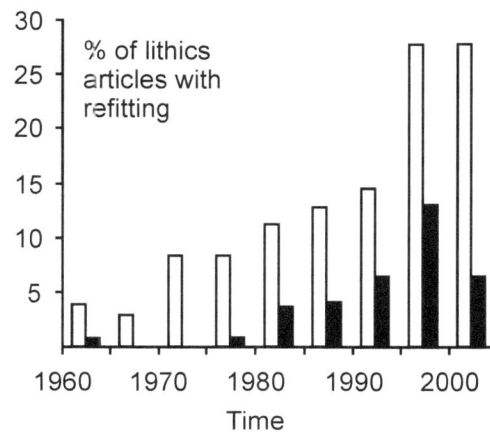

Figure 7 *Bar chart of the preponderance of articles with a refitting component as a percentage of all articles that include lithic analysis. The blue bars indicate all refitting articles, the red ones only articles that employ refitting in addressing a question.*

Gallia Préhistoire

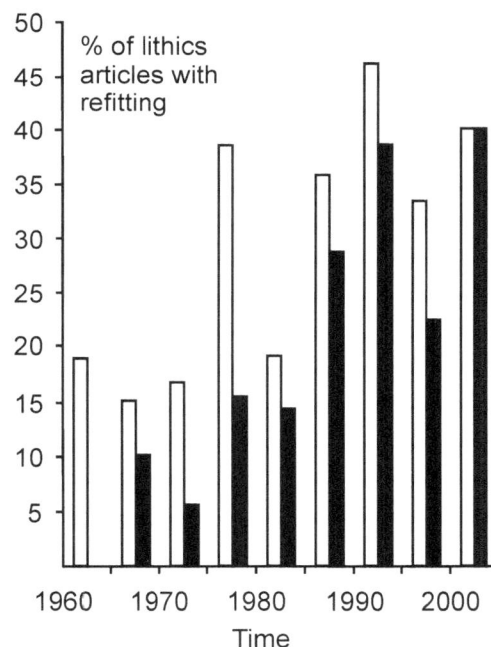

Figure 8 *Diagram of the preponderance of articles with a refitting component as a percentage of all articles dealing with lithic analysis. The gray bars indicate all refitting articles, the black ones only articles that employ refitting in addressing a question.*

These data from the BSPF and GP coincide very well with the onset of the currently reigning theoretical paradigm in French prehistory. Indeed, the

'Contemporary Era' following the initial leadership of Leroi-Gourhan is marked by a substantial increase in the use of refitting, increases that fall predominantly in the areas of technological and spatial analysis exactly as would be expected from the discussion of the theoretical paradigm. Further it is interesting to note that out of all articles dealing with refitting the focus on taphonomy is low. There seems to be an understanding that the mere presence of refits speaks to the taphonomic integrity of the site. While there is something to be said for this interpretation, the reverse, an absence of refits is not entertained as evidence against a sites 'undisturbed' character. Both these assumptions should be up for critical evaluation. As mentioned earlier, the prevalence of refits relative to the time investment in refitting can tell us a lot about the taphonomic history of a site as well as the character of the site occupation. Quarrying sites for example will have a different 'refitability' than do specialized retooling locations. Also the initial assumption of an undisturbed site should be reversed into the assumption that a site is disturbed unless it is proven that the site is impacted only mildly by post depositional disturbance. In this last case refits are one of a number of lines of evidence that could be used to make the case (see Dibble et al. 1997 for a number of others).

American Journals

For the journals AA and PA the pattern is very different (Figures 9 and 10). First, there are no real trends as can be seen in the French journals. Rather the use of refitting in addressing archaeological questions seems to come and go, like the pattern evident in the period before 1965 in Figure 5. Secondly, it must be noted that the overwhelming majority of papers with a refitting component have been classified as such because of break refits – notably the refitting of broken projectile points. Those articles that do use a substantial refitting component are very different as well. Articles in the GP and the BSPF with refitting components typically have a substantial amount of refits and use those fairly extensively in the analysis. The articles in the PA, contrast with this pattern in that they typically have a very limited number of refits. Further the refitting component is never very extensive. AA differs somewhat from the PA in this regard leaning closer to the pattern in the French journals. These patterns, however, do not show up when refitting components are scaled on a presence/absence scale. While this illustrates that refitting is even less ubiquitous in the United States than the data at first seem to indicate, the PA's articles do convey an integration of a number of different approaches in each article, however briefly. This, of course, should be commended. Indeed, the use of multiple lines of evidence to make a point is crucial[12]. Fortunately, this approach

_____

[12] For a theoretical consideration of this point, see Wylie 1992, for a practical application see De Bie et al. 2002.

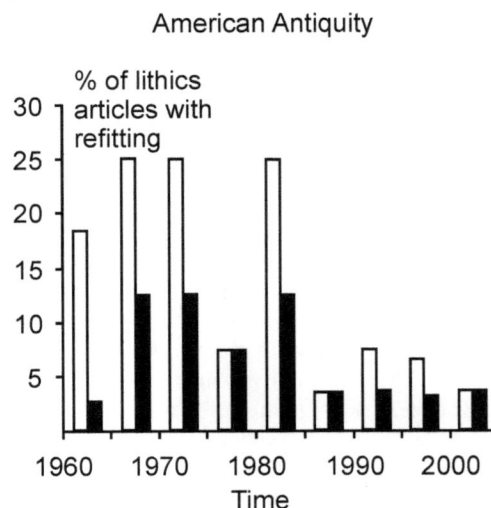

Figure 9 *Diagram of the preponderance of articles with a refitting component as a percentage of all articles dealing with lithic analysis. The white bars indicate all refitting articles, the black ones only articles that employ refitting in addressing a question.*

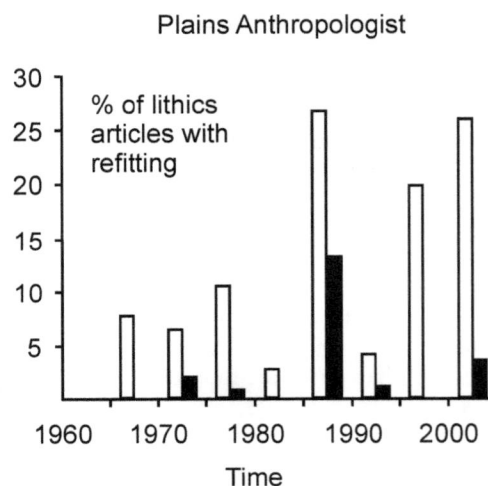

Figure 10 *Diagram of the preponderance of articles with a refitting component as a percentage of all articles dealing with lithic analysis. The white bars indicate all refitting articles, the black ones only articles that employ refitting in addressing a question.*

seems to be gradually increasing in European research. AA articles show a similar pattern as do the PA's ones when it comes to the intermittent use of refitting. On the other hand when refitting is used, that use is more often substantial than in the PA. Articles in American Antiquity often have an explicit theoretical or methodological focus as well as a broader range of regions represented than do either of the French journals or the PA. This contributes to the patterns observed with respect to refitting.

Relating the paradigms of the New World with the pattern as evidenced in Figures 9 and 10 is not a straightforward task. First of all the pattern in both journals does not match up very well at all. Second, many of the articles in AA are related to Paleolithic research and as such reflect a complex mix of perspectives. When we focus on the PA only it becomes clear that many of the early substantial uses of refitting are by the hand of a single researcher, George Frison. He is a processual archaeologist, but it does not seem warranted to link his use of refitting as demonstrating an increase in refitting due to the shift to a processual paradigm. Also no link with postprocessual archaeology can be made as the articles in the PA tend to remain engaged in a processual theoretical framework. Perhaps the increasing use of refitting in Europe and subsequent publications of highly positive papers on refitting can account for the change. Certainly Current Anthropology and, with it, the 1979 article on Meer II (Cahen et al. 1979) as well as some articles in AA are widely available to New World archaeologists. However, only one Plains Anthropology article using refitting from this time period (Bamforth 1985) cites the 1979 Cahen et al. paper. The pattern then, does not relate directly to either the New World theoretical framework or the increased use of refitting in the New World.

DISCUSSION

It has become clear in the previous section that there are some important differences between the Old World and the New World in the use of refitting. Why might this be the case? Differences can first be linked to the archaeological record itself and, second, to differences in general approaches to archaeology.

As highlighted in the background section of this chapter, there are three kinds of refits. Each of these goes hand in hand with particular questions that *can* be addressed using refitting[13]. The archaeological record of the Old World is mostly based on blank producing technologies. This record is ideally suited for production sequence refits, which in fact predominate much of Old World refitting. The New World on the other hand is not dominated by blank producing technologies, but rather by core/tool technologies. In other words, the tools are not made on blanks as is typically the case in the Old World, but on the cores themselves. Indeed, the New World in general, and the Plains region of the New World, in particular, are characterized by the use of bifacial technologies during most of its prehistoric periods. Such technologies cannot be refitted using production sequence refits, but rather must be refitted primarily by fitting tiny resharpening flakes onto the bifaces, before potential

larger flakes can be fit onto these tools. In essence, New World archaeologists are stuck with the most difficult type of refits: resharpening/modification refits.

In this light it becomes understandable that refitting has not seen the widespread, even standardized use in the New World as it has in the Old World. This difference further helps to explain the rather significant discrepancy between the abundance of papers with unsubstantial refit components, those with break refits, and those with substantial refit components. Finally, it should be mentioned that the likelihood of finding break refits among the not so abundant, but highly prized projectile points is probably much higher than the likelihood of finding break refits among ordinary blanks in Old World assemblages. As such differences in the archaeological record can account for much of the observed differences between the Old and New World[14].

A second element that might explain some of the differences are the dominant theoretical perspectives. The *chaîne opératoire* approach, for example, fits very well with the use of refitting, while that is not necessarily true of a processual perspective. In the latter approach there is a general dislike for singular phenomena. Typically refits cannot support any pattern with a robust sample size leading researchers to favor data derived from large numbers of individual artifacts. Postprocessual archaeologies on the other hand might fit better with refitting evidence as refit sets contain the exact decisions made by one or multiple agent(s) in deep time, highlighting the intricacies of a specific set or sets of events. However, it is too early to evaluate if these theoretical reasons for a good match are having an effect on particular research paths chosen.

Certainly one New World complaint that has been made of refitting is the lack of theoretical grounding the method

[13] Production sequence refits, for example, are ideal when one wants to address technological questions with regard to the reduction sequence being employed at a site.

[14] In this light, it is quite understandable that an alternative to physically refitting assemblages, while still trying to employ the benefits the refitting method offers, has been developed in the New World. This method is called Minimum Analytical Nodule Analysis (MAN analysis) (Kelly 1985; Frison 1974; Ingbar and Larson 1992; Larson and Kornfeld 1997). The idea of a MAN analysis is to sort the lithic artifacts by nodule. That is, dividing the raw material at the site in as finely distinguishable groups as possible. Within and between closely related groups, refits are then sought in an attempt to further narrow the groups (in the case of between group fits). The constituents of these groups are then analyzed in detail. While this method may have some severe problems due to the inability to recognize more or less correct analytical nodules, these problems should be easily assessed in some relatively straightforward experiments. MAN analysis then could become a viable alternative to lithic refitting.

Utsav Schurmans

has received (Larson and Ingbar 1992). This critique is to a certain extent well-taken and reflects one of the fundamental differences between the Old and New World approaches to archaeology. Archaeology in the U.S. remains largely grounded within a strong hypothetico-deductive approach (e.g. Binford 1962). In continental Europe on the other hand, the strong theoretical grounding that goes hand in hand with such a hypothetico-deductive approach is often lacking. As Audouze and Lerou-Gourhan (1981: 174) argue in their article, archaeology, at least in France is methodology driven, not theory driven. As such the approach remains inductive – data driven (Audouze and Leroi-Gourhan 1981). This difference is very clear to the student, such as myself, who has received training in both the Old and New Worlds. For example, a typical complaint of an Old World archaeologist towards the New World archaeologist is that they know all the theories, but when you give them a box of material, they do not know what to do with it. Why bother with everlasting theory when some real archaeology needs to be done? These differences in the approach to archaeology, more than specific theoretical differences, are at the basis of differences between Old and New World.

Interpretations of lithic refitting in the Old World can be easily fit within a standard division of questions addressed (taphonomy, production sequence technology, tool manufacturing technology, and spatial organization) – indeed these standard uses of refitting were formulated by Old World archaeologists (Cahen 1987, Cziesla 1990), In the New World approaches to refitting fit such a division much less easily. However, some part of this can be related to more theoretical differences related to inductive versus deductive approaches to archaeology. The work of Morrow (1996) and that by Bamforth and Becker (2000) are good examples of this for the New World. Morrow addresses mobility and uses an approach which includes the distinction between 'orphans' and 'ghosts.' Not only does he try to address a question (mobility) that is rarely tackled in Europe, he also devises a new theoretical framework complete with expectations against which he can test the archaeological material. Similarly, Bamforth and Becker (2000) bring in the arguments built around core to biface ratios used by Parry and Kelly in their well-known article correlating higher mobility with fewer cores and a more curated technology (Parry and Kelly 1987). Again, this approach allows the archaeologists to set up some expectations against which the archaeological material can be tested. Such an approach is foreign to most Old World archaeologists. They have some questions and start refitting – hence holding a symposium on lithic refitting (Schurmans and De Bie 2001) is greeted with initial distrust, what new could there possibly be to talk about?

Having highlighted some of the differences it seems important to talk about some similarities as well. In

essence many of the primary concerns of the 'Contemporary Era' paradigm, for lack of a better phrase, are identical to those of processual archaeology. There is a strong concern with process, most notably technological (see Shott 2003). Further, there is an explicit hierarchy in inference (see the ladder of inference, Hawkes 1954), giving priority to natural and technological explanations over social and religious ones (Audouze and Leroi-Gourhan 1981) – an argument very close to that advocated, or at least practiced, by Binford (1962). I sometimes wonder what good the often-strong opposition and all too easy generalizations about Old World archaeologists does us (see e.g. Clark 1997; Clark 1993; Clark 1991)? Exposing our biases is a good thing, but repeatedly arguing against a paradigm (the Bordesian paradigm) that has been replaced for quite sometime now, or simply claiming that nothing has changed with the adoption of a 'chaîne opératoire' paradigm, seems unjustified. Yes, it is true, the current French approach to archaeology is not exactly aligned with New World archaeology, but New World approaches themselves are far from unified. When all is said and done however, both Old and New World archaeologists can agree on what a good excavation is. So in the end, the theoretical issues notwithstanding, we should be able to work together effectively.

CONCLUSION

In this chapter I argue that the use of refitting is very different in the Old and New World. In comparing two journals from the U.S. and two French journals it became clear that French archaeologists have used refitting much more systematically since the 1980s. Indeed, refitting can be considered a standard practice. Furthermore, the kind of questions being asked and the kinds of refits actively pursued have changed dramatically throughout the history of the method in Europe. The focus shifted from an almost exclusive emphasis on break fits, to one that increasingly included production sequence refits and modification refits. Parallel with these shifts are changes in the questions addressed with refitting. Among the relatively late additions are the reconstruction of spatial organization, taphonomic considerations, and the technology of tool modifications. In the U.S. refitting has seen a moderate increase as well, but the prevalence is nowhere near that of France. This, I argued is strongly related to the kinds of refits New World archaeologists are typically forced to deal with – namely resharpening or modification refits. These differences in turn have an impact on the questions asked.

Besides the differences in the archaeological record there are some theoretical differences that play out in specific refitting research. New World research is typically much more sophisticated on a theoretical level. Springing from this has been an alternative to lithic refitting, MAN analysis (Larson and Kornfeld 1997). This type of analysis could be a viable alternative for refitting and should be employed more often. A further exciting line of reasoning that has been followed, albeit hesitatingly, in the New World is an attempt to devise a framework that would allow us to better deal with the information that can be gained from the absence of refits at a site. When we as archaeologists want to be serious about such advances we need to be particularly diligent in recording the time spend on refitting as well as the methodology used in looking for refits. Relatively absent from both the Old and New World are the use of refitting to address taphonomic questions, an observation that is unsettling given the demonstrated potential of refitting in this kind of research.

Finally, this chapter has shown the importance in distinguishing between the different types of refits. One hopes that knowledge of the significance of these differences will lead to an increased documentation of the percentages of refits in each category at sites so that others are given as many tools as possible to evaluate the research presented. Methods used in De Bie and Caspar (2000a: 26-28) in the illustration of the spatial layout of refitted sets is particularly effective. Similarly, it is hoped that in the illustration of refitted sets themselves all is done to ensure easy and complete reading of the technological sequence. All too often, valuable work is lost because of poorly illustrated/ described publications. In the end Old and New World archaeologists could learn a tremendous amount from collaboration in working on refitting both on a theoretical level and in the methodological aspects of refitting.

Refitting and its alternatives deserve a prominent place among the methodological toolkit of archaeologists for numerous reasons. These include the potential of refitting to speak to the taphonomy of a site as well as the behavioral information that can be gained from such studies. At the same time it should be stressed that refitting should only be one of a myriad of lines of evidence employed (see e.g. Wylie 1992; De Bie et al. 2002) in an attempt to better understand our prehistoric past.

BIBLIOGRAPHY

ALLAIN, J. 1952 L'histoire d'un burin double, hypotheses technologiques. *Bulletin de la Société Préhistorique Française* 49: 218-222.

ANDREFSKY, W. 1998 *Lithics: Macroscopic Approaches to Analysis*. Cambridge manuals in archeology. Cambridge University Press, New York.

ARTS, N. & E. CZIESLA 1990 Bibliography (1880-1988) on the subject of refitting stone artifacts. In *The Big Puzzle. Internation Symposium on Refitting Stone Artefacts*, edited by E. CZIESLA, S. EICKHOFF, N. ARTS & D. WINTER. Studies in Modern Archaeology, Vol 1. Holos, Bonn.

AUDOUZE, F. & A. LEROI-GOURHAN 1981 France: a continental insularity. *World Archaeology* 1: 170-189.

BAMFORTH, D. B. 1985 The Technological Organization of Paleo-Indian Small-Group Bison Hunting on the Llano Estacado. *Plains Anthropologist* 30:243-257.

BAMFORTH, D. B. & M. S. BECKER 2000 Core/Biface Ratios, Mobility, Refitting, and Artifact Use-Lives: A Paleoindian Example. *Plains Anthropologist* 45(173): 273-290.

BERGMAN, C. A., M. B. ROBERTS, S. N. COLLCUTT & P. BARLOW 1990 Refitting and Spatial analysis of Artefacts from Quarry 2 at the Middle Pleistocene Acheulean Site of Boxgrove, West Sussex, England. In *The Big Puzzle. Internation Symposium on Refitting Stone Artefacts*, edited by E. CZIESLA, S. EICKHOFF, N. ARTS & D. WINTER, Studies in Modern Archaeology, Vol 1. Holos, Bonn, pp. 265-282.

BINFORD, L. 1962 Archaeology as anthropology. *American Antiquity* 28: 217-225.

BINFORD, L. 1978 Dimensional Analysis of Behaviour and Site Structure: Learning From an Eskimo Hunting Stand. *American Antiquity* 43: 330-361.

BINFORD, L. 1979 Organization and Formation Processes: Looking at Curated Technologies. *Journal of Anthropological Research* 35: 255-273.

BINFORD, L. & J. SABLOFF 1982 Paradigms, Systematics and Archaeology. *Journal of Anthropological Research* 38: 137-153.

BODU, E., C. KARLIN & S. PLOUX 1990 Who's who? The Magdalenian Flintknappers of Pincevent (France). In *The Big Puzzle. Internation Symposium on Refitting Stone Artefacts*, edited by E. CZIESLA, S. EICKHOFF, N. ARTS & D. WINTER, Studies in Modern Archaeology, Vol 1. Holos, Bonn, pp. 143-164.

BOLDURIAN, A.T., G.A. AGOGINO, P.H. SHELLEY & M. SLAUGHTER 1987 Folsom Biface Manufacture, Retooling, and Site Function ant the Mitchell Locality of Blackwater Draw. *Plains Anthropologist* 32: 299-311.

BORDES, F. 1980a Savez-vous remonter les cailloux à la mode de chez nous. *Bulletin de la Société Préhistorique Française* 77: 232-234.

BORDES, F. 1980b Question de contemporanéité: l'illusion des remontages. *Bulletin de la Société Préhistorique Française* 77: 131-133.

BOSINSKI, G. 1966 Der paläolithischen Fundplaz Rheindahlen, Zeigelei Dreesen-Westwand. *Bonner Jahrbücher* 166: 318-343.

BOSINSKI, G. 1979 *Die Ausgrabungen in Gönnersdorf 1968-1976 und die Siedlungsbenfunde der Grabung 1968*. Der Magdalénien-Fundplatz Gönnersdorf, 3. Franz Steiner GMBH, Wiesbaden.

CAHEN, D. 1976 Das Zusammensetzen geschlagener Steinartefakte. *Archäologisches Korrespondenzblatt* 6: 81-93.

CAHEN, D. 1980a Question de contemporanéité: L'apport des remontages. *Bulletin de la Société Préhistorique Française* 77: 230-232.

CAHEN, D. 1980b Pour clore le débat. *Bulletin de la Société Préhistorique Française* 77: 234.

CAHEN, D. 1987 Refitting stone artefacts: why bother? In *The Human Uses of Flint and Chert*, edited by G. d. G. SIEVEKING & M. NEWCOMER, Cambridge University Press, Cambridge, pp. 1-9.

CAHEN, D. & L.H. KEELEY 1980 Not less than two, not more than three. *World Archaeology* 12(2): 166-180.

CAHEN, D., L.H. KEELEY & V. F. NOTEN 1979 Stone Tools, Toolkits, and Human Behavior in Prehistory. *Current Anthropology* 20: 661-686.

CAHEN, D. & J. MOEYERSONS 1977 Subsurface Movements of Stone Artefacts and their Implications for the History of Central Africa. *Nature* 266: 812-815.

CAHEN, D. & P. VAN BERG 1979 Un habitat danubien à Blicquy, vol. 1. Structures et industrie lithique. *Archaeologia belgica* 221.

CELS, A. & E. DEPAUW 1885 Considérations sur la taille du silex, telle qu'elle était pratiquée à Spiennes à l'âge de la pierre polie. *Bulletin de la Société d'anthropologie de Bruxelles* 4: 246-252.

CLARK, G.A. (editor) 1991 *Perspectives on the Past: Theoretical Biases in Mediterranean Hunter-Gatherer Research*. University of Pennsylvania Press, Philadelphia.

CLARK, G.A. 1993 Paradigms in Science and Archaeology. *Journal of Archaeological Research* 1: 203-234.

CLARK, G.A. 1997 Middle-Upper Paleolithic transition in Europe: an American perspective. *Norwegian Archaeological Review* 30(1): 25-33.

CLOSE, A.E. 1996 Carry that Weight: the Use and Transportation of Stone Tools. *Current Anthropology* 37(3): 545-553.

COMMONT, V. 1909 *L'Industrie Moustérienne dans la Région du Nord de la France*. Congrès Préhistorique de France.Compte rendu de la cinquième session - Beauvais. Bureaux de la Société Préhistorique de France, Paris.

CZIESLA, E. 1990 On refitting of stone artefacts. In *The Big Puzzle. International Symposium on Refitting Stone Artifacts*, edited by E. CZIESLA, S. EICKHOFF, N. ARTS & D. WINTER, Studies in Modern Archaeology, 1. Holos, Bonn, pp. 9-44.

DE BIE, M. & J.-P. CASPAR 1997 La signification des outillages lithiques dans les industries a Federmesser.Observations sur la variabilité des burins et des pièces laminaires ou lamellaires a modification latérale dans le gisement de Rekem (Belgique). *Bulletin de la Société Préhistorique Française* 94(3): 361-372.

DE BIE, M. & J.-P. CASPAR 2000a *Rekem. A Federmesser Camp on the Meuse River Bank, vol 1 and 2*. University Press, Leuven.

DE BIE, M., U. SCHURMANS & J.-P. CASPAR 2002 On Knapping Spots and Living Areas: Intra-Site Differentiation at Late Paleolithic Rekem. In *Recent Studies in the Final Palaeolithic of the European Plain*, edited by B. V. ERIKSEN & B. BRATLUND, Aarhus University Press, Aarhus, pp. 139-164.

DE MORTILLET, G. 1881 *Musée Préhistorique*, Paris.

DE MUNCK, E. 1893 Observations nouvelles sur le Quaternaire de la région de Mons-Saint-Symphorien-Spiennes. Présentation de pieces: Nucléi de l'époque paléolithique sur lequels se pappliquent plusieurs éclats. *Bulletin de la Société d'anthropologie de Bruxelles* 11: 198-210.

DIBBLE, H.L., P.G. CHASE, S.P. MCPHERRON & A. TUFFREAU 1997 Testing the Reality of a "Living Floor" with Archaeological Data. *American Antiquity* 62: 629-651.

DIBBLE, H.L. & A. DEBÉNATH 1991 Paradigmatic differences in a collaborative research project. In *Paradigmatic Biases in Circum-Mediterranean Hunter-Gatherer Research*, edited by G.A. CLARK, University of Pennsylvania Press, Philadelphia, pp. 217-226.

DIBBLE, H. L. 1995 Biache Saint-Vaast, Level IIA: A comparison of analytical approaches. In *The Definition and Interpretation of Levallois Variability*, edited by H.L. DIBBLE & O. BAR-YOSEF, Prehistory Press, Madison, pp. 93-116.

ELOY, L. 1951 Nouvelles reconstitutions du travail du silex dans un atelier omalien. *Bulletin de la Société Préhistorique Française* 48: 29-30.

ELOY, L. 1952 Un ensemble de deux tablettes de nucléus et de quatre lames provenant du XIXe atelier omalien du Bois de Tavelay, a Dommartin. *Bulletin de la Société Préhistorique Française* 49: 607-609.

ELOY, L. 1957 Quelques cas de fractures de lamesen silex avec préparation d'encoches dans l'Omalien. *Bulletin de la Société Préhistorique Française* 54: 464-466.

ENLOE, J. G. & F. DAVID 1992 Food Sharing in the Paleolithic:Carcass Refitting at Pincevent. In *Piecing Together the Past:Applications of Refitting Studies in Archaeology*, edited by J. L. HOFMAN & J. G. ENLOE, BAR International Series 578. BAR Publishing, Oxford, pp. 296-315.

FRANKEN, E. 1983 Rohmaterial, zusammensetzungen und Bearbeitungstechnik. In *Die Steinartefakte von Gönnersdorf*, edited by E. FRANKEN & S. VEIL, Der Magdalénien-Fundplatz Gönnersdorf, 7, Wiesbaden, pp. 1-169.

FRISON, G. 1968 A Functional Analysis of Certain Chipped Stone Tools. *American Antiquity* 33:149-155.

FRISON, G. 1970 The Kobold Site, 24BH406: A Post-Althithermal Record of buffalo-Jumping for the Northwestern Plains. *Plains Anthropologist* 15(47): 1-35.

FRISON, G. (editor) 1974 *The Caspar Site: A Hell Gap Bison Kill on the High Plains*. Academic Press, New York.

GRYBA, E. M. 1987 A Stone Age Pressure Method of Folsom Fluting. *Plains Anthropologist* 32: 53-66.

HAMAL-NANDRIN, J. & J. SERVAIS 1929 Contribution à l'étude de la taille du silex aux différentes époques de l'Age de la Pierre. Le Nucléus et ses différentes transformations. *Bulletin de la Société Préhistorique Française* 26: 541-552.

HAWKES, C. 1954 Archaeological Method and Theory: Some Comments from the Old World. *American Anthropologist* 56: 155-168.

HINOUT, J. 1985 Le gisement épipaléolithique de la Muette I, commune du Vieux-Moulin (Oise). *Bulletin de la Société Préhistorique Française* 82: 377-388.

HOFMAN, J. L. 1981 Refitting of Chipped Stone Artefacts as an Analytical and Interpretative Tool. *Current Anthropology* 22(6): 691-693.

HOFMAN, J. L. 1992 Putting the Pieces Together: An Introduction to Refitting. In *Piecing Together the Past: Applications of Refitting Studies in Archaeology*, edited by J. HOFMAN & J. G. ENLOE, BAR International Series 578. BAR Publishing, Oxford, pp. 1-20.

HOFMAN, J. L. & J. G. ENLOE (editors) 1992 *Piecing Together the Past: Applications of Refitting Studies in Archaeology*. BAR Publishing, Oxford.

HOLMES, W. 1894 Natural History of Flaked Stone Implements. In *Memoirs of the International Congress of Anthropology*, edited by C. S. WAKE, Schulte, Chicago, pp. 120-139.

HOLMES, W. H. 1897 Stone Implements of the Potomac-Chesapeake Tidewater Province. *Bureau of American Ethnology Annual Report* 15: 13-13152.

JOHANSEN FRISS, K. 1918 Affaldspletterne ved Thorsø Strand. *Aarbørger For Nordisk Oldkyndighed Og Historie* 3(8): 173-176.

KELLEY, H. 1954 Contribution a l'etude de la technique de la taille levalloisienne. *Bulletin de la Société Préhistorique Française* 51: 149-169.

KELLY, R. 1985 *Hunter-Gatherer Mobility and Sedentism: A Great Basin Study*, Unpublished PhD dissertation, University of Michigan.

KUHN, T. S. 1962 *The structure of scientific revolutions.* University of Chicago Press, Chicago.

LARSON, M. & E. INGBAR 1992 Perspectives on Refitting: Critique and a Complementary Approach. In *Piecing Together the Past: Applications of Refitting Studies in Archaeology*, edited by J. HOFMAN & J. G. ENLOE, BAR International Series 578. BAR Publishing, Oxford, pp. 151-162.

LARSON, M. & M. KORNFELD 1997 Chipped Stone Nodules: Theory, Method, and Examples. *Lithic Technology* 22(1): 4-18.

LEROI-GOURHAN, A. & M. BREZILLON 1966 L'Habitation Magdalenienne No. 1 de Pincevent près Montereau (Seine-et-Marne). *Gallia Préhistoire* 9: 263-385.

LEROI-GOURHAN, A. & M. BREZILLON 1972 Fouilles de Picevent. Essai d'analyse ethnographique d'un habitat magdalénien. *Gallia Préhistoire* 2 (VIIe supplément).

LINDAUER, O. 1992 Ceramic Conjoinability: Orphan Sherds and Reconstructing Time. In *Piecing Together the Past: Applications of Refitting Studies in Archaeology*, edited by J. HOFMAN & J. G. ENLOE, BAR International Series 578. BAR Publishing, Oxford, pp. 210-216.

LOUIS, M. 1935 Contribution à l'étude de la taille du silex. *Bulletin de la Société Préhistorique Française* 32: 616-621.

MAREAN, C. W. & S. Y. KIM 1998 Mousterian Large-Mammal Remains from Kobeh Cave: Behavioral Implications for Neanderthals and Early Modern Humans. *Current Anthropology* 39 (supplement): 79-113.

MILLS, B. J., E. CAMILLI & L. WANDSNIDER 1992 Spatial Patterning in Ceramic Vessel Distributions. In *Piecing Together the Past: Applications of Refitting Studies in Archaeology*, edited by J. HOFMAN & J. G. ENLOE. BAR International Series 578. BAR Publishing, Oxford.

MORROW, T. M. 1996 Lithic refitting and archaeological site formation processes: a case study from the Twin Ditch Site, Greene County, Illinois. In *Stone Tools: Theoretical Insights into Human Prehistory*, edited by G. H. ODELL, Interdisciplinary Contributions to Archaeology. Plenum Press, New York, pp. 345-373.

MÜLLER, S. 1897 *Nordische Altertumskunde. Nach Funden und Denkmalern aus Danemark und Schleswig. Bd.1: Steinzeit - Bronzezeit*, Straßburg.

ODELL, G. H. 2004 *Lithic Analysis*. Manuals in archaeological method, theory, and technique. Kluwer Academic/Plenum Publishers, New York.

PARRY, W. J. & R. L. KELLY 1987 Expedient Core Technology and Sedentism. In *The Organization of Core Technology*, edited by J. R. JOHNSON and C. MORROW, Westview Press, Boulder, pp. 284-304.

PETRIE, W. M. F. 1892 *Medum*, London.

PIGEOT, N. 1987 Eléments d'un modèle d'habitation magdalénienne (Etiolles). *Bulletin de la Société Préhistorique Française* 84(10-12): 35864.

PIGEOT, N., Y. TABORIN & M. OLIVE 1976 Problèmes de stratigraphie dans un site de plein-air: Etiolles. *Cahier du Centre des Recherches Préhistoriques de l'Université de Paris* 1(5):5-27.

POPLIN, F. 1976 *Les Grands vertébrés de Gönnersdorf, fouilles 1968*. Der Magdalenien-Fundplatz Gönnersdorf, 2. Fr. Steiner Verlag, Wiesbaden.

RASMUSSEN, J. P. 1918 Affaldspletter fra stenaldertilhugning. *Aarbørger For Nordisk Oldkyndighed Og Historie* 3(8): 151-172.

ROBERTS, M. B. & S. A. PARFITT 1999 *Boxgrove : a Middle Pleistocene hominid site at Eartham Quarry, Boxgrove, West Sussex*. English Heritage Archaeological report, 17. English Heritage, London.

SACKETT, J. R. 1991 Straight Archaeology French Style:The Phylogenetic Paradigm in Historic Perspective. In *Perspectives on the Past: Theoretical Biases in Mediterranean Hunter-Gatherer Research*, edited by G. A. CLARK, University of Pennsylvania Press, Philadelphia, pp. 109-139.

SCHALLER-ÅHRBERG, E. 1990 Refitting as a Method to Separate Mixed Sites: a Test with Unexpected Results. In *The Big Puzzle. International Symposium on Refitting Stone Artifacts*, edited by E. CZIESLA, S. EICKHOFF, N. ARTS & D. WINTER, Holos, Bonn, pp. 611-622.

SCHURMANS, U. & M. De BIE 2001 *Fitting Rocks. The Big Puzzle Revisited* – symposium held at the 2001 U.I.S.P.P. Meetings, Liège, Belgium.

SHARER, R. J. & W. ASHMORE 1993a *Archaeology: Discovering Our Past*. Mayfield Publishing Co, Mountain View, California.

SHOTT, M. J. 2003 *Chaîne Opératoire* and Reduction Sequence. *Lithic Technology* 28: 95-105.

SINGER, C. A. 1984 The 63-kilometer fit. In *Prehistoric quarries and lithic production*, edited by J. E. ERICSON & B. A. PURDY, Cambridge, pp. 35-48.

SMITH, W. 1894 *Man the Primeval Savage*, London.

SPURRELL, F. 1880 On the Discovery of the Place where Palaeolithic Implements were Made at Crayford. *Quarterly Journal of the Geological Society* 36: 544-549.

SULLIVAN, A. P. 1989 The Technology of Ceramic Reuse: Formation Processes and Archaeological Evidence. *World Archaeology* 21(1): 101-114.

TEXIER, J.-P. 1984 Un debitage experimental de silex par pression pectorale a la bequille. *Bulletin de la Société Préhistorique Française* 81(1): 25-27.

THIEME, H. 1983 Mittelpaläolitishce Siedlungsstrukturen in Rheindahlen (BRD). *Ethnographisch-Archäologische Zeitschrift* 24: 362-374.

THIEME, H. 1990 Wohnplatzstrukturen und Fundplatzanalysen durch das Zusammensetzen von Steinartefakten: Ergebnisse vom mittelpaläolithischen Fundplatz Rheindahlen B1 (Westwand-Komplex). In *The Big Puzzle. Internation Symposium on Refitting Stone Artefacts*, edited by E. CZIESLA, S. EICKHOFF, N. ARTS & D. WINTER, Studies in Modern Archaeology, Vol 1. Holos, Bonn, pp. 543-568.

TIXIER, J. 1980 Raccords et remontages. In *Préhistoire et Technologie Lithique*, pp. 50-56. CNRS, Paris.

TODD, L. C. & G. FRISON 1992 Reassembly of Bison Skeletons from the Horner Site: A Study in Anatomical Refitting. In *Piecing Together the Past: Applications of Refitting Studies in Archaeology*, edited by J. HOFMAN & J. G. ENLOE. BAR International Series 578. BAR Publishing, Oxford, pp. 63-82

VAN NOTEN, F. 1978 *Les chasseurs de Meer*. Dissertationes archaeologicae Gandenses. v. 18. De Tempel, Brugge.

VAN PEER, P. 1992 *The Levallois Reduction Strategy*. Monographs in World Archaeology 13. Prehistory Press, Madison.

VAN RIPER, A. B. 1993 *Men among the Mammoths: Victorian Science and the Discovery of Human Prehistory*. University of Chicago Press, Chicago.

VEIL, S. 1983 Die retuschierten Steinwerkzeuge und die Abfälle ihrer Herstellung. In *Die Steinartefakte von Gönnersdorf*, edited by E. FRANKEN & S. VEIL, Der Magdalénien-Fundplatz Gönnersdorf, 7, Wiesbaden, pp. 171-437.

VIGNARD, E. 1934 Triangles et Trapezes du Capsien en connexion avec leurs microburins. *Bulletin de la Société Préhistorique Française* 31: 457-459.

VILLA, P. 1982 Conjoinable Pieces and Site Formation Processes. *American Antiquity* 47: 276-290.

VILLA, P. 1983 *Terra Amata and the Middle Pleistocene Archaeological Record of Southern France*. University of California Press, Berkeley.

VOLKMAN, P. 1983 Boker Tachtit: Core Reconstructions. In *Prehistory and Paleoenvironments in the Central Negev,Israel. Volume III: The Avdate/Aqev Area, Part 3*, edited by A. E. MARKS, Southern Methodist University Press, Dallas, pp. 127-190.

WYLIE, A. 1992 The Interplay of Evidential Constraints and Political Interests: Recent Archaeological Research on Gender. *American Antiquity* 57(1): 15-35.

Address of the author:

Utsav SCHURMANS
Department of Anthropology
University of Pennsylvania
3260 South Street
Philadelphia, PA 19104
United States of America

utsav.schurmans@gmail.com

PARTAGE D'UNE EXPERIENCE DE *REMONTOLOGUE*

Pierre BODU

Résumé

Le remontage du matériel lithique est une méthode à ce point efficace qu'elle a occasionné de multiples rencontres où l'on débattait de ses applications et le Big Puzzle de 1987 en est une éclatante manifestation. Des symposium ont été organisés qui traitaient des modalités de représentation des liaisons mises en évidence par ces remontages. Ce texte, inspiré de travaux de remontage menés sur le site magdalénien de Pincevent (Seine-et-marne, France) se veut une contribution légèrement provocante à la discussion sur l'intérêt et les limites de la méthode.

Abstract

Lithic refitting is an effective method and as such has been the subject of several round-table discussions. A prime example of such a discussion was the Big Puzzle conference in 1987. Symposia have been organized where the interpretation of links demonstrated by refits formed the subject of discussion. This text, the result of refit work on the Magdalenian site of Pincevent (Seine-et-Marne, France), is written as a slightly provocative contribution to the discussion on the advantages and limits of refitting.

Cette courte note se veut avant tout le prélude à une discussion fournie plus qu'une véritable démonstration de l'intérêt des remontages, ce dont personne ne doute plus. M'appuyant notamment sur l'exemple de Pincevent, je vais tenter de montrer en quoi, cette méthode a su être efficace sur ce gisement mais aussi les limites qu'elle y a rencontrées. Usant d'autres exemples, j'enrichirai la démonstration de l'intérêt et des limites des remontages.

Depuis près de 40 ans, le gisement magdalénien de Pincevent (Seine-et-Marne, France) fait l'objet de fouilles scrupuleuses et développées tant au plan diachronique qu'au plan synchronique (Leroi-Gourhan et Brézillon 1966; Leroi-Gourhan et Brézillon 1972).

Claudine Karlin en 1964 lors de l'étude de l'habitation n°1 de Pincevent (Seine-et-Marne) avait lancé "la mode" et systématisé ce qui devait devenir une véritable méthode d'étude des séries lithiques (Karlin in Leroi-Gourhan et Brézillon 1966; Cahen et al. 1980). Un peu moins de 40 ans plus tard et 4500 m2 fouillés plus loin, nous avons pu appliquer cette méthode au plus vaste sol d'occupation magdalénien du gisement de Pincevent, le niveau IV20. Les premiers résultats de cette réflexion

avaient été présentés dans le cadre du symposium: "The Big Puzzle" en 1987 (Bodu et al. 1990).

Lors de ma thèse soutenue en 1994 (Bodu 1994) il m'a été donné de documenter plus encore les comportements techniques mais aussi économiques et spatiaux d'un groupe de magdaléniens de Pincevent. En réalisant un taux de remontages de plus de 90% sur le matériel lithique provenant d'une zone du niveau IV20, j'ai en effet pu sérieusement traiter des modalités techniques et économiques du débitage, inscrire l'outillage au sein de son système de production mais également discuter de l'organisation spatiale des activités concernant la taille du silex et l'utilisation des produits obtenus. Quelques inférences sur la composition du groupe ont également pu être avancées s'inspirant des travaux de Nicole Pigeot menés à Etiolles (Pigeot 1987) ou de ceux de Sylvie Ploux développés à Pincevent (Ploux 1989).

A travers quelques exemples pris dans cette étude particulière mais aussi en m'inspirant d'exemples extérieurs, je discuterai ici de l'intérêt de la méthode des remontages mais également de ses limites fusse t'elle appliquée à hauteur de 90% d'une industrie lithique. La trame essentielle du discours s'appuie donc sur Pincevent, mais, mon argumentation tire également partie d'un certain nombre de réflexions menées sur d'autres gisements.

Avant d'entreprendre ce petit tour de la question de l'intérêt des remontages à Pincevent, il me semble qu'il convient d'aborder quelques points de discussion qui peuvent paraître assez provocateurs dans le cadre de cette publication sur les remontages. J'espère qu'ils seront le prélude à une discussion ultérieure animée.

La pratique "forcenée" de cette méthode d'étude des séries lithiques m'a conduit à me poser la question de son intérêt et c'est en grande partie pour cela que le titre de ma contribution est volontairement interrogateur. Evacuons d'emblée le rôle essentiel des remontages pour tester l'homogénéité des niveaux, des sols d'occupation. Ce type de question ne s'est pas posé à Pincevent dans la mesure où chaque niveau d'occupation est séparé du précédent ou du suivant par une nette sédimentation. La méthode est cependant porteuse d'informations considérables notamment pour les contextes d'abri et des travaux récents comme ceux de J.-G Bordes à Caminade (Bordes 2000) ou plus anciens tels les remontages réalisés sur le matériel châtelperronien de la grotte du renne à Arcy-sur-Cure ont permis de relativiser l'homogénéité des ensembles étudiés et par conséquent de pondérer certaines interprétations d'ordre palethnographique ou même technique. Ainsi à Arcy-sur-Cure, les premiers remontages ont permis d'identifier des mélanges entre les différents niveaux châtelperroniens (Bodu 1990), et dans la mesure où une vive polémique est engagée à propos de l'outillage et des parures en os chatelperroniens (y a t'il ou non une contamination due à l'occupation aurignacienne située plus haut dans la stratigraphie?), il serait courageux de tenter des remontages entre les différents niveaux archéologiques (ne serait-ce que pour démontrer que les mélanges entre le Châtelperronien et l'Aurignacien sont limités et que par conséquent l'hypothèse d'une industrie et d'une parure osseuse châtelperronienne est loin d'être incongrue) (White in Schmider 2002).

Pour en revenir à notre propos, en fait personne ne nie l'intérêt évident des remontages pour une bonne lecture technologique des séries lithiques notamment. C'est sans doute la méthode la plus performante et en particulier pour les industries mal connues sur un plan technique. L'usage des remontages à tout va me semble cependant trouver une limite lorsque l'on aborde des séries abondantes (de l'ordre de plusieurs milliers de pièces) pour lesquelles les résultats du remontage de quelques blocs (et encore le plus souvent partiels) peuvent être érigés en termes de norme pour le débitage. L'un des dangers d'un tel usage c'est qu'à partir de quelques exemples, pas forcément les plus significatifs, on définit les grands critères techniques d'une série. J'ajouterai à cela que les remontages les plus aisément complets sont en fait ceux qui concernent des ensembles débités peu ponctionnés au niveau de leurs supports, donc peut-être les moins réussis et ce faisant les moins caractéristiques de la façon de faire du groupe.

Sachons donc utiliser la méthode du remontage à bon escient, mais, sans doute, cela est-il plus facile à dire qu'à faire. Ainsi à l'issue de la thèse de Nicole Pigeot qui concernait Etiolles (Pigeot 1987), thèse qui a été essentielle entre autres pour la compréhension de ce gisement magdalénien, on peut estimer qu'un syndrome de "Remontologie" a "frappé" toute une génération d'étudiants mais aussi d'archéologues professionnels. Chacun dans son coin a tenté de recoller entre eux les petits fragments de roche taillée, sans toujours se poser la question de l'utilité de cette opération, longue, laborieuse, coûteuse en temps avec pour corollaire des résultats qui bien souvent étaient décevants, tant en terme technique, qu'économique ou spatial. Ce qui l'emportait et peut-être l'emporte encore chez certains d'entre nous, c'est d'obtenir les taux de remontages les plus importants ou d'avoir les ensembles remontés les plus esthétiques. Un challenge en quelque sorte…Quoi alors des informations essentielles que l'on attend de la méthode?

Cette remarque me semble à ce point vraie que bien souvent l'obsession du remontage, empêche une lecture fine des artefacts, le remontage mental tel que l'a défini J. Pélegrin, qui pourrait conduire à des interprétations ou tout du moins des observations similaires à propos des méthodes et des techniques de débitage. Ainsi, il me semble que lorsque j'ai réalisé ma thèse, il n'était pas nécessaire d'obtenir les remontages les plus complets, j'irai même jusqu'à dire de faire des remontages pour documenter les aspects techniques généraux de l'industrie lithique. Je bénéficiai alors certes d'un fonds de connaissances sur le débitage magdalénien accumulé par mes aînés qui me permettait cette élipse. Nous allons voir qu'à Pincevent les intérêts de l'utilisation de cette méthode sont sans doute ailleurs. En revanche pour d'autres ensembles lithiques, les remontages s'avèrent totalement incontournables pour la compréhension des schémas opératoires directeurs.

Pensons ainsi à la nécessité absolue de réaliser à court terme des remontages d'armatures sur des burins du Raysse, afin de témoigner définitivement qu'un certain nombre d'entre eux ont été utilisés comme des nucléus à lamelles et non comme des burins et pour appuyer ce que certains de nos collègues et notamment Laurent Klaric de l'Université de Paris I, ont proposé après par une lecture technologique fine des "burins" et des armatures gravettiennes (Klaric et al. 2002)

De même, lorsque avec François Bon nous avons étudié la série aurignacienne d'Arcy-sur-Cure, une lecture attentive des artefacts nous a permis de proposer l'hypothèse d'un débitage de lames rectilignes scandé d'enlèvements de lames volontairement outrepassantes destinées à cadrer une surface laminaire centrale (Bon et Bodu 2002). Faute de temps et en raison de l'importante quantité de silex nous ne l'avons pas fait, mais, nous aurions apprécié de confirmer cette proposition par des remontages physiques.

J'évoquerai rapidement un troisième exemple pour asseoir cette idée: A Lailly, gisement découvert lors des travaux de l'Autoroute A5 dans le nord de l'Yonne (Bodu et al. 1999), a été découverte une industrie lithique particulière. Pour aller rapidement, on dira qu'elle était composée de lames élégantes et larges sur lesquelles l'outillage, dominé par des grattoirs, est réalisé. L'industrie prudemment rapportée à l'Aurignacien en raison de la présence de ces grattoirs carénés et d'une lamelle dufour type roc-de-Combe, aurait pu être décrite comme étant une industrie de type exclusivement laminaire, les supports des grattoirs carénés provenant des sous-produits de ce type de débitage. Là où le remontage mental avait suggéré peut-être une origine autre de ces supports, les remontages physiques ont clairement montré qu'il existait un mode opératoire sophistiqué de production d'éclats épais pour la fabrication des grattoirs carénés. Dans ce cas précis, il est évident que les remontages ont joué un rôle essentiel. On peut penser que la démarche est tout autant intéressante pour d'autres industries mal documentées au plan technique, je pense notamment à certains débitages d'éclats de l'âge du fer ou à des débitages apparemment peu organisés du Badegoulien dont les remontages ont montré une autre complexité que celle attendue. Là le remontage mental préconisé par J. Pélegrin n'est pas toujours suffisant pour atteindre le degré de précision dans l'observation, offert par le remontage physique.

Un troisième exemple de l'intérêt de la méthode des remontages pour des indications d'ordre technique concerne cette fois-ci Pincevent. Permettons nous alors une présentation rapide du site et du matériel concerné.

Découvert en 1964, le gisement magdalénien de Pincevent, localisé à 80 km au sud-est de Paris, est fouillé chaque année depuis près de 40 ans (Leroi-Gourhan et Brézillon 1972) Le site localisé en plaine d'inondation sur les bords de la Seine semble avoir été choisi par les magdaléniens il y a près de 14000 ans, lors de campements saisonniers pour une chasse sélective du renne. Vers la fin du Bölling, les magdaléniens sont revenus au moins à 15 reprises et ces passages répétés d'été et d'automne ont été soigneusement fossilisés par les limons de débordement du fleuve. Parmi ces 15 niveaux d'occupation, l'un plus particulièrement, celui que nous appelons le IV20, a été fouillé sur une vaste surface (4500 m2) ce qui en fait à l'heure actuelle le plus vaste campement magdalénien connu en Europe (Bodu 1996; Julien et al. 1987). Situées sur un même dépôt limoneux, une quinzaine de structure d'habitat forment la trame de ce vaste campement. Quelques foyers plus éphémères, aux densités de vestiges moins importantes sont associés aux gros foyers d'habitat longtemps utilisés, souvent réaménagés et entourés d'artefacts nombreux et diversifiés. Pour nous, la pauvreté des premières s'explique par le caractère éphémère des activités qui se sont développés dans ces unités, dépendantes, comme l'ont montré les remontages, d'unités plus pérennes.

A Pincevent, l'un des principaux intérêts des remontages est d'avoir démontré que l'ensemble de ces structures étaient contemporaines alors que leur localisation sur un même lit d'inondation le laissait présager sans en être véritablement une démonstration. Mais nous aurons l'occasion de revenir sur cet aspect. Au sein de ce vaste campement, nous avions choisi dans le cadre de la thèse de n'étudier qu'une partie réduite d'une surface d'environ 600 m2 qui présente une dizaine de structures d'habitat d'importance diverse et près de 5000 fragments de silex. A terme, notre travail nous a amené à prendre en compte la totalité des silex découverts sur le niveau IV20, soit près de 50000 fragments, ne serait-ce que parce que les remontages ont montré une circulation relativement intense de nombreux éléments de silex à l'intérieur du campement (Bodu 1996).

Revenons en à l'intérêt des remontages concernant les méthodes et technique de taille à Pincevent. C'est plus à un niveau de détail que nous avons retrouvé cet intérêt et non au niveau des grandes lignes du schéma opératoire, déjà décrites (Bodu et al. 1990). Pour cela nos remontages se sont avérés relativement redondants par rapport aux informations précédemment acquises. Remonter les blocs de Pincevent pour en décrire le schéma conceptuel ne nous semble plus tout à fait utile à moins de montrer qu'il existe une évolution des méthodes et techniques de débitage à travers les différents niveaux d'occupation magdalénienne. Les remontages ont cependant permis d'éclairer quelques détails techniques et notamment celui-ci: la tendance du débitage magdalénien, en particulier celui de Pincevent est de produire des lames et des lamelles, supports privilégiés de l'ensemble de l'outillage. Rares sont les outils réalisés sur des éclats. Parmi ceux-ci on observe fréquemment des perçoirs ou micro-perçoirs fabriqués sur des éclats plutôt fins, à profil légèrement convexe. A l'opposé, certains nucléus à lames et lamelles sont fréquemment abandonnés alors que les derniers négatifs sont des éclats parfois réfléchis. Là où une étude des supports n'a permis que de préciser le type d'objet sur lequel ont été faits les perçoirs sans permettre d'affirmer leur origine au sein de la chaîne opératoire, les remontages ont montré que ces éclats ne correspondaient pas du tout à des sous produits du débitage laminaire ou lamellaire, mais qu'il s'agissait bien de produits de première intention, volontairement extraits en fin d'exploitation de nucléus à lamelles.

Un autre exemple permet de souligner l'importance des remontages au plan technique, même pour des industries maintenant bien documentées sur cet aspect. Il s'agit plus particulièrement des techniques au sens restrictif proposé par l'équipe de Valentine Roux. Dans le schéma magdalénien final classique, à une mise en forme réalisé à la pierre et probablement en partie au bois de cervidé succède une étape nommée le plein débitage à l'intérieur de laquelle on situe l'enlèvement des produits de première intention accompagné de phases d'entretien et de réaménagement des convexités. Le détachement des lames et des lamelles s'effectue habituellement au percuteur de bois de cervidé, les séquences de réaménagement étant le plus souvent réalisées à la pierre. En regardant un certain nombre de lames, nous nous étions aperçu qu'elles étaient débitées à la pierre et par conséquent, nous les avions considérées comme des sous produit d'un débitage laminaire débité plus classiquement au bois. Des remontages de Pincevent montrent que certains blocs sont en fait exclusivement débités à la pierre, plein débitage y compris. Signe d'un faible niveau de technicité ou débitage expédient de quelques supports suffisants pour une activité ciblée?

A Pincevent, ce sont également les remontages qui ont permis d'associer en deux ensembles débités distincts, différentes lames au talon ocré découvertes autour d'un même foyer. Nous avons interprété la présence systématique de ce colorant sur les talons comme le témoignage de l'usage d'un abraseur ou d'un percuteur ocré proposant même que ces deux nucléus avaient été taillés par le même individu (Baffier et al. 1991).

Un dernier exemple illustrant l'intérêt des remontages au plan technique mais aussi économique correspond à ce que l'on appelle le rythme du débitage. Les remontages permettent de suivre pas à pas l'enchaînement des gestes, l'aspect semi-tournant du débitage magdalénien, ils éclairent le rôle des deux plans de frappe. Surtout, ils documentent de façon inédite ce que l'on appelle les débitages intercalés. Jacques Pélegrin, il y a de cela près d'une dizaine d'année, avait proposé l'existence d'un débitage de lamelles intercalées pour le site magdalénien de Verberie, qui consistait en une production de lamelles intercalées au sein d'un débitage de lames prépondérantes, ces quelques lamelles exploitant des dièdres apparents à la rencontre de deux négatifs de lames. Cette déduction se nourrissait d'une observation fine de produits indépendants par la méthode du remontage mental. A Pincevent, des remontages conséquents ont montré que cette version de production de lamelles parallèlement à une autre version qui se marque par un débitage de lamelles privilégié accompagné de quelques lames courtes prédéterminantes. Dans ce dernier cas, ce sont les lamelles qui sont numériquement les plus nombreuses et les quelques lames obtenues considérées comme des sous-produits rejoignent rarement l'outillage.

Cet autre exemple de l'intérêt technique des remontages nous permet d'aborder l'aspect économique de l'activité de taille du silex: En 1964, Claudine Karlin (Leroi-Gourhan et Brézillon 1966) avait bien montré l'intérêt des remontages pour l'estimation de la productivité d'un débitage en terme quantitatif et en terme qualitatif. Dans l'exemple de l'habitation n°1, elle avait en particulier décrit l'histoire d'un bloc producteur de grattoirs et de becs. Cette approche de la spécialisation ou de la non spécialisation des débitages est maintenant chose courante. Les remontages que j'ai pu mener à Pincevent ont bien évidemment mis en évidence cet aspect. Dans la mesure où ces remontages ont été réalisés à hauteur de 90 % de l'industrie lithique de l'ensemble étudié, des informations inédites ont pu être obtenues. Je pense ainsi à la mise en évidence de vides pertinents à l'intérieur de certains remontages qui caractérisent des produits emportés hors de l'unité productrice.

De ce dernier exemple, on voit bien que les remontages à Pincevent ont permis d'atteindre une dimension spatiale, ou plutôt plusieurs dimensions spatiales. Je m'explique: Passons rapidement sur les résultats relativement triviaux de la mise en évidence de la zone de débitage pour un bloc et de la dispersion des produits obtenus au sein même de l'unité. Cette première étape de l'analyse

spatiale est à la base de la structuration de l'espace habité. Dans la mesure où l'on rend dynamiques des objets en les réintégrant au sein d'une chaîne opératoire et qu'on leur attribue un statut (support, déchets, outil) on peut également interroger les concentrations composées de ces objets et tisser ou non des relations entre elles. Un seul exemple pour illustrer cela nous permet de discuter des modalités de couverture, de la protection de l'espace habité. On sait qu'à Pincevent le modèle théorique du Pr A. Leroi-Gourhan s'inspirait d'exemples ethno-graphiques. Il n'est cependant pas impossible que les différentes unités de Pincevent n'aient pas connu le même type de protection, pour peu qu'elles en aient connu une: au nord d'un foyer, une limite nette convexe des artefacts laissait penser avant remontage, qu'il avait existé une super-structure du type tente au-dessus ou légèrement décalée du foyer. En tissant des liens "permanents" entre une zone qui aurait été alors intérieure et une zone extérieure, les remontages montrent que l'hypothèse de la tente n'est pas valide pour cette unité particulière. L'hypothèse qui convient le mieux pour cet exemple est la présence d'une ou plusieurs peaux directement posées sur le sol et dont le négatif est encore visible après enlèvement par les magdaléniens ou destruction. Sinon, comment expliquer la multiplicité de ces circulations alors qu'une paroi dressée les aurait largement compromises?

L'étape ultérieure d'analyse spatiale est lorsque l'on peut mettre du sens derrière ces déplacements. Sur un autre exemple, on voit en effet le mouvement des tailleurs au sein d'une même unité montrant en cela qu'à un seul bloc peuvent correspondre plusieurs postes de taille et zones de rejet. Ceux-ci peuvent résulter du déplacement d'un seul individu mais être également liés à la reprise par un second tailleur d'un bloc précédemment abandonné. Le changement d'individu se notera alors par une différence de traitement dans la taille du bloc, le plus souvent par une péjoration de la qualité, qui montre que le nucléus a été récupéré après une première exploitation par un tailleur moins performant.

A une échelle plus importante on peut suivre le déplacement des artefacts lithiques au sein d'une partie du campement. La mise en évidence de circulations de lames, de lamelles beaucoup plus exceptionnellement d'éclats entre différentes unités proches dans l'espace pose différentes questions en fonction de la nature des objets qui ont circulé, de leur quantité et de l'existence ou non d'une double circulation.

Prenons l'exemple d'un autre foyer de Pincevent dont le caractère annexe est mis en avance par sa faible structuration et sa faible durée d'utilisation. Les remontages montrent que le lieu apparaît comme un centre éphémère de production de lames destinées à un usage extérieur vers d'autres unités. Seuls deux blocs y ont été débités essentiellement pour une production de lames. La presque totalité de ces deux productions est utilisée à l'extérieur vers des unités proches. Des absences significatives dans les remontages de ces deux blocs démontrent pour le moins que certains supports ont connu un déplacement plus lointain dans ou à l'extérieur du gisement (posons nous simplement la question de savoir avec quoi les magdaléniens découpaient-ils en premier dégrossissage, les rennes sur les lieux d'abattage?). Cet exemple illustre clairement un des aspects de l'organisation d'un campement magdalénien. La structuration plus ou moins forte des foyers, le nombre de vidanges, la quantité de vestiges abandonnés nous donnent une idée de l'importance de l'unité et de son rôle plus ou moins prépondérant dans le campement. Les remontages tissent des liens de contemporanéité, de dépendances, de voisinage entre ces unités plus ou moins proches, montrant avec cet exemple qu'installé à proximité d'unité plus pérenne, il existe des foyers dits satellites à vocation purement technique, destinés dans le cas qui nous occupe ici à procurer des supports à une partie du campement.

L'exemple suivant agrandit la maille spatiale et va nous permettre, tout en concluant d'aborder le dernier intérêt des remontages à Pincevent, l'aspect chronologique, celui de la démonstration de la contemporanéité entre les différentes structures découvertes sur le même lit d'inondation: Ici un foyer très structuré et de nombreuses fois utilisé a accueilli quelques activités qui se sont appuyées sur des outils, produits ou non localement. L'essentiel de son activité de taille (2 ou 3 blocs au maximum) a pour vocation d'approvisionner le reste du campement: les plus beaux supports acquis de l'un des meilleurs débitages du campement ont été exportés vers au moins 3 unités distantes de plusieurs mètres voire plusieurs dizaines de mètres. Cette relation n'est pas à sens unique puisque des supports débités à l'extérieur sont venus également approvisionner cette unité.

Cela signifie que des tailleurs parmi les meilleurs du campement peuvent être amenés à tailler pour le groupe. Sans parler véritablement de spécialistes, on peut penser que la reconnaissance par le groupe d'une capacité à tailler d'un individu, capacité que les autres n'ont pas, incline ce dernier à alimenter le campement en supports de meilleure qualité. Nous frôlons ici le domaine des relations sociales sans pouvoir toutefois plus en dire. D'autres remontages montrent qu'il n'y a pas que les spécialistes qui se déplacent sur de longues distances. Un autre exemple concerne un bloc débité dans un premier temps de façon médiocre dans une unité et retrouvé dans une seconde unité, trente mètres plus loin, où il est également débité de façon médiocre. Les façons de faire dans les deux endroits sont les mêmes, les outils obtenus de ce bloc dans les deux unités sont les mêmes: ceci nous incite à penser que c'est l'individu qui s'est déplacé et non pas uniquement ses produits, ce qui tisse ainsi des liens très forts de contemporanéité entre les deux unités impliquées.

Du particulier nous passons au général. En fait c'est à partir de l'ensemble de ces liaisons que nous sautons de l'histoire individuelle à la vie du groupe. Dans la mesure où les circulations bi-directionnelles de produits lithiques sont multiples et variées à l'intérieur du campement, on peut considérer enfin, et ça n'est pas le moindre intérêt des remontages à Pincevent, que l'ensemble des unités découvertes sur le même lit d'inondation sont contemporaines. La démonstration tangible de cette contemporanéité fait que l'on peut parler pour la première fois d'un véritable campement de chasseurs magdaléniens. En effet, les remontages unidirectionnels ne démontraient nullement la contemporanéité de deux structures et il avait même été dit à propos des pierres de foyers remontées entre deux locus qu'elles matérialisaient un emprunt fait auprès d'un foyer abandonné par de nouveaux arrivants sur le site, soucieux de construire une nouvelle structure de combustion. Cette interprétation n'est plus valide actuellement pour le niveau IV20 de Pincevent où les remontages de silex, de pierres mais aussi d'os sont multiples et où ils témoignent tous d'une étroite symbiose entre l'ensemble des unités, traduisant sans doute des relations de voisinage, de parenté, de complémentarité.

Un petit clin d'œil pour finir ce texte: nous venons de parler ici de relations entre unités à l'intérieur d'un campement. Une échelle d'analyse spatiale plus large nous intéresse désormais même si nous sommes conscient des difficultés que son approche suscite. Il s'agit de l'échelle territoriale. De la même façon que les magdaléniens de Pincevent sont arrivés sur le site avec des supports prêts à être utilisés, ils ont emporté avec eux, vers leur prochain campement quelques lames et lamelles retouchées provenant de Pincevent. Suivant l'excellent travail de raccord de Marie-Isabelle Catin entre les sites magdaléniens de Monruz et Champréveyres en Suisse (Cattin 1992), peut-être établirons-nous un jour des relations physiques entre Pincevent et les nombreux gisements contemporains que nous connaissons maintenant dans le Bassin parisien.

BIBLIOGRAPHIE

BAFFIER D., S. BEYRIES & P. BODU 1991 Histoire d'ocre à Pincevent: la question des lames ocrées. In *Rencontres Internationales d'Archéologie et d'Histoire d'Antibes. 25 ans d'Etudes technologiques. Bilan et perspectives*, pp. 215-234.

BODU P. 1990 L'application de la méthode des remontages à l'étude du matériel lithique des premiers niveaux châtelperroniens de la grotte du Renne à Arcy-sur-Cure (Yonne). In *Paléolithique moyen récent et Paléolithique supérieur ancien en Europe. Colloque internationale de Nemours. 1988, Mémoires du Musée de préhistoire d'Ile-de-France, 3*, pp. 309-312.

BODU P. 1991 Pincevent, site magdalénien. Les premiers chasseurs dans la vallée de la Seine. *Les Dossiers d'Archéologie* 164, pp. 60-67.

BODU P. 1994 Analyse typo-technologique du matériel lithique de quelques unités du site magdalénien de Pincevent (Seine-et-Marne): applications spatiales, économiques et sociales. Thèse de Doctorat, Université de Paris I, Sorbonne.

BODU P. 1996 Les chasseurs magdaléniens de Pincevent; quelques aspects de leurs comportements. *Lithic Technology* 21: 48-70.

BODU P., V. DELOZE, V. KRIER, J.L. LOCHT, P. DEPAEPE & E. TEHEUX 1999 Un gisement du Paléolithique supérieur sur la commune de Lailly-Le Domaine de Beauregard (Yonne). In *Occupations du Paléolithique supérieur dans le sud-est du Bassin parisien*, M. Julien & J.-L. Rieu (eds.), Paris, Documents d'Archéologie Française, 78, pp. 162-195.

BODU P., C. KARLIN & S. PLOUX 1990 Who's Who? The Magdalenian Flint Knappers of Pincevent. In *The big puzzle. International symposium on refitting stone artefacts*, E. CZIESLA, S. EICKHOFF, N. ARTS & D. WINTER (eds.). Holos, Bonn, pp. 143-163.

BON F. & P. BODU 2002 Analyse technologique du débitage aurignacien. In *L'Aurignacien de la grotte du Renne. XXXIVe supplément à Gallia Préhistoire. B. Schmider (ed.), pp. 115-133.
BORDES, J.-G. 2000 La séquence aurignacienne de Caminade revisitée: l'apport des raccords d'intérêts stratigraphique. *Paléo* 12: 387-408.

CAHEN D., C. KARLIN, L.-H. KEELEY, & F.-L. VAN NOTEN 1980 Méthode d'analyse technique, spatiale et fonctionnelle d'ensembles lithiques. *Helinium* 20: 209-259.

CATTIN M.-I. 1992 Un raccord entre deux sites magdaléniens. *Revue de Préhistoire Européenne* 1: 35-42.

JULIEN M., C. KARLIN & P. BODU 1987 Pincevent: où en est le modèle théorique aujourd'hui? *Bulletin de la Société Préhistorique Française* 84 (10-12): 335-362.

KARLIN C., P. BODU & J. PELEGRIN 1991 Processus techniques et chaînes opératoires: comment les préhistoriens s'approprient un concept mis au point par les ethnologues. In *Observer l'action technique. Des chaînes opératoires, pour quoi faire?* H. Balfet (ed.), C.N.R.S., pp. 101-117.

KLARIC L., T. AUBRY & B. WALTER 2002 Un nouveau type d'armature en contexte gravettien et son mode de production sur les burins du Raysse (La Picardie, commune de Preuilly-sur-Claise, Indre-et-Loire). *Bulletin de la Société Préhistorique Française* 99(4): 751-764.

LEROI-GOURHAN A. & M. BRÉZILLON 1966 L'habitation magdalénienne n°1 de Pincevent près Montereau (Seine-et-Marne). *Gallia-Préhistoire* 9(2): 263-385.

LEROI-GOURHAN A. & M. BRÉZILLON 1972 *Fouilles de Pincevent: Essai d'analyse ethnographique d'un habitat magdalénien (la section 36), VIIe supplément à Gallia-préhistoire.*

PIGEOT N. 1987 *Magdalénien d'Etiolles , Economie de débitage et organisation sociale (l'unité d'habitation U5). XVe supplément à Gallia Préhistoire.*

PLOUX S. 1989 Approche archéologique de la variabilité des comportements techniques individuels. Les tailleurs de l'unité 27-M 89 de Pincevent. Thèse de préhistoire, Université de Paris X, Nanterre.

PLOUX S., C. KARLIN & P. BODU 1991 d'une chaîne l'autre: normes et variations dans le débitage laminaire magdalénien. In *Préhistoire et Ethnologie. Le geste retrouvé. (Techniques et Cultures 17-18)*, editions de la Maison des Sciences de l'Homme, pp. 81-114.

SCHMIDER. B. (ed.) - 2002 - *L'Aurignacien de la grotte du Renne*. XXXIVe supplément à Gallia Préhistoire.

Address of the author:

Pierre BODU
UMR 7041, ARSCAN, MAE.
21 allée de l'Université.
92023. Nanterre cedex
France

bodu@mae.u-paris10.fr

BENEFITING FROM REFITTING IN INTRA-SITE ANALYSIS: LESSONS FROM REKEM (BELGIUM)

Marc DE BIE

Abstract

The procedure of refitting is most beneficial when it is fully embedded in an integrated research program. Refitting can help to entangle a wide variety of research topics often also touched upon by other research methods such as petrography, attribute analysis, and usewear. The late Palaeolithic site of Rekem serves as a case study in this respect. The lithic material from this large camp site offers excellent refitting potential (some 2500 artefacts are conjoined), allowing for a detailed study of reduction strategies and spatial distributions. With regard to lithic technology, the refitting data provide better insights into both reduction methods and knapping styles as well as into the processes of tool manufacture, use, maintenance and discard. Derived from these data, the method also contributes to the study of social aspects (skills of the artisans) and economic features (the material 'output' of the various sequences and its role in further activities). On a spatial scale the results of refitting can be used to measure the degree of vertical dispersal and to assess the disturbance on the site by natural post-depositional processes. Most importantly, however, the mapping of refits supplies insight into the horizontal patterning of human activities both in and between the various loci of the site. At Rekem, such patterning shows the relationship between manufacturing process and artefact discard and elucidates the transport patterns of various kinds of artefacts and tool types.

Résumé

Pour être au plus rentable, une analyse de remontages doit intégralement s'inscrire dans un vaste programme de recherche. Ces remontages peuvent alors contribuer à une série de questions de recherche qui elles-mêmes font l'objet d'analyses spécifiques telles que la pétrographie, l'analyse des attributs, la tracéologie, etc. L'étude du site Paléolithique final de Rekem peut servir comme d'exemple de pareils cas. Le matériel lithique de ce vaste campement a offert d'excellentes possibilités de remontage (environ 2500 artefacts de remontés), ce qui a permis une étude en profondeur de stratégies de réduction et de distributions spatiales. En ce qui concerne la technologie lithique, les remontages ont apporté une meilleure compréhension des méthodes de réduction et des styles de débitage, mais aussi de processus de façonnage, d'utilisation, d'entretien et d'abandon des outils. Sur la base de ces données, la méthode nous a également renseigné sur des aspects sociaux (savoir-faire des artisans) et économiques (le rendement matériel des différents séquences et leur rôle dans les activités). Sur le plan spatial, les résultats des remontages pouvaient être utilisés pour mesurer le degré de dispersion verticale des artéfacts et pour évaluer la perturbation sur le site des processus naturels post-dépositionnels. Finalement, la cartographie des remontages s'est avérée instructive sur l'organisation spatiale des activités dans et entre les différentes zones du site. A Rekem, cette analyse spatiale en outre a démontré une relation entre les processus de production et d'abandon des artéfacts et a révélé des modèles de transport pour les différentes catégories d'artéfacts et d'outils.

INTRODUCTION

The principal goal of this paper is not to offer new evidence of actual refitting work, but merely to reflect on limits, merits and benefits of this procedure, based on extensive refitting experience. The fully published analysis of the late Palaeolithic camp site of Rekem (De Bie & Caspar 2000) serves as an example.

In fact, since the pioneering work in the 1970's and 1980's (Leroi-Gourhan & Brézillon 1972, Cahen 1976, 1978, Bordes 1980, Villa 1982, Cziesla 1986), lithic refitting has become a standard procedure in many site reports, essentially contributing to two major research topics: lithic technology and spatial analysis. In NW-Europe, both aspects are well-studied at Late Palaeolithic open air sites in France (e.g. Pincevent, Etiolles, Marsangy, Verberie, Rueil-Malmaison; Leroi-Gourhan & Brézillon 1972, Audouze et al. 1981, Pigeot 1987, Ploux 1989, Schmider n.d., Bodu 1994, 1995), Germany (e.g. Andernach, Gönnersdorf, Niederbieber; Bosinski & Hahn 1972, Eickhoff 1990, Bolus 1992), Great-Britain (e.g. Hengistbury Head; Barton 1992), the Netherlands (e.g. Oldeholtwolde; Johansen & Stapert 2004) and Belgium (e.g. Meer, Orp; Cahen 1978, Vermeersch et al. 1987). That the technique is beneficial does not need to be proven anymore. But while the value of refitting has become obvious to most prehistorians, we believe its capacity is only rarely benefited from to its full potential. In our view, the procedure of refitting is actually most compelling when fully embedded in an extensive research program, especially within the context of an intra-site analysis. In that case, refitting can help to entangle a wide variety of research topics, including lithic technology and spatial patterning, but also aspects such as tool use, style, and typology. These aspects are generally studied with specific methods (e.g. attribute analysis, mapping, and usewear analysis). We believe these should not operate in isolation. An intra-site analysis in our view is most rewarding in a network of intermingling part-studies, steadily inquiring and stimulating each other (Figure 1). Working on one aspect of the study provokes research questions to be dealt with from a different angle. In the end, this process generates a detailed picture of the

other stones, in all about 25.000 pieces. A group of 12 artefact concentrations in the central area of the excavations, called habitation zone 1, presents a particular layout. A range of larger sites in this zone is aligned along a western line, while a series of smaller scatters occurs in the East (De Bie & Caspar 2000).

The combined research results depict the Late Palaeolithic settlement at Rekem as a relatively large

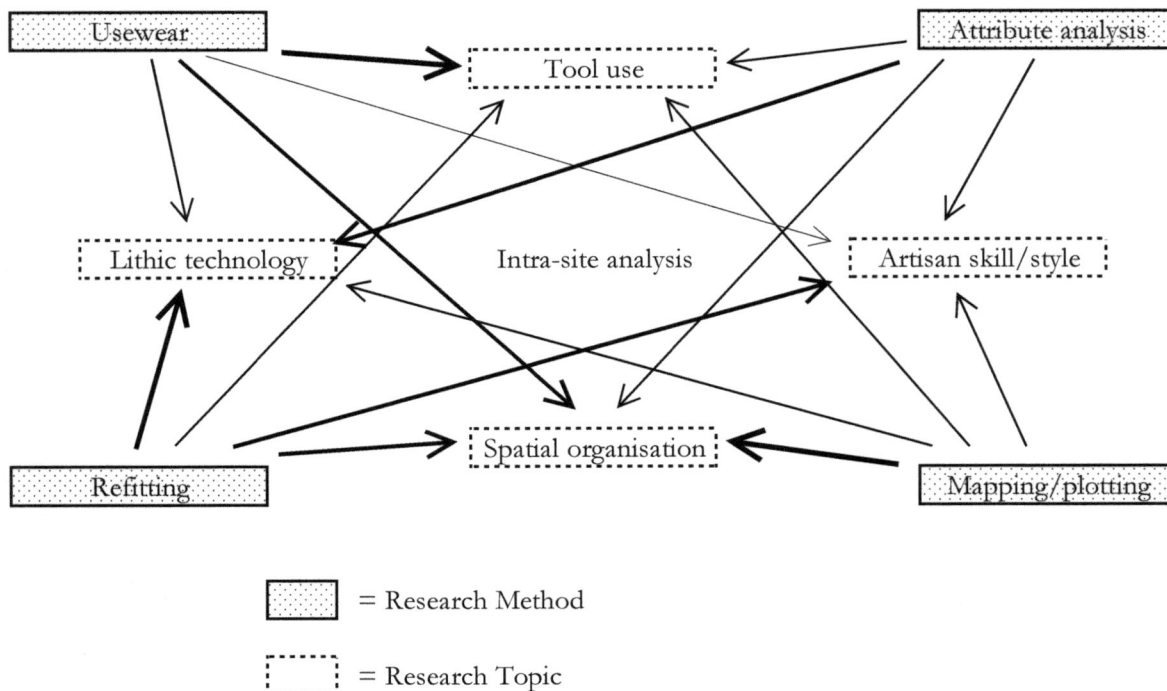

Figure 1 *Model of integrated research strategy for intra-site analysis, as adopted at Rekem. Heavier arrows reflect more important contribution. Input: record of lithic material. Output: insight into sequence of human activities in Late Palaeolithic camp.*

variety of human handling, and eventually sheds light on social organisation and/or ritual behaviour in a hunter-gatherer settlement.

In this paper, we provide various examples of the contribution of refitting in such an approach. First, however, we present the site of Rekem and the picture we were able to gain after such extensive site analysis.

REKEM

The Late Upper Palaeolithic *Federmesser* site of Rekem, Belgium, dates to about 13.500 years ago. Over an area of 1.7 ha on a sand dune along the river Meuse, 16 distinct concentrations of artefacts were recorded. Apart from some rare resin glue attached to a projectile point, scraps of charcoal, and fragments of red ochre, the site delivered exclusively lithic material, mainly flint, but also

camp area with, on the one hand, widely spaced settlement units representing residential areas where a sequence of processing and maintenance activities occurred and, on the other hand, some isolated knapping spots, either reserved for tool manufacture, or else lacking tool-production altogether (Figure 2).

For instance, the manufacturing of projectile points occurred in small knapping spots. At such tool production places, the spatial layout of the flint working process perfectly corresponds with parallels from knapping experiments and ethnoarchaeological contexts. Disposal of used projectile points, on the other hand, took place at the larger residential areas. Here, the topographical location of used projectile points, depends on their state of fragmentation. Short basal fragments were pressed out of the shaft adhesive and dropped near the hearth area, while longer specimens were pulled out and thrown to the periphery (Caspar & De Bie 1996).

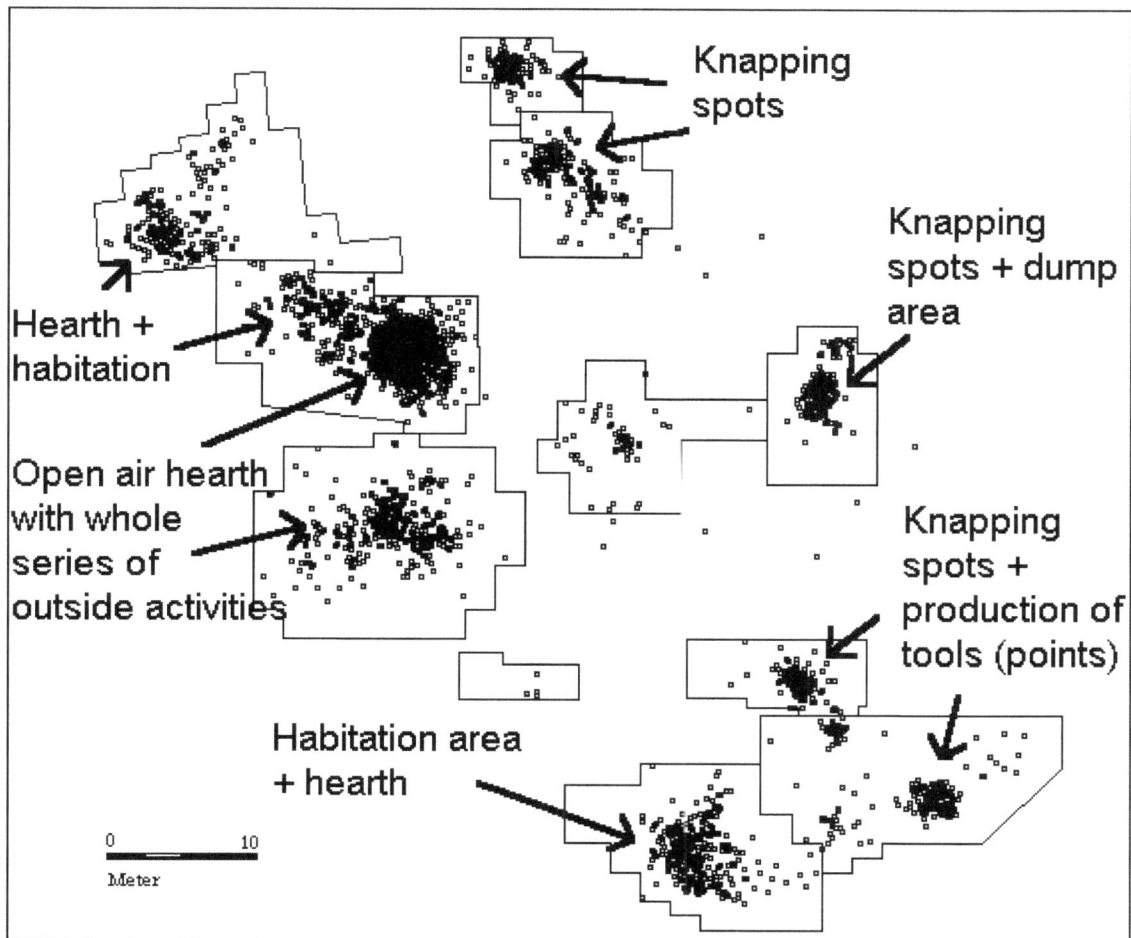

Figure 2 *General interpretation of Rekem Habitation zone 1.*

In these large and dense concentrations, the hearth area seems to have attracted a sequence of activities related to the procurement of game (maintenance of hunting gear), butchering and food processing activities, hide fleshing and dehairing, dry hide working, and various aspects of bone or antler work. Notwithstanding this amalgamation of refuse-producing activities in a single place, each performance appears to have preserved specific intra-locus spatial patterning. With regard to the scrapers, for instance, the location of the scraping activity and the organisation of manufacture and resharpening, varied according to the physical state of the hides at the time of working. Fresh hide scraping and dry hide work occurred in separate areas at each side of the hearth. In the case of dry hide work, the production and resharpening of the scrapers was moreover spatially segregated from the scraping activity, presumably to avoid depositing retouch waste on the hide located outside the main concentration.

In short, the site is organised into more or less distinctive activity or disposal areas to such an extent that the ultimate content of each site sector is different. In the following sections, we would like to highlight the key role of refitting in the emergence of these insights.

REFITTING RESULTS AT REKEM

The lithic material at Rekem offers excellent refitting potential. The refitting program took several years, but was repeatedly interrupted. Unfortunately, there has been no systematic recording of the time invested in this operation and we are not able to accurately recalculate the man hours involved. It is also obvious that more work can be done, but the actual state of the database is presumably a good representation of all potential conjoinments on both flint and other rocks.

3.1. ROCKS

In this paper, we do not profoundly discuss the refitting results of the non-flint stones (as sandstones, quartzes, and quartzite). These so-called 'rocks', essentially confined to the large concentrations, were intensely employed as structural elements, in hearths or dwellings. They are mostly burned. Many also show intentionally trimmed edges and seem to have functioned as individual tools. The fragmentation of the non-flint rock remains is generally intense. The refitting results show that they were an extremely mobile class of objects, travelling both within and between different loci.

In contrast to the refitting of the flint artefacts, the refitting of the rock remains can generally be considered as more or less exhaustive. The physical variation between these remains is usually sufficient to allow the quick recognition of related fragments. The inclusion of all the small fragments into the refitting objective, however, is often not only unrealistic, in some instances the refitting of certain rock debris also has limited interpretative value (e.g. the small debris of burnt quartzes). Still, at Rekem, refit quota of rocks are quite high (i.e. from 54% to 64%) in the large residential areas. Far fewer fragments could be refitted at most of the small loci, where the fragments seem either to have been imported as such, or are the result of trimming, assuming that the rock tools were subsequently removed.

3.2. FLINT

With regard to the flint artefacts, at Rekem habitation zone 1, 521 refitting groups, totalling 2311 artefacts could be realised. In proportion to the total inventory (and excluding the small chips), the refitting artefacts represent 21% of the entire flint assemblage of habitation zone 1. Some 82% of the refitting artefacts are involved in debitage refits, sometimes combined with a fracture conjoinment (14%), a tooling refit (3%), or, exceptionally, both. Simple tooling refits represent 6%; 11% of the refitting artefacts are connected in a break only. The achievements of the refitting work have not been equally successful at the various loci. The refitting rates range from 13% (at *locus* 6) to 63% (at *locus* 15).

In terms of artefact types, the best results are gained for debris (93% has been refitted), and cores (59%). Good scores are also obtained for edge-damaged pieces (43%), tooling waste products (35%), and core rejuvenation products (33%). Still above average are the refitting results for the tools (24%), but there are major differences among the various tool types, ranging from 10% for projectile points to 41% for burins. While dominating the refits in absolute numbers, only 18% of the entire population of blade(let)s and (laminar) flakes could be conjoined.

The precise significance of this quantitative divergence is not obvious. For instance, 'simple' flakes and blade(let)s, without distinctive features, are generally not easily refitable. Conversely, tools may have received preferential treatment during the refitting process: while this was not consciously intended, tools are looked at more often (typology, microwear), and may thus eventually have a better chance of being recognised and refitted.

Despite the fact that the results may thus to a certain degree be an artefact of the refitting process itself, the variety in refitting rates for different tool types, for instance, strongly indicates that this variation must also have a systemic meaning. In this scenario then, refits even help us better evaluate the etic categories we have constructed and through which we try to understand the dynamic processes in the past. In the following, we address some other major contributions of refitting to various research topics.

THE CONTRIBUTIONS OF REFITTING TO TECHNOLOGICAL ANALYSES

The merits of refitting as a heuristic tool in studies of lithic technology have since long been recognised and acknowledged (Cahen *et al.* 1980, Cziesla *et al.* 1990, Julien 1992). At Rekem, even an advanced techno-morphological analysis of knapping waste alone, would have rendered a limited and sometimes even inadequate picture of the debitage technology. This is particularly well illustrated by the confrontation of the detailed techno-morphological analysis of the cores with the dynamic analysis of the refitted sequences. In fact, the information obtained from a static analysis of the knapping waste on the one hand, and from refitting on the other, may be even more divergent in a lithic assemblage that has an extremely flexible debitage (like at Rekem) than in an industry with a more strictly organised, recurrent and uniform technology (like for instance in the Magdalenian).

First of all, size, morphology, and quality of the original nodules selected for exploitation, and the degree of their reduction, can hardly be reconstructed without refitting. At Rekem these features appear to be highly variable. It seems that the *Federmeser* people were not too much concerned with real 'selection' procedures, but rather exploited a wide range of raw materials, an observation that contrasts significantly with the strategy adopted by former Magdalenian groups nearby, who intentionally searched for large good quality flint nodules.

Second, refitting brought to light the observation that - except in case of rapid abandonment - the technical attributes of the cores do not necessarily reveal the actual manufacturing process applied. The initial shaping of the cores in particular is often obliterated by posterior reduction, as successive stages of the knapping sequence by nature remove traces of earlier exploitation. Evidence of lateral trimming, for instance, frequently observed in the refitted sequences, was repeatedly erased from the abandoned core, by the posterior laminar exploitation of the flanks. The initial position of a crest on the core table (central or close to one of the edges), as well as its actual role in the sequence (e.g. displacement of 'natural' ridge, correction of flaking accidents etc.) can also only be reconstructed from the refitting analysis. Major divergences can equally be observed between the morphologically defined rejuvenation products, and the actual role they played in the reduction sequence. For example, not all flakes of a platform preparation procedure necessarily correspond with morphologically defined tabular flakes. The information where exactly flakes belong within a reduction process, can thus not be read correctly from an inventory table. Only re-fitting it into its original context can provide information about the provenance, its contribution to the reduction process, and thus the original technological significance.

Also the character of the 'full debitage', however, can often not be reconstructed from the appearance of the abandoned core alone. The direction(s) of exploitation, for instance, can hardly be adequately inferred from the negative removals on the core tables or from the number of preserved striking platforms. In fact, refitting shows that the knapping direction repeatedly changed in the course of the reduction sequence, often without leaving any traces on the discarded core. It is obvious that only the act of refitting can highlight factors such as the rhythm of these changes, the actual output of single laminar generations and the precise successions of the various stages of the reduction sequence.

The type of production also cannot always be accurately inferred from the core table. For instance, the gradual reduction of 'blade cores' results in an over-emphasis of abandoned core tables with traces of bladelet production.

Another aspect where only refitting can help to gain insights, concerns the productivity of the reduction sequences, not only the output in absolute terms (i.e. all artefacts produced in each production sequence), but also the real productivity of the sequence, in terms of serviceable 'economic' output. This can be estimated by listing the refitted tools, 'adequate' blanks and, if such is the case, artefacts with traces of use-wear. Various refits reveal a serial production of one tool type, sometimes with a certain tendency towards the 'monopolisation' of blanks from reduction sequences. For instance, 33 burins could be refitted with at least one other burin in the same refit-set. On the other hand, there is plenty evidence for the association of burins with other tool types in a single conjoinment. Sometimes, the functional analysis then shows that diverse tools from such compositions were employed in a similar task.

The causes for the abandonment of a knapping sequence, as inferred from the core analysis, can equally be fine-tuned by the refitting results. It appears, for instance, that the plunging of blanks on the core table did not automatically lead to the rejection of a core, as knappers occasionally took advantage of the additional convexity created by heavy overpassing, or started exploiting the opposite side of the core. On the other hand, the hinging

of flakes is confirmed as a cause of discard, as is the absence of useful ridges on globular cores.

Finally, refitting certainly contributes to a general evaluation of the 'quality of knapping' at Rekem. This evaluation can be made through an assessment of various quantitative and qualitative aspects of the reduction processes, such as raw material selection, the shaping of the core, the general organisation and standardisation of the knapping process, the emergence of flaking accidents and possible corrections, the stage of core abandonment, the quantity, quality and size of the output, and so on.

Our initial goal in this assessment was to build a database that would allow us to distinguish a range of technical levels and possibly relate these with the knapping skills of individual artisans as, for example, demonstrated for Magdalenian assemblages of the Paris basin (Pigeot 1987; Ploux 1989). However, in the course of this exercise at Rekem, we realised that several criteria used in this assessment are in fact quite ambiguous. The intensive preparation and rejuvenation of the striking platform, for instance, on the one hand could point at an advanced level of technical know-how while, on the other hand, it could equally refer to a knapper who failed to execute an efficient, economic laminar production without constant renewal of the platform (and thus unfavourable reduction of the core table length). With regard to the quality of the raw material selection, it is obvious that poor selection does not necessarily have to be ascribed to inexperienced knappers. In fact, small, irregularly shaped stones could perhaps only be exploited by competent knappers, and only with a 'simple' reduction strategy. Since such ambiguity can be revealed for many of the criteria used to establish the 'quality' of knapping, this aspect of the analysis should be treated with some caution. We merely intend to open the 'knapping skill debate' with regard to the Federmesser industries.

In short, numerous refits at Rekem provide pertinent evidence and help in establishing a fine-grained picture of the technology. The lithic industry is characterised by a poorly elaborated blade technology, aiming at the production of short unstandardised blades and laminar flakes using direct hard hammer percussion. Flint knappers exploited a wide range of stones, in terms of quality, size, and morphology and clearly possessed divergent levels of technical skill. Whatever the initial form of the stone, the artisans always tried to take advantage of its appearance in a most profitable way. The output of this flexible procedure was extremely versatile, both in terms of quality (unstandardised products), and in quantitative terms, ranging from half of the core volume being exploited, to a reduction index of 90 %. While a production of 100 blanks seems to have been a maximum output, reduction processes generated on average some 50 items. In spite of the overall basic level of technical expertise, and the apparent lack of rigid procedural templates, the artisans at Rekem clearly possessed a divergent level of technical skills. Still, although possible social aspects in terms of specialisation and correlated apprenticeship may have guided flint knapping, it seems to have been a fairly elementary practice, of domestic rather than of prestige character.

THE CONTRIBUITION OF REFITTING TO UNDERSTANDING LITHIC 'CONSUMPTION': TOOL DESIGN AND TOOL USE

Within the context of a habitation site, it may be postulated that flint knapping primarily serves to generate blanks destined for tooling and/or use. It is therefore interesting to find out what blanks were desired for tooling or use, or, in other words, what 'endproducts' were intended to result from the knapping process. Answering this question is not as easy as it may seem. In fact, tool-fabrication by definition implies the modification of a blank. To some extent, these modification processes always obliterate the true dimensions of the original blanks. The more a tool is used and resharpened, the less evidence it will retain of the original nature of its blank. Whether a short endscraper was initially made on a flake, a laminar flake or a blade is often hard to define from the tool itself, found as an abandoned specimen.

Refitting can help here in the following circumstances: 1) refitting of (re)sharpening flakes (and fragments) can occasionally lead to a reconstruction of the original blank (at Rekem, this was only possible with burins); or 2) refitting of the tool in its original position in the reduction sequence can make its initial form visible on the negative removals of the 'neighbour' blanks (this was possible with all tool categories). The results for Rekem are shown in Figure 3.

In dimensional terms, more than two thirds of these tools (40/56) appear to be made on blades (L>2W), a ratio that is not at all compatible with the general artefact inventory. Altogether, the refitted reduction sequences show that, on average, nearly 1 blade out of 4 was modified into a tool, while less then 1 flake out of 12 was selected for tool production. So-called laminar flakes are situated in between, but tend towards the blades. These differences must not be ascribed to the refitters' impact, as refit rates for flakes and blades are on the whole quite similar. Therefore, the results can truly be seen as a reflection of the actual choices made by the toolmakers.

However, differences appear when the tool types are considered separately. Though the number of reconstructed blanks of backed pieces is limited, an outspoken preference for narrow blades (somewhere between 13mm and 18mm wide, and 40mm to 60mm

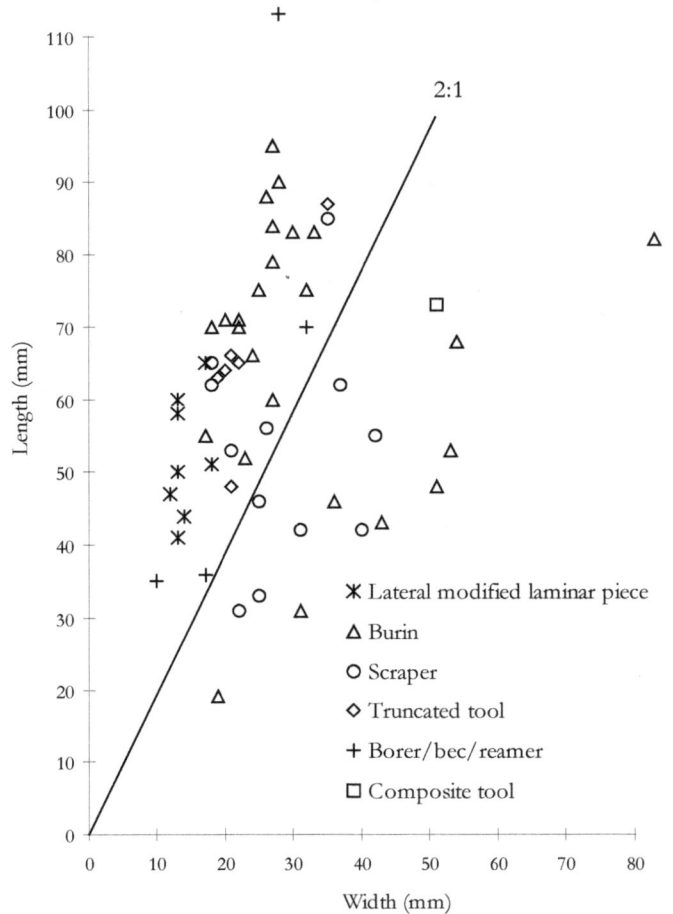

Figure 3 *Rekem 1984-86. Dimensions of original blanks of various tool types, reconstructed by refitting.*

long) seems to exist. Burins are also preferentially made on blades (17/25), though certainly not exclusively. Burin blanks are mainly characterised by their large size. Scrapers, to the contrary, appear to be made on flakes (7) rather then on blades (5). The other tool types are only minimally represented. On the whole, the refitting work reveals that while a preference exists for laminar elements, selection criteria are not rigidly adopted when blanks are chosen for tooling. Several examples in fact reveal a choice of quite irregular blanks or thick cortical pieces for modification, whereas more 'regular' blanks from the same reduction sequence are sometimes ignored.

The extensive refitting results, in combination with a detailed techno-morphological examination of all tools and their waste products and with systematic use-wear analyses, shed light on the use-lives (i.e. stages of manufacture, repair, use and discard) of various types of tools at Rekem in a dynamic approach, allowing us to address questions as: How do the tool-types 'emerge'? What processes of shaping, modification, and use affect and 'create' them during their 'active life'? Why are they eventually discarded? The 'active life' or 'biography' refers to the time-span when these tools are 'conceived' (created) and 'consumed' (used and (re)modified) in the systemic context. An accurate assessment of these manipulations may lead to a more acute cognition of tools. We give two examples to illustrate this point.

BURINS

Burins in their 'final form', frequently preserve remnants of earlier features, testifying to some of the transformations that occurred in the course of their biographies. In most cases, however, the tools as such do not allow for a complete reconstruction of a former state. For such information, one has to fall back on the refits again.

At Rekem, the refitting of burins with tool waste (principally spalls) and with fragments of their blanks, allows for a detailed examination of the processes related to the fabrication, use, and the 'consumption' of these tools. In all, 66 burins, or more than one quarter of the items from habitation zone 1, could be conjoined with at least 1 burin spall, implying a total number of 95 spalls. In 9 cases this even led to the physical reconstruction of the original blank. In all, 124 previously unknown phases of the burins' biographies before final discard could be illustrated. This calculation only comprises the physically reconstructed evidence, and does not take into account the numerous phases that can be perceived as 'negative' information in these reconstructions. In fact, more than 10 phases can sometimes be reproduced for a single tool if such 'negative evidence' is equally included.

Firstly, the refits reveal the impact of the successive rejuvenations on the burin length (Figure 4). At Rekem, the mean length of the blanks is reduced by about 3 cm from the most completely reconstructed items to the ultimately abandoned tools. Certain dihedral and atypical Lacan burins have refitted spalls that show a deviation of about 2cm between the final burin phase and the proximal end of the refitted spall. If truncation and spall removal were employed accurately to refresh the worn burin ends, these tools potentially had a prolonged use-life.

Secondly, the reconstructed phases allow for an analysis of burin 'biographies' in great detail. The refitting of the burin spalls, retouch flakes and fragments confirms that burins are a very 'dynamic' category of tool indeed. In the course of the 'use-resharpening-reuse' cycles, they can frequently be classified as different 'types': 104 phases of the physically reconstructed burin biographies portray a 'new' burin edge and these reconstructions do not necessarily represent the same type of burin edge as those preserved on the discarded item. Eleven refitted phases of the tool biographies do not even belong to the burin category at all, but to a different tool class, especially becs. This "alliance" between burins and becs can probably be explained by the use of these tools on

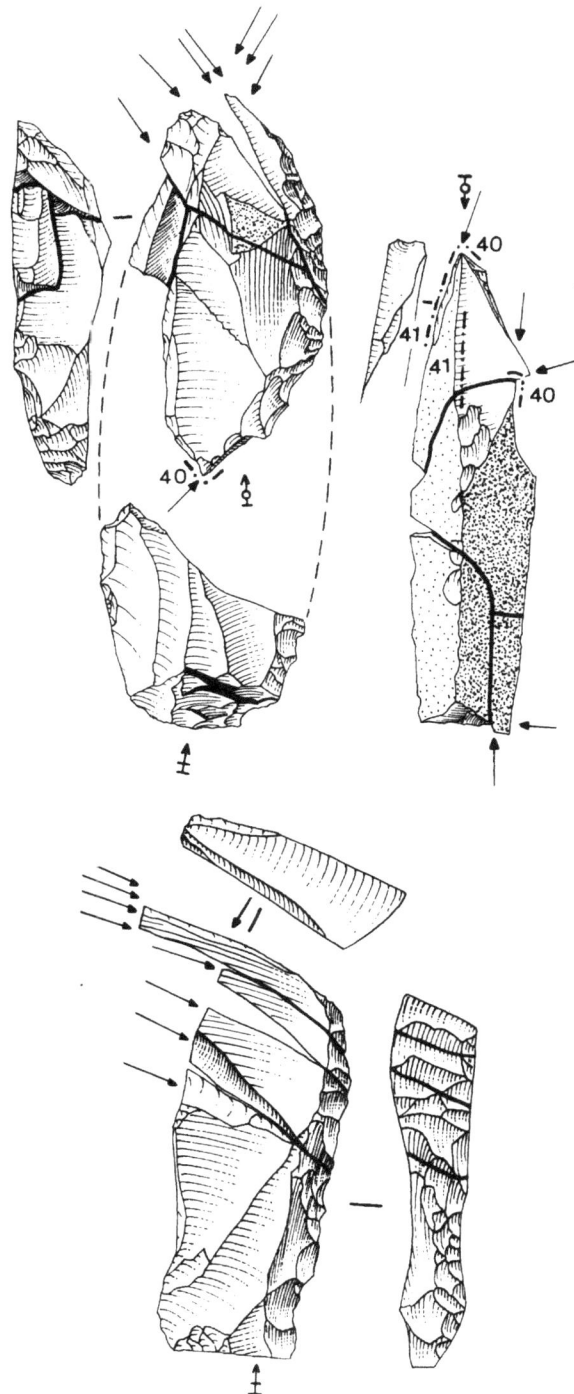

Figure 4 *Examples of burins refitted with tool waste at Rekem, revealing repeated transformation of the implements. Also note the significant decrease in size. Codes 40 and 41 refer to the presence of usewear traces generated by cutting or grooving on hard animal matter (bone or antler).*

37

similar contact material. The burin blow in some cases also serves as a useful technique to rejuvenate a bec.

The exploration of the 'evolution' of the burins thus illustrates that the actual form of these tools, in the sense of present-day typology, is largely determined by the precise moment of abandonment. That is, if one wants to explain variability in burin typology (rather than just describe it), one has to consider the question of why burins are actually discarded. Various converging causes contribute to the abandonment of burins. They mainly consist of an interplay of functional aptitudes (e.g. burin facet orthogonality, type of action), and technical modalities (i.e. rejuvenation opportunities). Other possible causes may also contribute. As the most obvious expedient tools at Rekem, burins are hardly curated (transported) or kept apart for successive tasks. Many, therefore, may be abandoned just because the task for which they are created is accomplished, or because the artisan leaves the working area for whatever reason, even if the burins are still potentially efficient or could be successfully rejuvenated.

The 'finished' form of the burins - in the typological sense – thus totally depends on the moment of abandonment and is frequently governed by 'exterior' reasons for their discard. The burin types at Rekem, therefore, do not reflect the consciousness of an artisan wishing to establish a preconceived form.

LATERALLY MODIFIED LAMINAR PIECES

A totally different pattern is observed regarding the fabrication and maintenance of laterally modified laminar pieces (LMP).

As mentioned earlier, refits show that the unmodified blanks selected for the fabrication of (slender) backed pieces are fairly standardised, and narrow blades rather than bladelets. It is only after modification of the entire edge (on average reducing the width of the original blades by about 3-4mm) that they become less than 12mm wide, and thus fall into the category of bladelets.

Due presumably to the high mobility of this tool class (as projectiles), only some 22 LMP are integrated into sequential refitting. Still, 3 loci especially (Rekem 1, 7, and 11), supply clear evidence of a serial production of LMP. In those cases, the 'finished elements' obviously left the area, and what remained are rejected pieces. Together, though, they provide at least an impression of the variability of type of tools generated during the LMP production process. At Rekem 7, for instance, a very specific flint nodule apparently served for the production of a range of LMP-types, all discarded on a very limited surface: 2 curved backed points, 1 rectilinear backed point, 1 obliquely truncated point, 2 backed bladelets, 2 fragments of a curved backed pointed blade, 1 rectilinear

backed pointed blade, 1 undulated backed pointed blade, and 4 backed blades or blades with marginal retouch. The fragments of these tools are all broken as a result of accidental breakage during retouching. Clearly, in a traditional typo-morphological approach, the variability observed in this series could have been easily explained as a mixture of various 'cultural traditions'.

The numerous point fragments and Krukowski microburins (accidental waste, produced involuntarily during the backing of points and bladelets), as well as the apical position of most trihedral points show how manufacturing the point-tip was a most delicate task and a frequent cause of fracture. Refitted pieces with a well-formed point-tip (rectilinear, bi-directional), and an incompletely backed lateral edge, suggest that creating the tip was also the first task. The special attention the point-tip received relates both to its fragility and its function as the missile's head.

As opposed to most other tool types, LMP were in general not subjected to "use-resharpening-reuse" cycles. They were designed to arm arrow shafts and then were normally abandoned when damaged as a result of their use. No use-wear traces have been found on Krukowski microburins that might suggest the retooling or resharpening of used missile points. On the whole, LMP can be regarded as implements that were generally only used once (or at most until they were damaged).

With regard to discard procedures, being arrow armatures, LMP are in the first place lost during the hunt, whereas base fragments may also be abandoned at the retooling areas in the residences. At the production places, however, LMP are either discarded as unfinished implements (when the 'appropriate design' could not be achieved any more, e.g. when the remnant part became too short or possibly too thick), or because of tooling accidents. In fact, at these loci, hardly any piece is abandoned in a 'finished' state (cf. above).

In conclusion, as opposed to most other tool types, LMP do generally not participate in "manufacture-use-rejuvenation-reuse" cycles. Throughout their entire use-life, these tools have to conform to more or less rigid schemes during the production and selection of blanks, as well as to particular design requirements during the shaping process. For instance, as arrow armatures hafted in a preconceived shaft, these tools must carefully respect criteria of efficacy regarding the penetrating potential of the point tip, the shape of the base, general outline, volume, and weight. Whenever the artisan fails to provide the future arrow armature with the necessary qualities, the project is given up. Flexibility in those cases is far more limited than in the production processes of other type of tools. It is obvious, again, that refitting plays a major role in recognising such patterns – if indeed the evidence is integrated in a much broader approach.

In short, whereas laterally modified laminar pieces are essentially 'designed tools', burins, as well as most other 'domestic tools' (scrapers, becs, composite tools), are primarily end-products of a use-rejuvenation process. They are 'transformation tools' in two ways: they are intensively transformed in the course of their use-lives and they serve to transform other materials (such as hide, bone, wood and stone). Their 'dynamic' character in a technological sense can be seen as a prolongation of the lithic reduction process that starts with the initial selection of the flint nodule and ends with the abandonment of exhausted, discarded implements. In a broad diachronic perspective, aspects of this entire process are constantly in evolution and therefore are characteristic of specific archaeological traditions. Refitting, in this perspective, also helps to deal with classical archaeological questions of culture history.

THE CONTRIBUTION OF REFITTING TO SPATIAL ANALYSIS

Whereas pioneers of the procedure have quickly realised that refitting can be extremely useful in spatial analysis, and while the integration has long since become a standard procedure, some comments on this topic may still be useful.

At Rekem, both the horizontal and vertical distribution of the artefacts was recorded in detail. Vertically, the artefacts were found scattered through a considerable depth of 40 to 70 cm. As artefacts from these variable depths could be conjoined (Figure 5), this vertical

distribution does not necessarily mean that the site had been occupied several times. Natural processes, such as burrowing animals and plant roots, displaced the abandoned tools from a single occupation vertically.

From a technical point of view, it is important to realise that refits can be mapped in many different ways and that the type of visualisation can have a considerable effect on the impression a reader gets from the maps (Figure 6). At Rekem, three major kinds of refit connections are distinguished on the maps (following Cziesla 1990): production sequences (debitage), modification sequences (resharpenings), and breaks. For debitage production sequences and tool modifications, arrows indicate the technological direction of the sequence from the outside to the inside, that is from the first flake removed to the abandoned core or from the first (re)sharpening flake (e.g. burin spall) to the final tool.

On earlier versions of the maps, we also indicated technological changes within the process, thus splitting the sequence into subsequences, corresponding with the major technological steps of the reduction process. It was hoped that these steps would also coincide with spatial moves. It soon became apparent, however, that in the (*Federmesser*) context at Rekem there is no indication at all for such correspondences and it was therefore decided to remove these additional signs on the final maps, in order to keep the maps legible. In other contexts, however, such additional information might of course be useful.

A production sequence line on the maps may in fact be

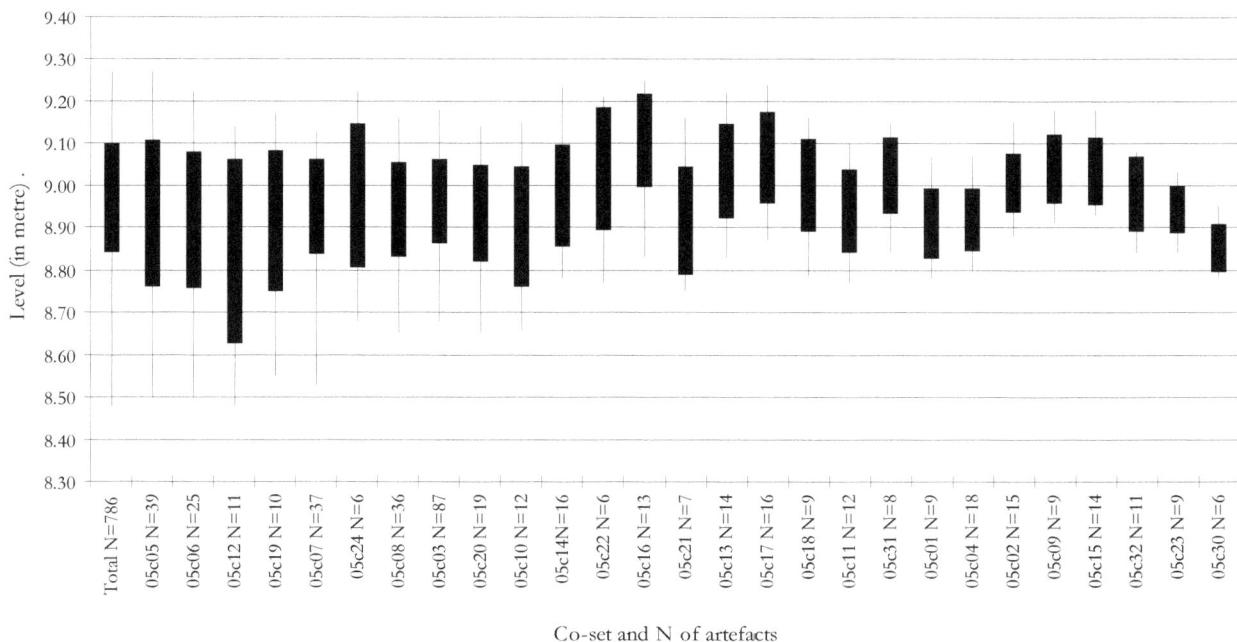

Figure 5 *Rekem 5. Vertical spread of refitted co-sets. Fine line gives maximum dispersion, bold line gives average dispersion ± 1 standard deviation. Ordering from left to right follows decreasing maximum spread.*

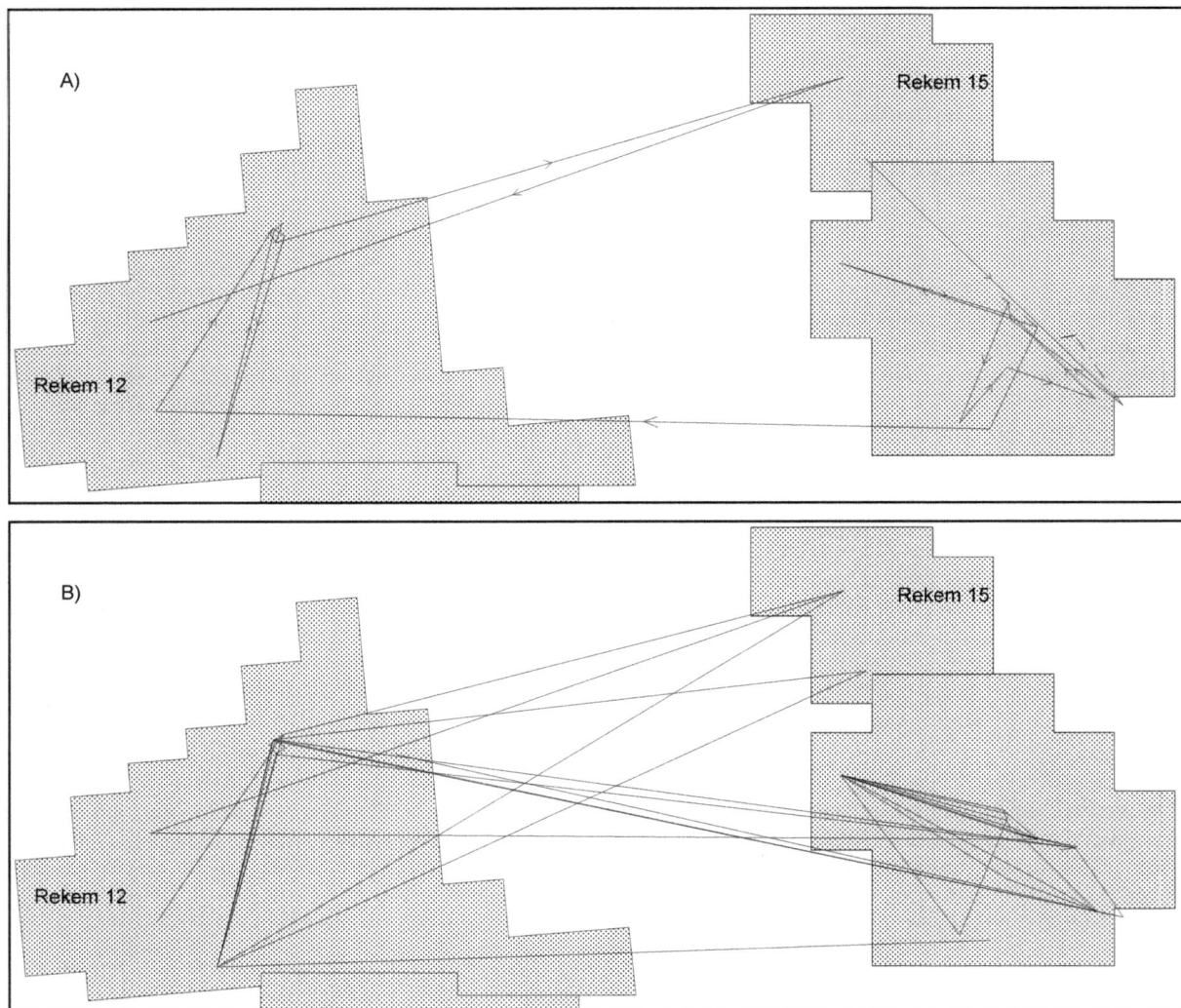

Figure 6 *A refitted co-set (16c01) as we choose to map it (example A) and the same refit portrayed in a different way (example B), in this case connecting every contacting surface (one type of line) . The latter representation seems to reveal a rather intense traffic between Rekem 16 and Rekem 12 and between Rekem 12 and Rekem 15. It is more likely, however, that there had been a single transport from the core, first exploited at Rekem 16 and then further reduced at Rekem 12. From both concentrations a single artefact then moved to Rekem 15. Such considerations are of course important for the assessment of the (chronological) relationship between different loci.*

seen as a trajectory followed by the core while being reduced and leaving detached blanks behind, until the core itself is eventually abandoned. A similar image can be used for a trajectory of subsequent tool modifications. Illustrating this in such a way agrees well with the general goal to reconstruct the sequence of events that occur at the site. Excavation maps only offer the last image, a 'frozen picture', after all the protagonists are gone and, with them, part of the setting. We start with this final picture, first rewind the movie by gluing pieces back together, and then switch to 'play', hoping that a meaningful 'story' will unfold.

Of course, this is a highly simplified image and should in fact only serve as a theoretical expedient. Blanks do not generally fall exactly on the spot where they are detached; modified and used pieces are transported at least once more and, many other systemic processes and post-depositional disturbances may alter the picture substantially. The goal of spatial analysis is to exactly reconstruct these processes.

One of the systemic processes that can be partly reconstructed with the help of the refits is the study of 'tool mobility', i.e. on questions with regard to the origin of the tool blanks ('support'). It is of course not feasible to track down the trajectory of every single tool, but at Rekem at least, it is possible to provide general indications on the provenance of the various tool classes. Systematic analysis of dorsal-ventral refitting results and of specific flint types by locus to some extent allow for a diagnosis on the origin of the blanks. Depending on the evidence, these determinations are qualified with varying degrees of certainty, as reflected in the description of the various situations that can be distinguished:

1. Tool refitted in a locally abandoned reduction sequence including debitage waste material.
2. Unrefitted tool, but the debitage waste material of this specific type of flint is refitting at the locus.
3. Unrefitted tool, but member of a specific type of flint that includes non-refitting debitage waste material at the locus.
4. Tool refitted in a dorsal-ventral refit but lacking debitage waste (i.e. only refitted with other tools).
5. Unrefitted tool of a common type of flint.
6. Unrefitted tool of a specific type of flint that lacks debitage waste material.
7. Tool refitted with artefacts from a different locus.

The interpretation of this classification with regard to the origin of the tool blanks (i.e. their production place) is as follows. For tools of groups 1, 2, and 3, the origins are considered 'local', i.e. blank production likely occurred on the same spot. However, when debitage waste in those cases is limited to just a few artefacts, their production place may still be located away from the locus ('extra-local'). The production place of members of group 4 cannot be determined from refitting alone. The interpretation therefore depends on its belonging to other groups as well. For group 5, the origin of the tool blank can not be determined either (can be local or not). Finally, for groups 6 and 7, the fabrication of the tool blanks is clearly extra-local (unless, of course, the piece is knapped locally from a prepared core that is taken away again after site abandonment). It should be noted that 'local production' in this stage of the interpretation also may include the occasional recycling of blanks knapped earlier but 'consumed' on the same spot in a later stage of occupation.

The application of this approach at Rekem reveals major differences in mobility for the various tool classes. The high rate of debitage refits for burins, for instance, contrasts sharply with the poor refitting evidence for projectiles (cf. above). Burins apparently are frequently abandoned in the area where they were manufactured, after utilisation and resharpening near the same spot. The local character of their 'production-use-discard' cycle is further corroborated by the numerous unrefitted burins made of specific flint types, associated with - generally

refitting - debitage waste material of the locus concerned (i.e. group 2 above). Notwithstanding the explicitness of this major trend, the production of burins is not exclusively local. In fact, some unrefitted pieces are also lithologically isolated, and therefore certainly intrusive. Three burins even refit within reduction sequences generated at distant loci.

This latter observation finally raises a major concern of spatial analysis in which refitting plays a key role: should a site like habitation zone 1 be regarded as a single-occupation camp? Inter-locus refitting is often forwarded as an important tool in establishing the contemporaneity of spatially separated (activity) areas within archaeological sites. At Rekem, a network of inter-unit relationships, connecting most of the concentrations within habitation zone 1 with refits of flint and/or other rock material, can be established (Figure 7). Most loci are connected although a succession of occupational episodes can not be fully ruled out.

But can refitting really tell us something here? It has long since been argued that this method does not offer clear-cut and unambiguous solutions to the problem of the contemporaneity of occupation. On the one hand, a paucity of inter-locus refits certainly does not exclude simultaneous occupation, as activities could of course be undertaken separately with no exchange of materials taking place. In fact, with respect to the flint material, such behaviour seems a hallmark of the artisans at Rekem. On the other hand, temporally discrete sites can become connected, as earlier deposits can be used by later inhabitants to gather useful material (mining), or, conversely, for the dumping of waste material.

It should be noted, however, that in both the latter cases, the abandoned locus becomes part of the activity space of the new settlement: it becomes respectively an extraction area or a dump area within the new context. In other words, if a network of inter-locus connections can be established, we can at least expect that the site provides a representative image of the general use of space in a settlement, even if fully continuous occupation cannot be proven. A site is always the material record of a sequence of activities. Since depositional processes always occupy a certain time span, any settlement is formed diachronically. While the objective precisely should be to reconstruct (part of) that dynamic, it will always be difficult to estimate the time-span of possible *hiati* in this process.

In the case of interrupted occupation, several possible scenarios can be conceived:

- In the case of long-term hiati, it is likely that any organic material (remnants of dwellings, organic floors, site 'furniture', etc.) disappears and that the detection of the abandoned site therefore becomes difficult. Moreover,

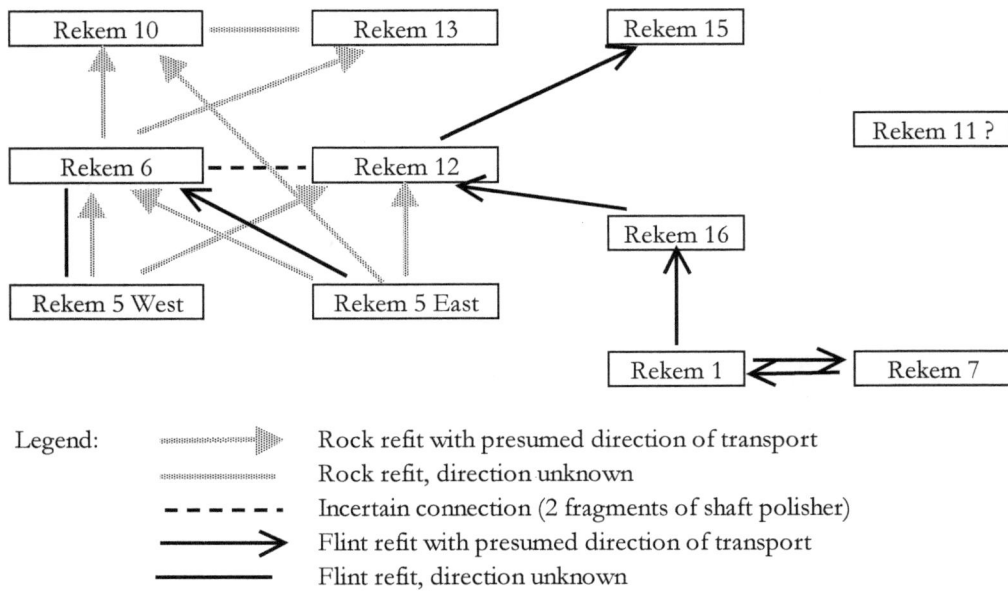

Figure 7 *Synthesis of inter-locus refitting. Inference of direction for rocks: transport of big slabs to destination (small fragments ar left at source locus).Inference of direction for flint: transport of tools or blanks to destination (debitage waste is left at source locus).*

it can be questioned whether in this scenario, the vegetation would not cover most lithic material as well. In this case, therefore, inter-locus refits become unlikely (though not impossible for larger (rock) remains).

- In the case of shorter intervals (e.g. seasonal reoccupation), it is possible that a certain restoration of the camp took place and that the activity pattern was largely resumed. But in such a scenario, a site like habitation zone 1 can in fact still be regarded as one settlement - though with interrupted occupation.

At Rekem, then, refitting certainly provides good arguments to accept that the loci at habitation zone 1 are at least broadly contemporary and fully representative of a single *Federmesser* settlement.

CONCLUSIONS

The variety of the research topics touched upon in this paper, shows that refitting is a powerful tool that definitely enhances the quality and strength of site studies. As for most intra-site analyses, at Rekem, the most compelling contribution of refitting resides in the study of the reduction strategies (for flint) and of the spatial distributions (for both flint and rocks). But, as demonstrated above, refitting can also still improve our understanding of more classical concerns such as the design and use of tools.

In terms of the entire *chaîne opératoire*, refitting not only provides better insights into flint knapping methods, but also into processes of tool manufacture, maintenance and

discard. At Rekem, several 'new' aspects of tool manufacture and consumption could indeed be documented, especially with regard to categories that generate typical and easily refitting tool waste, such as burins and backed pieces. Even when refits document only part of the rejuvenations and transformations of these tools at the site, they provide solid evidence about the dynamic aspects of these tool types. In combination with the results of the functional and spatial analyses, they show for instance that most of the burins at Rekem are clearly expedient transformation tools that are used, rejuvenated, and abandoned at the same spot where they are manufactured. Laterally modified pieces, conversely, are conditioned by specific design requisites and are extremely mobile.

On a spatial scale, the mapping of refits supplies important insights into horizontal patterning both in and between the various loci, as it shows the relationship between the manufacturing process and artefact discard, and as it elucidates the transport patterns of both flint artefacts and rock fragments. An extensive refitting project, especially in combination with the exhaustive usewear results, thus also helps in answering the question on the value of so-called disturbed living floors. In fact, it appears that the post-depositional disturbance processes at Rekem generally failed to blur fine-grained spatial patterns connected with past human activities.

Although refitting would without any doubt be useful in any assemblage, choices will have to be made in view of the time needed for effective refitting. In other words, the cost/benefit balance will have to be considered for every individual site. On the cost side, rather practical issues such as raw material variability (distinctive flint types can be refitted more easily), artefact size (cf. problem of refitting microlithic industries) and cost of the working hours (e.g. help from unpaid volunteers, in the future perhaps automated refitting) will play a role, whereas on the benefit side, the range of research topics to which refitting can contribute, as well as the novelty of the insights it can produce will have to be considered. Of utmost importance is to balance the efforts put into refitting with the share of other research methods, as their contribution fundamentally fuels the impact of refitting (and vice-versa). At Rekem the benefits of the refitting analysis largely outweighed the costs.

BIBLIOGRAPHY

AUDOUZE F., D. CAHEN, L.-H. KEELEY & B. SCHMIDER 1981: Le site magdalénien du Buisson Campin à Verberie (Oise), *Gallia Préhistoire* 24: 99-143.

BARTON R.N.E. 1992: *Hengistbury Head, Dorset. Volume2: The Late Upper Palaeolithic & Early Mesolithic sites,* Oxford University Committee for Archaeology Monograph 34, Oxford.

BODU P. 1994: *Analyse typo-technologique du matériel lithique de quelques unités du site magdalénien de Pincevent (Seine-et-Marne). Applications spatiales, économiques et sociales,* Thèse de Doctorat, Université de Paris I.

BODU P. 1995: Le site à Federmesser du "Closeau" à Reuil-Malmaison (Hauts-de-Seine - France), *Notae Praehistoricae* 15: 45-50.

BOLUS M. 1992: *Die Siedlungsbefunde des späteiszeitlichen Fundplatzes Niederbieber (Stadt Neuwied). Ausgrabungen 1981-1988. Monographien Römisch-Germanisches Zentralmuseum* 22, DR. Rudolf Habelt GMBH, Bonn

BORDES F. 1980: Question de contemporanéité: l'illusion des remontages, *Bulletin de la Société Préhistorique Française* 77: 132-133.

BOSINSKI G. & J. HAHN 1972: Der Magdalénien-Fundplatz Andernach (Martinsberg). In: *Beiträge zum Paläolithikum im Rheinland,* Rheinische Ausgrabungen 11, Bonn: pp. 81-257.

CAHEN D. 1976: Das Zusammensetzen Geschlagener Steinartefakte, *Archäologisches Korrespondenzblatt* 6: 81-93.

CAHEN D. 1978: Remontage de l'industrie lithique. In: F. VAN NOTEN, *Les Chasseurs de Meer.* Dissertationes Archaeologicae Gandenses, 18, De Tempel, Brugge, pp. 59-72.

CAHEN D., C. KARLIN, L.H. KEELEY & F. VAN NOTEN 1980: Méthodes d'analyse technique, spatiale et fonctionelle d'ensembles lithiques, *Helinium* 20: 209-259.

CASPAR J.-P. & M. DE BIE 1996: Preparing for the Hunt in the Late Paleolithic Camp at Rekem, Belgium, *Journal of Field Archaeology* 23: 437-460.

CZIESLA E. 1986: Uber das Zusammenpassen geschlagener Steinarte-fakte, *Archäologisches Korrespondenzblatt* 16: 251-265.

CZIESLA E. 1990a: *Siedlungsdynamik auf steinzeitlichen Fundplätzen. Methodische Aspekte zur Analyse latenter Strukturen,* Studies in Modern Archaeology 2, Holos, Bonn.

CZIESLA E., S. EICKHOFF, N. ARTS & D. WINTER (editors) 1990: *The Big Puzzle. International Symposium on Refitting Stone Artefacts, Monrepos, 1987,* Studies in Modern Archaeology 1, Holos, Bonn.

DE BIE M. & J.-P. CASPAR 2000: *Rekem. A Federmesser Camp on the Meuse River Bank.* Archeologie in Vlaanderen 3 & Acta Archaeologica Lovaniensia 10, Zellik & Leuven, 2 vol.

DE BIE M., U. SCHURMANS & J.-P. CASPAR 2002: On knapping spots and living areas: intrasite differentiation at Late Palaeolithic Rekem. In *Recent studies in the Final Palaeolithic of the European plain. Proceedings of a U.I.S.P.P. Symposium, 14.-17. October 1999,* edited by B. V. ERIKSEN & B. BRATLUND. Jutland Archaeological Society Publications 39, Aarhus University Press, Århus, pp. 139-164.

EICKHOFF S. 1990: A spatial analysis of refitted flint artefacts from the Magdalenian site of Gönnersdorf, Western Germany. In *The Big Puzzle. International Symposium on Refitting Stone Artefacts, Monrepos, 1987,* edited by E. CZIESLA, S EICKHOFF, N. ARTS & D. WINTER, Studies in Modern Archaeology 1, Holos, Bonn, pp. 307-330.

JOHANSEN L. & D. STAPERT 2004: *Oldeholtwolde. A Hamburgian family encampment around a hearth,* Balkema Publishers, Lisse.

JULIEN M. 1992: Du fossile directeur à la chaîne opératoire. Evolution de l'interprétation des ensembles lithiques et osseux en France. In *La Préhistoire dans le monde,* edited by J. GARANGER,. Nouvelle Clio, Paris, pp. 163-193.

LEROI-GOURHAN A. & M. BREZILLON 1972: *Fouilles de Pincevent: Essai d'analyse ethnographique d'un habitat magdalénien,* Paris, CNRS, VIIe supplément à Gallia Préhistoire.

PIGEOT N. 1987: *Magdaléniens d'Etiolles. Economie de débitage et organisation sociale,* Supplément à Gallia Préhistoire 25, Paris.

PLOUX S. 1989: *Approche archéologique de la variabilité des comportements techniques individuelles: l'exemple de quelques tailleurs magdaléniens de Pincevent,* Thèse de Doctorat, Université de Paris X, Nanterre.

SCHMIDER B. n.d. *Marsangy. Un campement des derniers chasseurs magdaléniens, sur les bords de l'Yonne,* Etudes et Recherches Archéologiques de l'Université de Liège 55, s.l.

VERMEERSCH P.M., N. SYMENS, P. VYNCKIER, G. GIJSELINGS & R. LAUWERS 1987: Orp, site Magdalénien de plein air, *Archaeologia Belgica* 3: 7-56.

VILLA P. 1982: Conjoinable Pieces and Site Formation Processes, *American Antiquity* 47: 276-290.

Address of the author:

Marc DE BIE
Flemish Heritage Institute & Vrije Universiteit Brussel
Geo-Institute, Prehistoric Archaeology Unit
Celestijnenlaan 200 E
B-3001 Heverlee,
Belgium

marc.debie@vub.ac.be

FITTING ROCKS. Lithic Refitting Examined.
Edited by Utsav SCHURMANS and Marc DE BIE

REFITTING AND TECHNOLOGY IN THE BRITISH LOWER PALAEOLITHIC: WHERE ARE WE?

Nick ASHTON

Abstract

This paper presents a review of how refitting of stone artefacts has affected our understanding and interpretation of technology in the British Lower Palaeolithic. It describes how it has altered our perceptions of core and flake working, with implications for how we interpret the wider Lower Palaeolithic record, but has so far contributed little to our understanding of biface manufacture.

Résumé

Cet article présente un aperçu sur l'apport des remontages d'artéfacts lithiques à la compréhension et l'interprétation de la technologie dans le Paléolithique inférieur britannique. On décrit comment cette procédure a changé nos perceptions concernant le travail des nucléus et des éclats, et les conséquences pour l'interprétation des industries du Paléolithique inférieur en général. De fait, jusqu'à présent, les remontages ont à peine contribué à la compréhension des processus de fabrication des bifaces.

INTRODUCTION

Refitting of stone artefacts has long been recognised as an important tool in Palaeolithic studies. As early as the 1890s Spurrell identified the refitting blades and cores from Crayford (1880; Cook 1986), while in the same decade Worthington Smith was refitting sequences of biface manufacture from Caddingon (1894; Bradley and Sampson 1978). It has only been in the last 30 years, however, that it has become a standard technique and deployed whenever suitable assemblages are identified.

The number of British Lower Palaeolithic sites containing refitting groups of artefacts is small. The sites of Boxgrove, Sussex (Roberts and Parfitt 1999), High Lodge, Suffolk (Ashton et al. 1992) - both OIS 13, Barnham, Suffolk (Ashton et al. 1998), Elveden, Suffolk (Ashton et al. 2000), Beeches Pit, Suffolk (Gowlett and Hallos 2000) and Swanscombe, Kent (Conway et al. 1996) - all OIS 11, are the sole representatives (with the possible exception of the poorly dated Caddington assemblage) of this type of information.

Refitting in Britain has been used to study three areas of research. The taphonomy of individual assemblages has led to assessment of the integrity of the context, the degree of movement, and on occasion enables an assessment of an approximate order of time that the assemblage represents - be it decades, centuries or millennia (Ashton 1992; Woor 1997; Ashton 1998a; Roberts 1999; Pope 2004).

The main benefit of taphonomy (or the natural post-depositional movement of artefacts) has been that where little movement has been demonstrated it has led to the second area of research - studies of the spatial distribution of artefacts and their refits. In Britain, there is no evidence from refitting of the movement of artefacts over a distance longer than 25m. There are, however, repeated patterns of artefact movement, much of this evidence given by the absence of specific refits against a background of more abundant refitting. The refitting patterns identified from the products of core working suggest a situational technology, where manufacture, use and discard, frequently take place in the same area (Ashton 2004), whereas the patterns from biface manufacture suggest slightly longer distances of movement, with hints of very limited curation of bifaces (Pope 2004). Beyond this, taphonomic studies have helped in the development of the Static Resource Model, in particular at the site of Barnham, where a variety in the resources in the surrounding landscape are interpreted as the primary influence on assemblage variation and location (Ashton 1998b).

The third area of research where refitting has contributed is the study of technology. It is this area that forms the main focus of this paper.

TECHNOLOGY

The technological repertoires of knappers from this period can neatly be divided into core and flake working and biface manufacture. Of the Lower Palaeolithic sites from Britain with refitting (see above), Boxgrove is unique in having a wealth of refitting groups of biface debitage, but relatively little core and flake working, whereas the other sites all contain refitting groups of flakes, sometimes with cores, but little refitting of biface debitage. Each knapping repertoire is treated separately below.

Biface manufacture

Analysis of biface manufacture has been largely based on experimental work (Bordes 1947; Knowles 1953; Crabtree 1970) and particularly on the tripartite system of knapping developed by Newcomer (1971). He described three stages of knapping from 'roughing out' as the initial working of the nodule with a hard stone hammer, followed by 'shaping' and 'finishing' as the middle and last stages of manufacture with the increasing use of a soft antler, bone or wood hammer.

Although refitting has confirmed that soft hammer flakes are the products of biface manufacture, the detailed refitting of biface manufacturing debitage from Boxgrove, has so far answered few other technological questions. In fact one of the answers that has perhaps emerged has been ignored; both analysis of flakes (Austin and Roberts 1999; Bergman & Roberts 1999) and experiments by Wenban-Smith (1989) suggest that the initial roughing-out stages are undertaken with a soft rather than hard hammer. Despite this, most experimenters still continue to use a hard hammer for the initial stages of biface manufacture (eg Wenban-Smith and Ashton 1998). Evidence from Barnham also suggests that a soft hammer was used from the initial stages (Ashton 1998c). Here, cortical and semi-cortical flakes bear many of the features of soft hammer debitage - diffuse bulb of percussion, a distinct lip, pronounced curvature in profile, distinct rippling towards the distal end, and a dorsal scar pattern showing increased flaking from the distal end. From initial examination, this seems also to be the case for Elveden (cf Ashton et al. 2000). In terms of the basic technological analysis of biface manufacture there is still much that can be done, and refitting would play a role in this. So far, however, the results have been limited. Future work might concentrate on the comparison between technological analyses, refitting studies and experimental assemblages, in order to understand better the various stages of biface manufacture, and lead to improved assessment of different areas of working in the landscape.

A further area to which refitting could contribute is the raw material versus resharpening debate (Ashton and McNabb 1994; McPherron 1994, 1995; White 1995, 1996, 1998; Ashton and White 2003), and both these against longstanding cultural interpretations. McPherron has argued that initial biface forms tend to be pointed and through resharpening attain an ovate planform. In contrast Ashton, McNabb and White argue that ovates are the optimal form and not constrained by raw material, whereas pointed forms are conditioned by the shape of the original nodule. Furthermore, they suggest that their manufacture is governed by certain rules (bifacial flaking; a sharp, durable cutting edge; broad symmetry; and good prehensile qualities) that define a mental construct, but that raw material constraints often prevent the optimisation of this construct.

One way of testing the models is through refitting, where the process of manufacture, and initial and intermediate stages in form can be analysed. If the resharpening model is correct then intermediate forms should show a progression from a pointed to ovate morphology, whereas if raw material has played a part, for pointed bifaces there

ought to be a correlation between original nodule shape and biface form.

Core and flake working

Previous descriptions of cores and core working in the British Lower Palaeolithic have relied on descriptions of the endforms of cores rather than the processes by which they were reached. Terms such as 'amorphous', 'shapeless and irregular' (Coulson 1990, 30) or 'crude' (Wymer 1985, 188) were deployed to describe their apparent lack of form, with the assumption that the endform of each core was a deliberate, rather than a byproduct of the knapping process. However, study of the refitting groups of cores and flakes from High Lodge, Barnham, Elveden and Swanscombe have contributed to a system of describing this type of technology. The importance of the system is that it reflects demonstrably what is happening on the cores, and provides a summary of the suite of gestures carried out by these early humans. Although this system has been summarised elsewhere (Ashton 1992; Ashton and McNabb 1996; Ashton1998c) it will be repeated briefly below.

The flaking of cores seems to be characterised by a series of removals that form a sequence, termed a core episode. Often several independent sequences or core episodes will be found on a single core, where the core has been turned and a different part has been worked. The methodology used here relies on identifying and summarising these core episodes. The simplest is a single removal (type A) which is one flake removed independently of other removals. If a single removal is followed by one or more removals in the same direction and from the same or adjacent platforms, then this is termed parallel flaking (type B). A single removal or a sequence of parallel flaking most often develops into a more complex sequence, termed alternate flaking (type C), where the core is turned and the proximal ends of the flake scar or scars act as the platform for one or more further removals. The sequence can develop further by the core being turned back to the original direction, with the second set of removals being the platform for one or more removals. By using this methodology, it is possible not only to describe and summarise the reduction processes for refitting groups, but also describe the final phases of knapping on individual cores.

Three examples of refitting demonstrate the methods

1. Barnham (Area I, Group B; Figure 1). This group consists of eight flakes (two broken on knapping into two pieces) and comprises one long sequence of alternate flaking (type C) in two directions (A and B). An initial missing flake was removed in direction A, followed by a single flake (229 and 129) in the same direction, and probably from the same platform. On knapping the flake broke laterally in two, and two small additional flakes

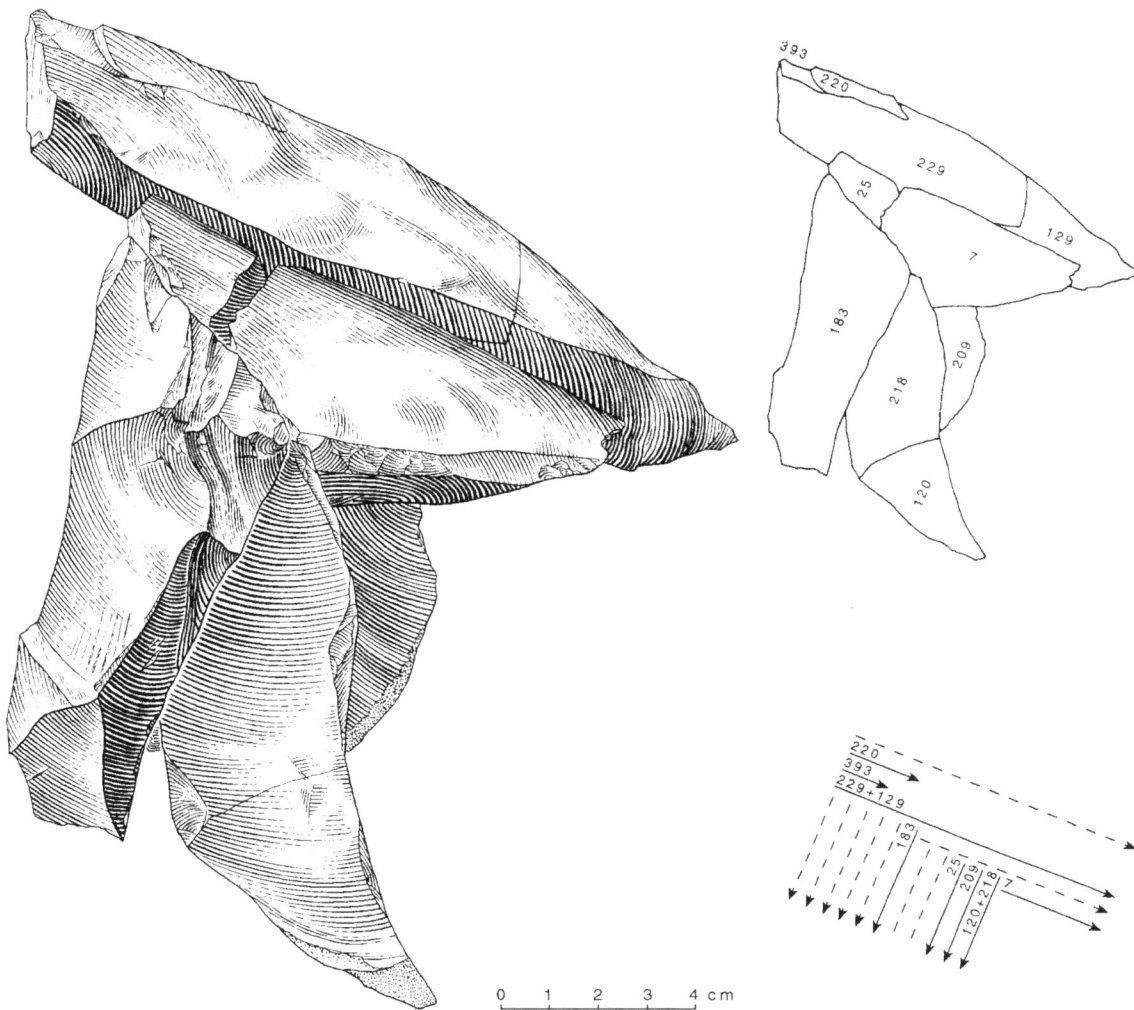

Figure 1. *Refitting Group B from Area I at Barnham, Suffolk, showing alternate flaking (type C).*

were removed probably spontaneously from the platform on the dorsal surface (220 and 393). The core was turned and six flakes were removed from direction B, five of which are missing, but the last flake being 183. The core was turned again to remove a missing flake in direction A, followed by two missing and three existing flakes in direction B (25, 209 and 218). The latter flake broke spontaneously on knapping (120). The core was turned once more to remove one flake (7) in direction A, which was retouched.

2. Swanscombe. (Complex 19, Group A; Figure 2). This is a slightly more complex group and consists of four large flakes (1184-1187) with evidence of ten previous removals. All the flakes appear to have been removed as a sequence of alternate flaking (type C) from either side of a ridge, the axis of which shifted slightly as knapping progressed. The flake scars are numbered sequentially in the probable order in which they were removed and are described as being removed from directions A and B.

Flakes 1 and 2 were both removed in direction A, and flake 3 from direction B probably after these removals. Flakes 4 and 5 were then removed from direction A and at this point the axis of the ridge shifted. The core was turned again with the removal of flake 6 from direction B and turned a further time to take off flakes 7, 8 and 9 from direction A. Flake 10 was removed from direction B, probably followed by one of the refitting flakes (1186) in the same direction. Flakes 1185 and 1184 were then removed from direction A and the core was turned a final time for the removal of flake 1187 from direction B. In this last phase it is possible that flake 1186 was removed after 1185 as there is no direct relationship between the two. The whole sequence involved at least six, and potentially eight, turns of the core with the removal of 14 flakes.

3. High Lodge. Bed C2, Group A; Figure 3). This is a far more complex sequence of refitting and includes four largely independent core episodes of alternate flaking

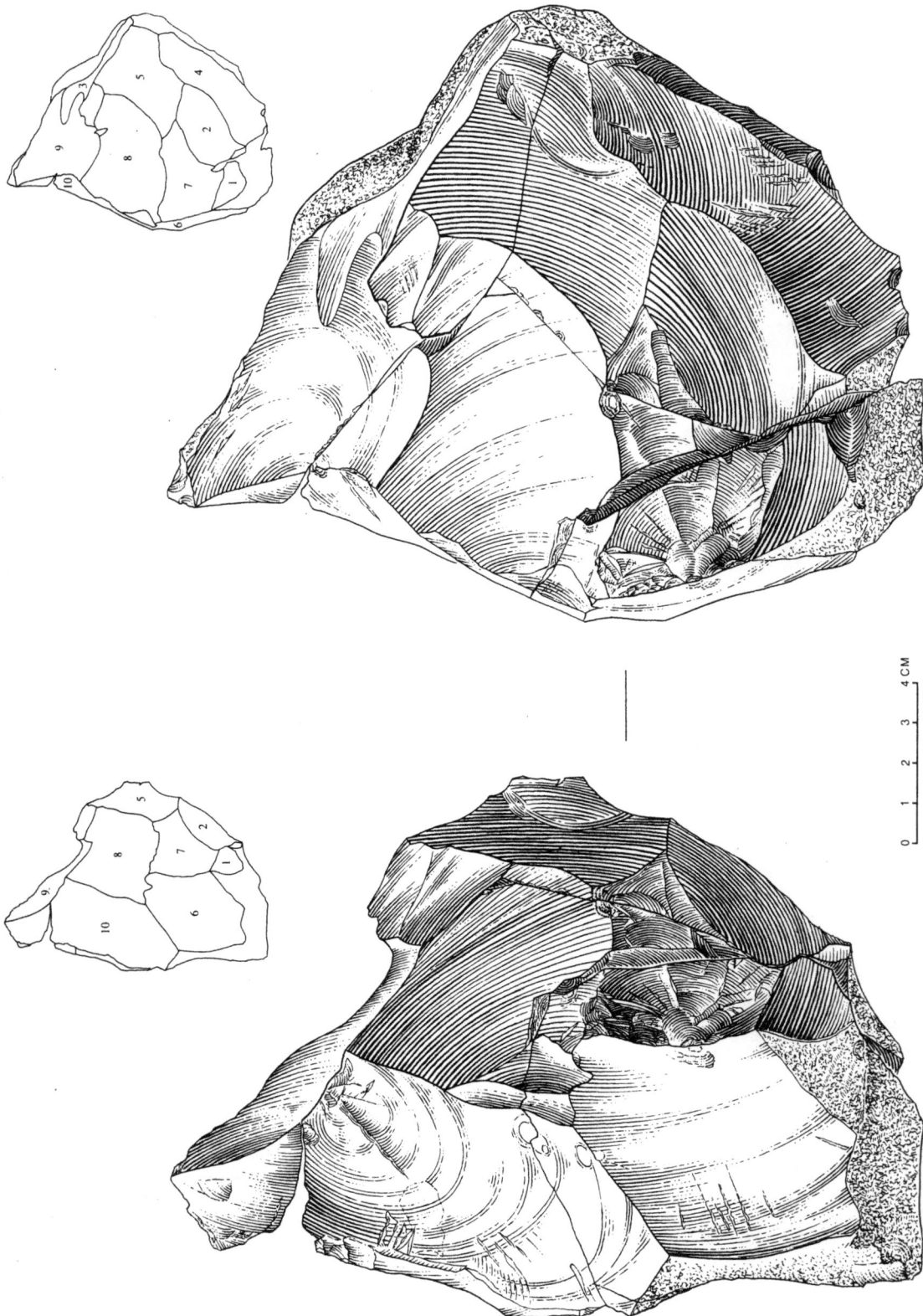

Figure 2. *Refitting Group A from Complex 19 in the Lower Loam at Swanscombe, Kent, showing alternate flaking (type C)*

(type C), all from the same core. The sequence of removals is best followed by referring to Figure 3.

These examples of refitting illustrate the difficulties of interpreting cores without the aid of refitting. However, the general patterns are still discernable on cores, which bear the scars of the final phase of knapping. As shown above, where longer sequences of flaking can be recognised through refitting, these nearly always consist of alternate flaking (type C), whereas the more truncated

sequences found on cores sometimes include parallel (type B) and single removal (type A) flaking.

This methodology has been applied to the cores from a range of sites from the British Lower Palaeolithic. Previous analysis of Clactonian and Acheulian

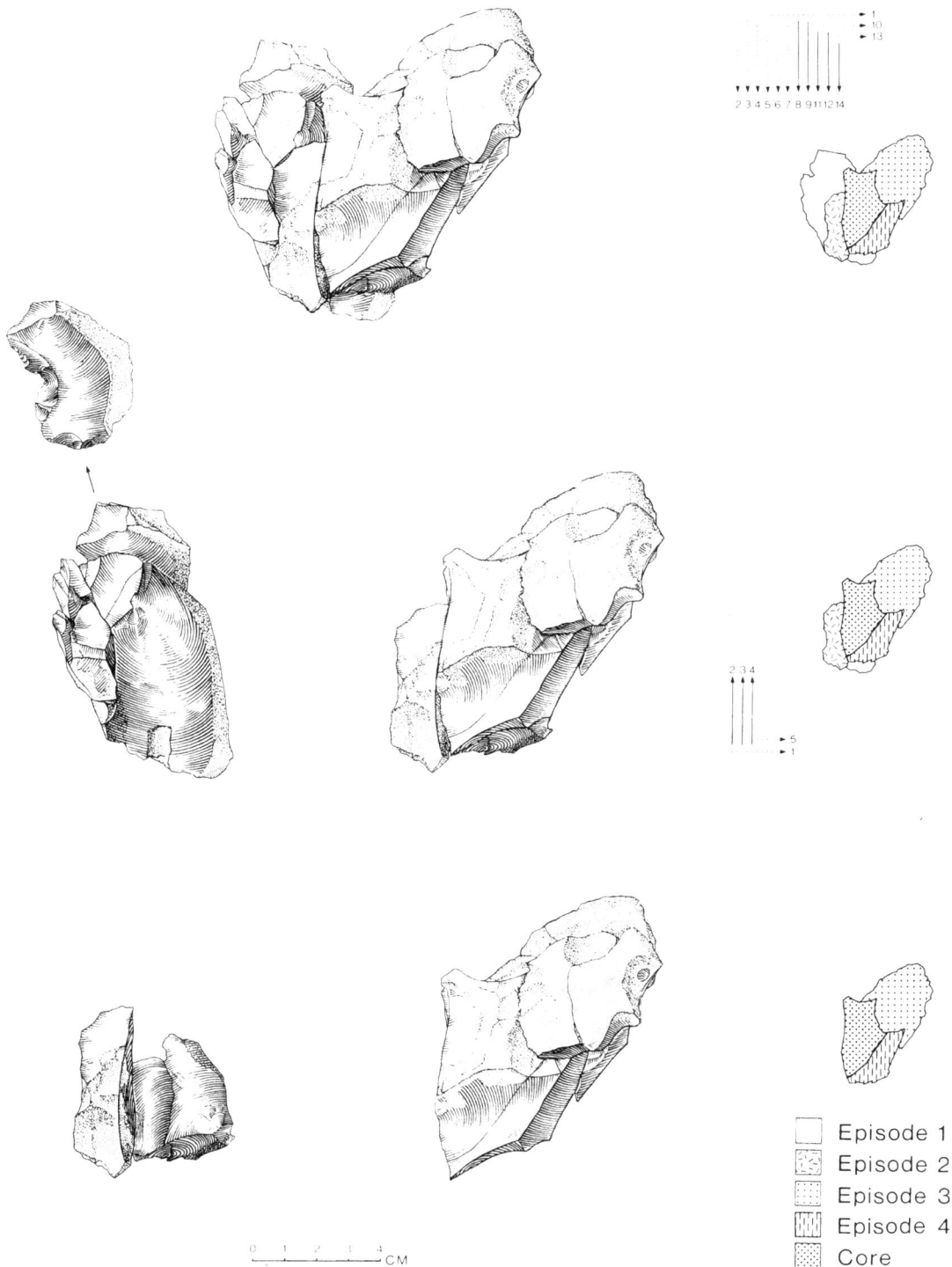

	Episode 1
	Episode 2
	Episode 3
	Episode 4
	Core

Figure 3. *Refitting Group A from Bed C2 at High Lodge, Suffolk, showing four core episodes of alternate flaking (type C) (the second part of the figure can be found on the next page).*

assemblages had suggested that differences exist in the core technology (eg. Warren 1922; Breuil 1932; Wymer 1968, 71; Roe 1981, 70). The use of this methodology has allowed less subjective analysis and suggests that there is little difference in the core working between these two assemblage types (McNabb 1992; Ashton 1992; Ashton and McNabb 1996; Ashton 1998a). This is shown graphically in Figure 4, where it can be seen that both industrial variants deploy the same range of knapping methods. This clearly makes an important contribution to the Clactonian-Acheulian debate, and supports other lines of evidence that suggest these assemblage types are variants of the same tradition.

Beyond this, the system of analysis shows that the use of these knapping techniques enables a flexibility in approach, so that the adoption of a particular strategy is dependant on the state of the evolving core. The turning of the core, the creation of a new platform, or the continued knapping of a sequence, all show an awareness of the properties of flint, and a direct reflection of human thinking. This flexibility, however, appears to be limited to a suite of gestures, and tied to certain rules of conduct. It might therefore also be described as a mental construct (see above) that guides the knapper through a finite set of choices, displaying a flexibility of approach, but within certain parameters.

CONCLUSIONS

These two very distinct technologies, of core and flake working and of biface manufacture, appear to display rather different aspects of human behaviour. On the one

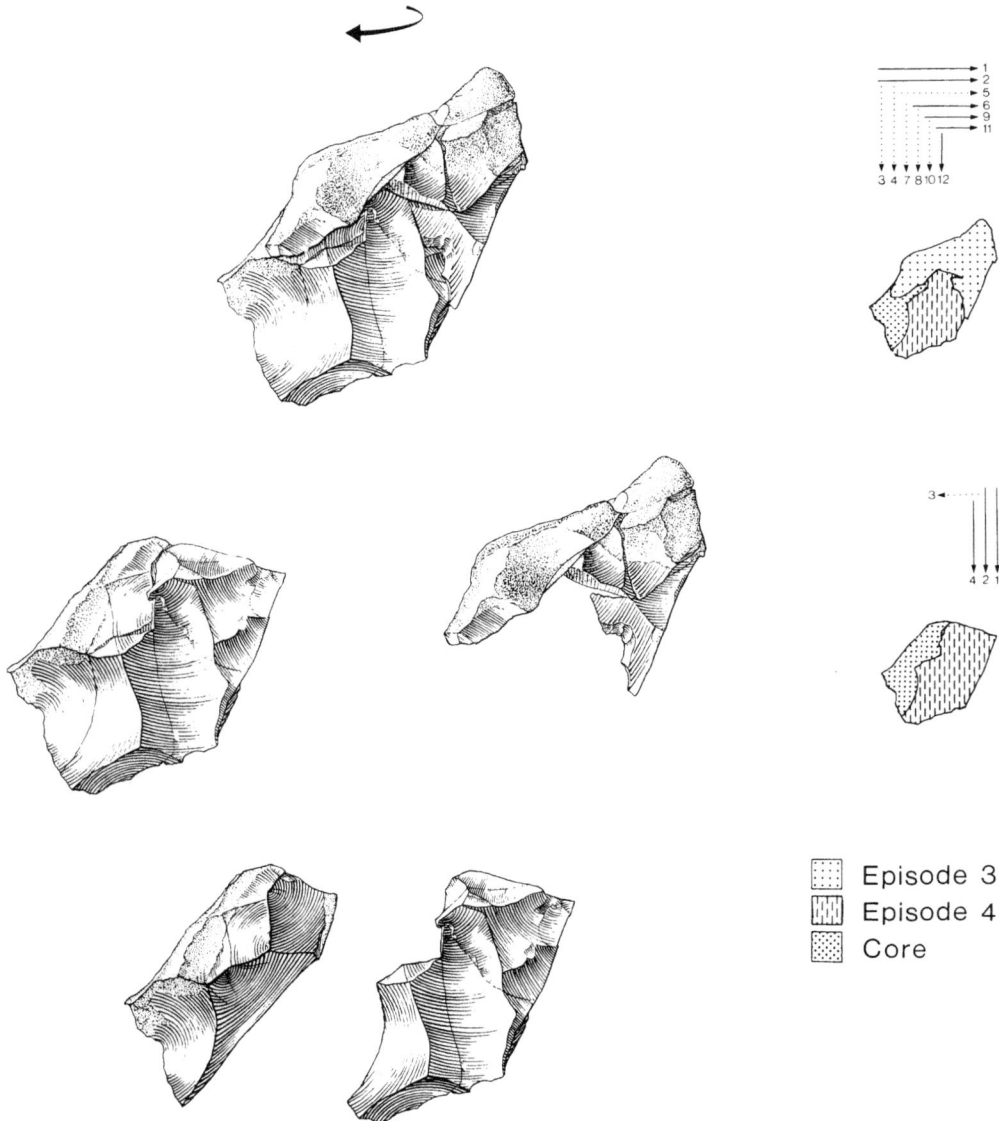

Figure 3 continued. *Refitting Group A from Bed C2 at High Lodge, Suffolk, showing four core episodes of alternate flaking (type C)*

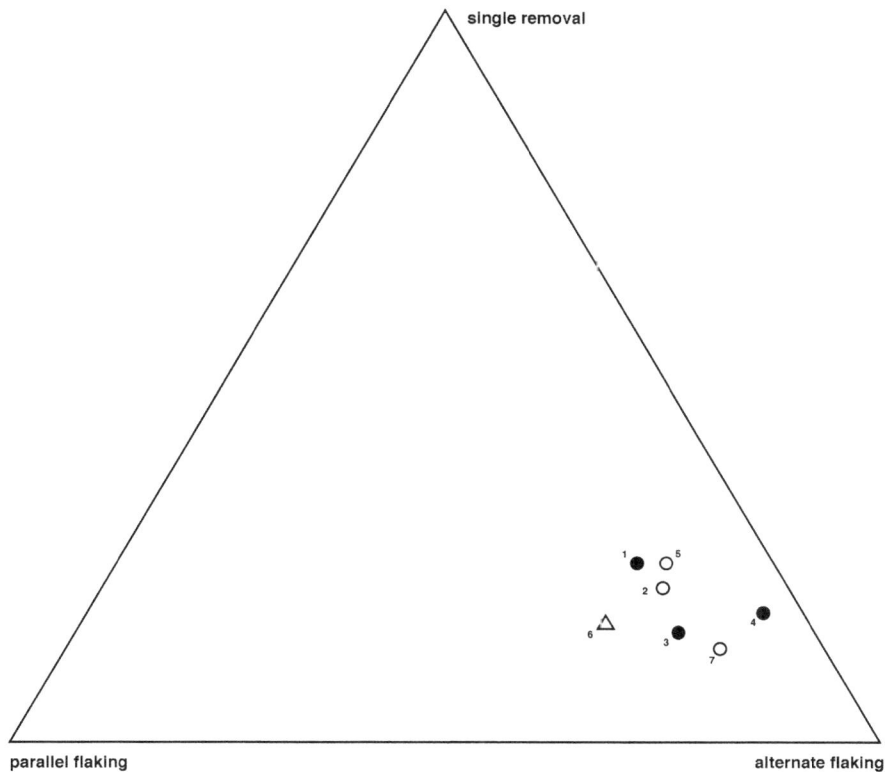

Figure 4. *Diagram showing relative proportions of Single removal, parallel flaking and alternate flaking from British Lower Palaeolithic sites. 1 = Barnham Area I; 2 = Barnham Area IV(4); 3 = Swanscombe Lower Gravel; 4 = Swanscombe Lower Loam; 5 = Swanscombe Lower Middle Gravel; 6 = High Lodge; 7 = Wansunt Pit, Darford Heath. Solid circles = Clactonian assemblages; open circles = Acheulian assemblages; triangle = High Lodge.*

hand there seem to be very specific suites of gestures for both technologies, that provide parameters within which the knappers operate - the mental constructs. With core and flake working these gestures are limited to parallel and alternate flaking, while with biface manufacture the gestures are argued to operate within parameters that maximise the cutting edge, but impose bifacial working and a degree of symmetry. Within these strictures, however, there is a flexibility in knapping, where with core working it is the shape of the evolving core that determines the next suite of gestures, while with biface manufacture, practical considerations such as prehensile qualities and conditioning by raw material lead to different solutions, but each within the parameters of the mental construct. How this can be interpreted for a greater understanding of human cognition, is work for the future.

ACKNOWLEDGEMENTS

I would like to thank Mark White for commenting on earlier drafts of this paper, to Phil Dean for the artefact illustrations, and to Stephen Crummy for the diagram.

BIBLIOGRAPHY

ASHTON, N.M. 1992 The High Lodge flint industries. In *Excavations at High Lodge, G. de G. Sieveking 1962-1968, J. Cook 1988,* edited by N.M. ASHTON, J. COOK, S.G. LEWIS & J. ROSE, British Museum Press, London, pp. 124-163.

ASHTON, N.M. 1998a The taphonomy of the flint assemblages. In *Excavations at the Lower Palaeolithic Site at East Farm, Barnham, Suffolk, 1989-94,* edited by N.M. ASHTON, S.G. LEWIS & S.A. PARFITT. British Museum Occasional Paper, 125, British Museum Press, London, pp. 183-204.

ASHTON, N.M. 1998b The spatial distribution of the flint artefacts and human behaviour. In *Excavations at the Lower Palaeolithic Site at East Farm, Barnham, Suffolk, 1989-94,* edited by N.M. ASHTON, S.G. LEWIS & S.A. PARFITT. British Museum Occasional Paper, 125, British Museum Press, London, pp. 251-258.

ASHTON, N.M. 1998c The technology of the flint assemblages. In *Excavations at the Lower Palaeolithic Site at East Farm, Barnham, Suffolk, 1989-94,* edited by N.M. ASHTON, S.G. LEWIS & S.A. PARFITT. British Museum Occasional Paper, 125, British Museum Press, London, pp. 205-235.

ASHTON, N.M. 2004 The Role of Refitting in the British Lower Palaeolithic: A Time for Reflection. In *Lithics in Action: papers from the conference Lithic Studies in the Year 2000,* edited by E.A. WALKER, F. WENBAN-SMITH & F. HEALY, Oxbow, Oxford, pp. 57-64.

ASHTON, N.M., J. COOK, S.G. LEWIS & J. ROSE (eds.) 1992. *Excavations at High Lodge, G. de G. Sieveking 1962-1968, J. Cook 1988.* British Museum Press, London

ASHTON, N.M., S.G. LEWIS, D. KEEN & S. PARFITT 2000 Excavations at Elveden, Suffolk (TL 809804). In *The Quaternary of Norfolk and Suffolk. Field Guide,* edited by S.G. LEWIS, C. WHITEMAN & R. PREECE, Quaternary Research Association, London, pp. 177-183.

ASHTON, N.M., S.G. LEWIS & S.A. PARFITT (eds.) 1998 *Excavations at the Lower Palaeolithic Site at East Farm, Barnham, Suffolk, 1989-94*, British Museum Occasional Paper, 125, British Museum Press, London.

ASHTON, N.M. & J. MCNABB 1994 Bifaces in perspective. In *Stories in Stone,* edited by N.M. ASHTON & A. DAVID, Lithic Studies Society Occasional Paper, 4, London, pp. 182-191.

ASHTON, N.M. & J. MCNABB 1996 The flint industries from the Waechter excavations. In *Excavations at Barnfield Pit, Swanscombe, 1968-72,* edited by B.

CONWAY, J. MCNABB & N. ASHTON, British Museum Occasional Paper, 94, British Museum Press, London, pp. 201-236.

ASHTON, N.M. & M. WHITE 2003 Bifaces and Raw Materials: Flexible Flaking in the British Early Palaeolithic. In *Multiple Approaches to the Study of Bifacial Technologies*, edited by M. SORESSI & H. DIBBLE University of Pennsylvania Press, Philadelphia, pp. 109-123.

AUSTIN, L.A. & M.B. ROBERTS 1999 Quarry 1 Area B. In *Boxgrove: A Middle Pleistocene Hominid Site at Eartham Quarry, Boxgrove, West Sussex*, edited by M.B. ROBERTS & S.A. PARFITT. English Heritage Archaeological Report, 17, English Heritage, London, pp. 339-354.

BERGMAN, C. & M.B. ROBERTS 1999 Quarry 2 Area A. In *Boxgrove: A Middle Pleistocene Hominid Site at Eartham Quarry, Boxgrove, West Sussex*, edited by M.B. ROBERTS & S.A. PARFITT. English Heritage Archaeological Report, 17, English Heritage, London, pp. 354-361.

BORDES, F. 1947. Etude comparative des différentes techniques de taille du silex et des roches durés. *L'Anthropologie* 51: 1-29.

BRADLEY, B. and C.G. SAMPSON 1986 Analysis by replication of two Acheulian assemblage types. In *Stone Age Prehistory: Studies in Memory of Charles McBurney*, edited by G.N. BAILEY & P. CALLOW, Cambridge University Press, Cambridge, pp. 29-45.

BREUIL, H. 1932. Les industries à éclats du Paléolithique ancien. I. Le Clactonien. *Préhistoire* 1: 125-90.

CONWAY, B., J. MCNABB & N.M. ASHTON (eds.) 1996. *Excavations at Barnfield Pit, Swanscombe, 1968-72*, British Museum Occasional Paper, 94. British Museum Press, London.

COOK, J. 1986. A blade industry from Stoneham's Pit, Crayford. In *The Palaeolithic of Britain and its Nearest Neighbours: Recent Trends*, edited by S.N. COLLCUTT, University of Sheffield, Sheffield, pp. 16-19.

COULSON, S.D. 1990. *Middle Palaeolithic Industries of Great Britain*. Studies in Modern Archaeology, 4. Holos, Bonn.

CRABTREE, D. 1970 Flaking stone with wooden implements. *Science* 169: 146-53

GOWLETT, J. and J. HALLOS 2000 Beeches Pit: Overview of the archaeology. In *The Quaternary of Norfolk and Suffolk. Field Guide*, edited by S.G. LEWIS, C. WHITEMAN & R. PREECE, Quaternary Research Association, London, pp. 197-206.

KNOWLES, F.H.S. 1953. *Stone-Worker's Progress*. Pitt-Rivers Occasional Papers on Technology, 6. Oxford.

MCNABB, J. 1992. *The Clactonian: British Lower Palaeolithic flint technology in biface and non-biface assemblages*. Unpublished PhD thesis. University of London.

MCPHERRON, S. 1994. *A Reduction Model for Variability in Acheulian Biface Morphology*. Unpublished Ph.D. dissertation, University of Pennsylvania.

MCPHERRON, S. 1995. A re-examination of the British biface data. *Lithics* 16: 47-63.

MITCHELL, J. 1995. Studying biface butchery at Boxgrove: roe deer butchery with replica handaxes. *Lithics* 16: 64-69.

NEWCOMER, M.H. 1971. Some quantitative experiments in handaxe manufacture. *World Archaeology* 3: 85-94.

POPE, M. 2004. Behavioural implications of biface discard: assemblage variability and land-use at the Middle Pleistocene site of Boxgrove. In *Lithics in Action: papers from the conference Lithic Studies in the Year 2000*, edited by E.A. WALKER, F. WENBAN-SMITH & F. HEALY Oxbow, Oxford, pp. 28-47.

ROBERTS, M.B.1999. Quarry 2 GTP17. In *Boxgrove: A Middle Pleistocene Hominid Site at Eartham Quarry, Boxgrove, West Sussex*, edited by M.B. ROBERTS & S.A. PARFITT. English Heritage Archaeological Report, 17. English Heritage, London, pp. 372-378.

ROBERTS, M. & S. PARFITT (eds.) 1999 *Boxgrove: A Middle Pleistocene Hominid Site at Eartham Quarry, Boxgrove, West Sussex*. . English Heritage Archaeological Report, 17. English Heritage, London.

ROE, D. 1981. *The Lower and Middle Palaeolithic Periods in Britain*. Routledge and Kegan Paul, London.

SMITH, W.G. 1894. *Man the Primeval Savage*. Stanford, London.

SPURRELL, F.J.C. 1880. On the discovery of the place where Palaeolithic implements were made at Crayford. *Quarterly Journal of the Geological Society of London.* 36: 544-8.

WARREN, H.S. 1922. The Mesvinian industry of Clacton-on-Sea, Essex. *Proceedings of the Prehistoric Society of East Anglia* 3 (4): 597-602.

WENBAN-SMITH, F.F. 1989. The use of canonical variates for determination of biface manufacturing technology at Boxgrove Lower Palaeolithic site and the behavioural implications of this technology. *Journal of Archaeological Science* 16: 17-26.

WENBAN-SMITH, F. & N. ASHTON 1998 Raw material and lithic technology. In *Excavations at the Lower Palaeolithic Site at East Farm, Barnham, Suffolk, 1989-94*, edited by N.M. ASHTON, S.G. LEWIS & S.A. PARFITT. British Museum Occasional Paper, 125. British Museum Press, London, pp. 237-244.

WHITE, M. 1995. Raw materials and biface variability in southern Britain: a preliminary examination. *Lithics* 15: 1-20.

WHITE, M. 1996. *Biface Variability and Human Behaviour: a Study from South-Eastern England*. Unpublished Ph.D. dissertation, University of Cambridge.

WHITE, M. 1998. On the significance of Acheulean biface variability in southern Britain. *Proceedings of the Prehistoric Society* 64: 15-44.

WOOR, F. 1997. *Contextual Analysis of the West Cutting at the Lower Palaeolithic site of Hoxne, Suffolk*. Unpublished BA dissertation, University of Cambridge.

WYMER, J.J. 1968. *Lower Palaeolithic Archaeology in Britain as Represented by the Thames Valley*. John Baker, London.

WYMER, J.J. 1985. *Palaeolithic Sites of East Anglia*. Geo Books, Norwich.

Address of the author:

Nick ASHTON
Department of Prehistory and Early Europe
British Museum
56 Orsman Road
London N1 5QJ

nashton@british-museum.ac.uk

REFITTING AT LAPA DO ANECRIAL: STUDYING TECHNOLOGY AND MICRO SCALE SPATIAL PATTERNING THROUGH LITHIC RECONSTRUCTIONS

Francisco ALMEIDA

Abstract

Lapa do Anecrial is a cave site located in central Portuguese Estremadura. Three field seasons already completed have provided a stratigraphic sequence spanning the transition from the Gravettian to the Solutrean. In Layer 2 (Terminal Gravettian - dated to c. 21, 500 B), the more extensively excavated, excellent post-depositional conditions have preserved several clusters of lithic artefacts and fauna, representing activities taking place around a hearth. The refitting studies, already concluded, reaffirm the excellent preservation of the site: more than 51% (92% in weight) of the lithic assemblage was refitted, making possible an almost complete view of the reduction sequences and strategies used.

This paper presents the various advantages of the application of refitting to the Lapa do Anecrial Layer 2 assemblage: both for lithic technology and spatial analysis. The main technological characteristics of the studied assemblage can be described in detail. The reconstructions show how a carinated thick-nosed bladelet production strategy was often associated (in the same block of raw material) with traditional prismatic bladelet technology. Such association, which results in high core to cobble ratios, was detected not only for flint, but also for quartz, a raw material usually considered as having inferior knapping qualities. The combination of lithic refitting with the tri-dimensional spatial patterning of the artefacts makes a first attempt to interpret the micro scale spatial organization of the short-term Terminal Gravettian occupation of Lapa do Anecrial possible.

Résumé

Lapa do Anecrial est un petit gisement de grotte situé en Estremadura, Portugal. Trois saisons de fouille ont révélé une séquence stratigraphique qui embrasse la période de transition entre le Gravettien et le Solutréen. La couche 2, datée par le radiocarbone d'environ 21, 500 BP, est la plus riche du point de vue archéologique, et présente des excellentes conditions post-dépositionales. Plusieurs concentrations de vestiges lithiques et fauniques se sont préservées au tour d'un foyer en cuvette. L'étude de remontages confirme la préservation excellente des distributions originelles de la couche 2 : le succès de remontage de l'industrie lithique est de 51% (92% en poids), ce que nous permet d'avoir une vision presque complète des différentes chaînes opératoires appliquées sur les différents blocs de matière-première.

Cette contribution présente les différents avantages de l'application de la méthode des remontages lithiques a l'ensemble lithique de la Couche 2 de Lapa do Anecrial: du point de vue de l'information technologique, et du point de vue de l'étude de l'organisation spatiale de l'habitat. Les caractéristiques technologiques peuvent, donc, être décrites en détail. Plusieurs remontages montrent l'association, parfois dans le même bloc de matière-première, d'une technologie carénée et d'une technologie prismatique pour la production de lamelles. Cette association, qui a comme résultat un ratio élevé entre nucleus et bloc original, a été détectée dans les blocs de silex, et aussi dans des blocs de quartz – une matière-première généralement considérée comme inférieure pour la taille. La combinaison des remontages avec la distribution spatiale des vestiges lithiques nous permet un premier essai d'interprétation a une échelle très précise de l'organisation de l'espace d'une occupation de grotte très éphémère du Gravettien Terminal de la Estremadura portugaise.

INTRODUCTION

Lapa do Anecrial is a cave site located in the Portuguese Estremadura, on the south slope of the Alvados' *polje*, at an altitude of 340 meters above sea level (Zilhão 1995, 1997; Zilhão *et al.*1999; Almeida 1998, 2000). The Alvados depression, along with the Minde one, forms one of the natural passageways between the Tagus basin and the Atlantic. The cave entrance faces north. The main chamber (Figure 1) has a horizontal area of approximately 100 square meters, with an average height of 6 meters. The walls are covered with carbonate concretions, and most of the surface is composed of a stalagmitic crust of variable thickness. Speleothems are ubiquitous in the chamber roof, and also in some areas of the floor. At the southwest corner of the cavity, an erosive funnel with a diameter of 1 to 1.2 meters provides access to a lower chamber. This erosive feature seems to be a result of water activity coming from the surface through a shaft just above this part of the cave (see profile view in Figure 1).

The discovery of the archaeological potential of Lapa do Anecrial dates back to the Summer of 1991, when a small test-pit (c. 50 square centimetres) was excavated in the northern part of the funnel. Three subsequent field seasons (1992, 1993, and 1995) have provided a stratigraphic sequence of importance for the transition from the Gravettian to the Solutrean in Central Portugal. The total excavated area was limited to an area of c. 9.50 square meters (Figure 1). In this area, the stratigraphic succession presented the following characteristics (Figure 2):

Layer Sc: Stalagmitic crust. Its thickness increases towards the erosive depression (south of the excavated area), as well as when approaching the centre of the chamber, where several stalagmites sometimes reach a height of over one meter. In the easternmost part of the excavated area (unit M21), the crust reaches a thickness of 40 cm, and joins another stalagmitic crust that underlies layer 0 (Figure2). The formation of the top stalagmitic crust probably dates to the Holocene, and

represents a general increase in both temperature and humidity in the cave's environment.

Layer 0: This layer is composed of brownish sands and silts with small limestone fragments, for the most part slightly rolled. The thickness of Layer 0 increases towards the cave entrance. It is likely that most of the finer sediments are a result of exogenous processes, either colluvial or aeolian. In the eastern half of unit K20, the base of layer 0 was *brecciated* (layer 0b in Figure 2). In units L-M20/21, this *breccia* gradually turns into a stalagmitic crust which, in the northwest corner of unit M21, reaches a thickness of c. 20 cm. Layer 0 was partially destroyed by rodent burrows. These burrows were responsible not only for the disturbance of layers 0 and 0b, but also affected some areas of Layers 1 and 3, especially in units K19 and L20. Both layers 0 and 0b are

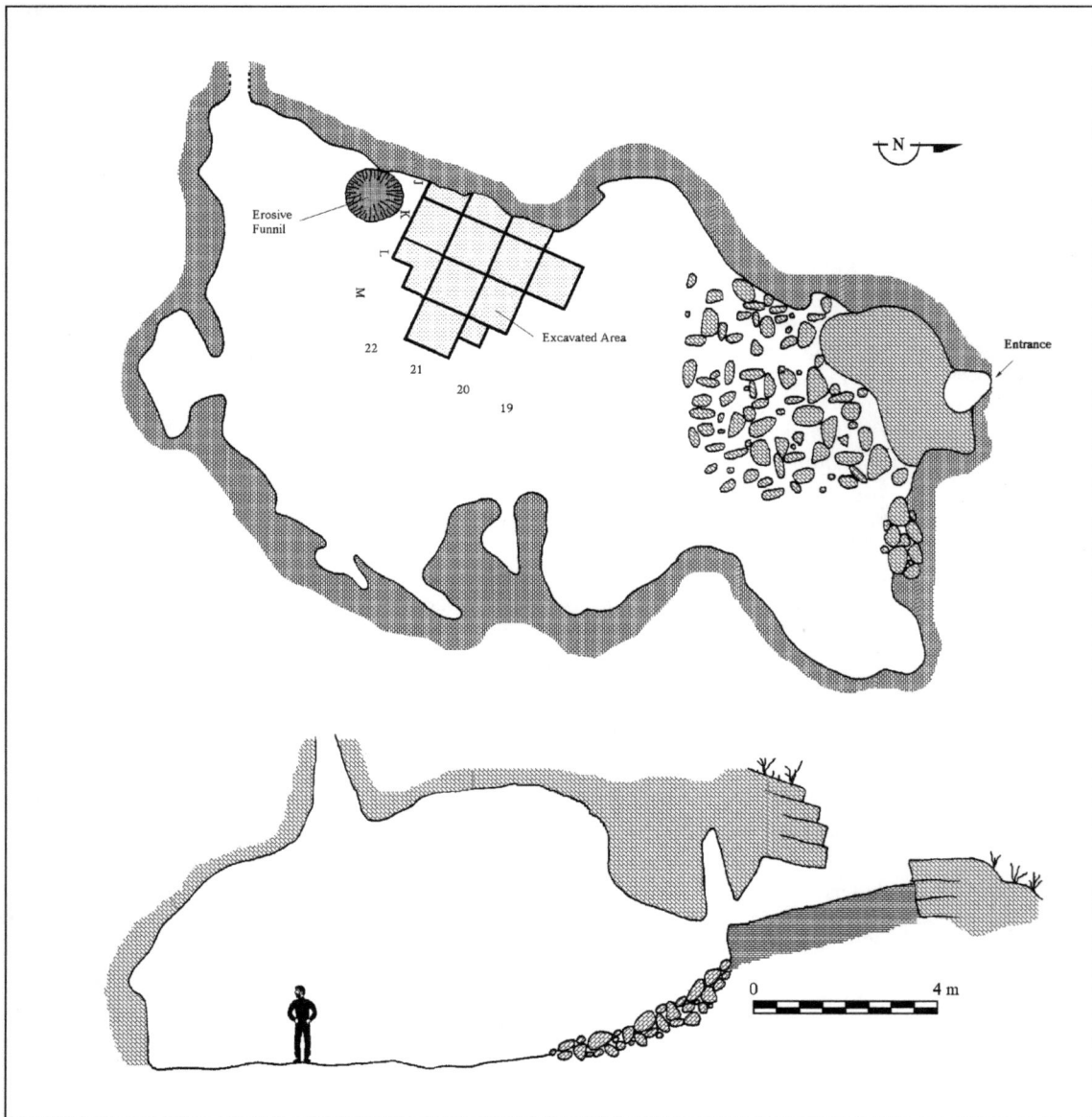

Figure 1. *Lapa do Anecrial: Plan and Profile views of the cave*

sterile, the first one having an average thickness of 30 cm, and the latter of 5 cm.

Layer 1: This is a sparse yellowish-brown sandy matrix, inside dense limestone *eboulis sec* of medium size (5 to 10 cm) with sharp edges, which result from frost weathering of the cave roof and walls. It is, indeed, still

a Shouldered Point preform) and an AMS absolute date of 20,520±100 BP (GrA-12019) concur to date this last occupation of Anecrial to the Last Glacial Maximum. Associated with this minimal artefact sample, four marine shells of *Littorina obtusata*, one of which was perforated, were collected. As for faunal remains, very few burned rabbit bones were recovered. The Solutrean occupation of

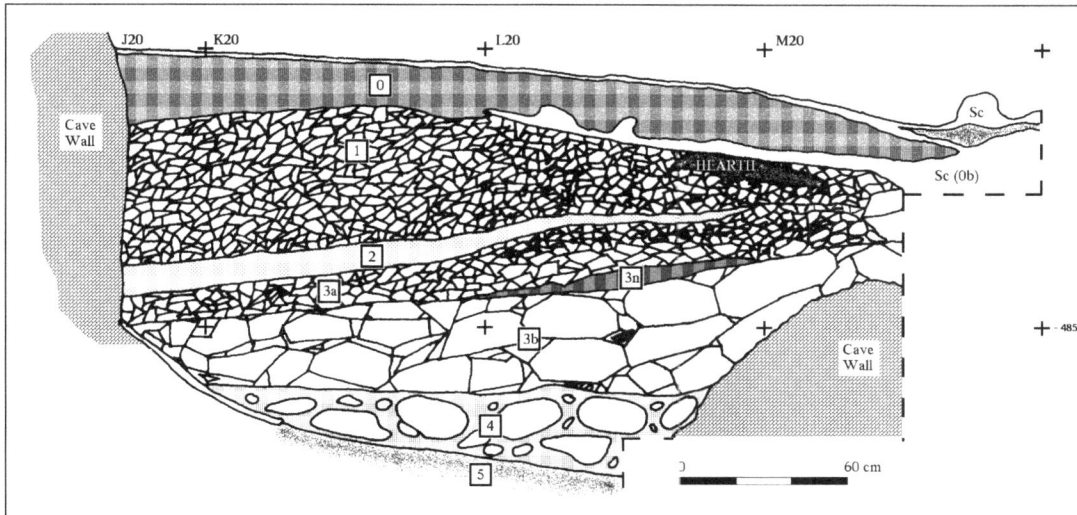

Figure 2. *Lapa do Anecrial. Section J-M20/21*

possible to notice some areas of the west wall of the cave where fractures with sharp and pointed edges are further evidence of this type of process. On the top part of Layer 1, several artefacts were recovered. These artefacts are related to a small hearth centred on the SW corner of excavation unit M20 and extending to the bordering areas of units L20, L21, and M21. They date to the Solutrean. Both the sedimentary characteristics of the layer, the typological characteristics of the flint artefacts recovered (one flint Laurel Leaf preform, showing heat treatment, and one flint retouched blade, corresponding probably to

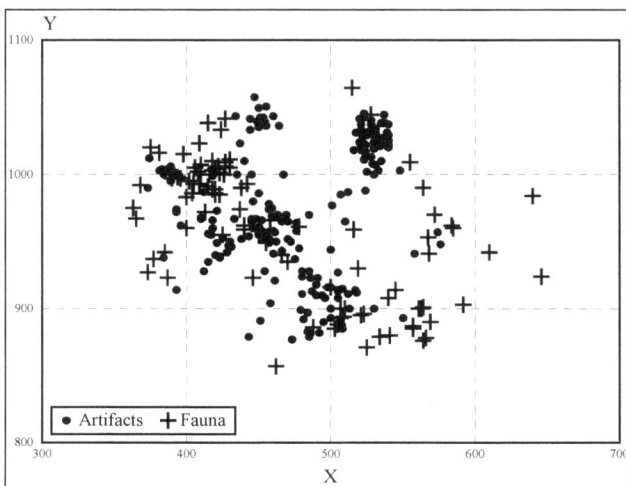

Figure 3. *Lapa do Anecrial Layer 2. Spatial distribution of artefacts and fauna.*

the cave seems to have been a very short one both in time and intensity. The northern part of the hearth was partially truncated by the burrow system already described for Layer 0. The average thickness of Layer 1 is 25 cm. At its base it was already possible to collect some artefacts related to the underlying Layer 2 archaeological occupation.

Layer 2: This layer is composed of yellowish-brown dry limestone fine sands, on top of a brownish sand/silt matrix that fills the voids of the underlying *eboulis* (Layer 3a). With an average thickness of 10 cm, this layer had an important archaeological occupation with an excellent post-depositional preservation. The general spatial patterns of both artefacts and fauna, associated with a hearth *en cuvette*, clearly indicate they are *in situ*. Most of the post-depositional processes (if any) related to Layer 2 seem to have been limited to small-scale vertical movements of some artefacts and charcoal fragments. Nevertheless, the horizontal spatial distribution seems to represent exactly the one that was present at abandonment. Although a slight slope towards the west is visible in Layer 2 (Figure 2), the artefact and faunal spatial distributions are independent of that inclination. Figure 3 shows how both artefacts and fauna were non-randomly scattered. The artefact spatial distribution is even clearer in showing how the organizational properties of Anecrial Layer 2 are almost pristine: the different blocks of raw material are clustered in small and generally segregated areas. The percentage of refitting success for the assemblage recovered in Layer 2 is also

Lapa do Anecrial Layer 2 Absolute Dating

Sample	Material dated	Origin	Lab and Sample #	Date BP
1	Charcoal	Hearth (Layer 2)	ICEN-964	21,560±680
2	Charcoal	Hearth (Layer 2)	OxA-5526	21,560±220
3	Charcoal	Layer 2	ICEN-963	23,450+1470/-1240

concomitant with an excellent post-depositional condition: over 51% (92% by weight) of the artefact sample was refitted. The area of the hearth was extremely rich in rabbit bones, and several charcoal samples from Layer 2 were already C14 dated (Table 1):

At two *sigma*, the three results are virtually identical, and Sample 2, obtained through the AMS method, can be considered as the most reliable and precise for Layer 2. Dating to c. 21,560 BP, the human occupation from Anecrial Layer 2 is clearly contemporaneous with what in France has been designated as "Aurignacian V". A traditional typological study of the Anecrial artefact sample agrees with such an attribution.

Layer 3a: Almost identical to Layer 1, and archaeologically sterile, this layer contains medium sized limestone *eboulis* (5 to 10 cm), with sharp edges and showing ubiquitous voids filled at the top with a brown matrix of sands and silts. Average thickness: 15 cm.

Layer 3n: This represents a thin concentration of fine sediments structurally identical to Layer 2. No evidence of archaeological remains was recovered, but some charcoal fragments were collected. A sample was AMS dated to 24,410±110 BP (GrA-12016).

Layer 3b: This layer has limestone *eboulis* of large dimensions (sometimes over 35 cm), with sharp edges, including some broken stalactites. It represents the beginning of the main period of frost weathering of the cave roof. From the cave entrance and, hence, the main source of finer sediments, the "dry" characteristics of Layer 3 tend to fade: while near the erosive funnel there is almost no matrix, at the northern part of the excavation, the various limestone blocks, although still showing sharp edges, are associated with a fine matrix of brown sands and silts. Average thickness: 30 cm. Sterile.

Layer 4: This layer contains rolled blocks of limestone (large dimensions - over 20 cm), inside a brown matrix of fine sands and silts. Average thickness: 18 cm. Sterile.

Layer 5: This red clay layer represents the geological substratum of the sequence. It lies directly on the cave floor. The general shape of this layer follows the cave floor morphology: in Figure 2 it is possible to visualize the general concave shape of the cave walls and floor,

showing that before the deposition of Layers 5 to 0, this area was probably related to a water channel.

The two archaeological occupations of Lapa do Anecrial (layers 1 and 2) seemed to have a very ephemeral character. While the occupation from layer 1 was characterized by the presence of a hearth and only two lithic artefacts, the Terminal Gravettian occupation from layer 2 was richer, with several clusters of lithic artefacts scattered around a hearth. Both the small vertical scatter of artefacts and fauna, and the spatial clustering of different raw materials from layer 2 suggested an excellent post-depositional preservation.

Soon after the study of the lithic assemblage from layer 2 started, it became clear that very few blocks of raw material had been knapped during what apparently seemed to be a short term occupation of the cave. Early attempts to refit some of the artefacts, by the end of the first field season, were successful enough for us to decide that the assemblage was adequate to apply systematically the refitting method, with all its consequent advantages. Thus, the refitting procedures continued on the material from the following field seasons, and were completed by the end of 1995. This paper presents the main technological and spatial patterns resulting from the application of refitting to the layer 2 assemblage.

LITHIC REFITTING OF THE LAPA DO ANECRIAL LAYER 2 ASSEMBLAGE

The assemblage from layer 2 of Lapa do Anecrial was the first archaeological lithic assemblage in the Portuguese Upper Palaeolithic where the application of refitting was performed systematically. Such application focused on three main archaeological problems: First, evaluate if the degree of post-depositional movement of artefacts was significant. Although the spatial distribution of both artefacts and fauna seemed to be completely independent of the slight slope of layer 2 (Figures 2 and 3), only the vertical scatter of conjoins would assure us that the post-depositional condition was pristine. Second, to clearly describe the technological characteristics of the assemblage, in the dynamic perspective that only refitting can provide. Through the reconstructions, we had the opportunity of clearly evaluate the reduction sequences and strategies of the various blocks of raw material, to analyse which stages of their respective chaînes opératoires were represented, in which state of exploitation did the blocks of raw material enter the cave, which artefacts were exported at abandonment, and if there were any "phantom tools" (Hofman 1992, Cahen & Keeley 1980), or "phantom cores". Last but not least, and since the assemblage was rich in carinated and thick-nosed elements, we had the chance to apply refitting to test the hypothesis that these types of artefacts might have served as bladelet cores (e.g. Sonneville-Bordes 1963, Delporte 1968, Bordes 1968, Tixier & Inizan 1981, Ferring 1980, 1988, Rigaud 1993, Lucas 1997, Zilhão 1995, 1997, Almeida 1998, 1999, 2000, Zilhão et al. 1999). Finally, the reconstructions would allow us to undertake the spatial patterns study much further than the single recognition of clusters or concentrations, allowing the detection of artefact movements between the various small clusters. This endeavour permitted us to detect some past organizational patterns at a very precise scale, a precision quite difficult to achieve if refitting had not been applied to the assemblage.

The combination of the three aforementioned objectives provided a much better understanding of the technological behaviour, and of the habitat organization of a small hunter-gatherer group, during a very ephemeral (possibly single-night) logistical occupation of a cave, during the beginning stages of the Last Glacial Maximum.

type and raw material, after the fracture reconstructions were completed. An attribute analysis was performed after this first stage of refitting (Almeida 2000).

As seen in Table 2, the main raw materials exploited in Anecrial were flint (76%) and quartz (22%). Quartzite is only represented by 10 artefacts, which, as the refitting procedures have shown, result from the knapping of a single block. Since Anecrial is at least 8 km away from any flint or quartz source, all the original volumes were imported and cannot be considered as immediately available. Taking this into consideration, the relatively high percentage of quartz use was not directly driven by distance to good flint sources. Such a pattern is typical of the Portuguese Terminal Gravettian, where a high exploitation of non-siliceous raw materials seems to be culturally driven (Zilhão 1995, 1997, Almeida 1998, 2000, Zilhão et al. 1997,1999).

The general good quality of the quartz cobbles exploited at Anecrial suggests a selection of good quality milky quartz at the source, a suggestion that is further reinforced by evidence (provided by refitting) for raw material testing. For the flint, the vast majority of the sample from Anecrial resulted from the exploitation of a type of grey flint so far very rare in other Estremaduran assemblages. Since almost no cortex was found in the three blocks of this flint, even after the reconstructions were complete, it

Table 2
General Inventory of Lapa do Anecrial Layer 2
Lithic Assemblage (after refitting of broken pieces)

ARTEFACT TYPE	RAW MATERIAL			
	Flint	Quartz	Quartzite	TOTAL
Cores	9*	14**	1	24
Flakes	102	35	6	143
Blades	5	4		9
Bladelets	80	11		91
Chunks	11	5	1	17
Chips	229	69	2	300
Core Tablets	12	2		14
Core Flanks	1			1
Burin Spalls	1			1
TOTAL	**445**	**131**	**10**	**586**

*Including 5 thick "scrapers"
**Including 9 thick "scrapers"

THE ASSEMBLAGE – TECHNOLOGICAL AND TYPOLOGICAL CHARACTERISTICS

Layer 2 has yielded a lithic sample that, although relatively small, provides important technological information on the lithic reduction strategies of the Estremaduran Terminal Gravettian. Table 2 summarizes the lithic assemblage from Anecrial Layer 2, by artefact

is difficult to establish if they were originally collected in secondary gravel deposits, or at primary geological raw material sources.

The sample of flint cores from Anecrial, as seen in Tables 2 and 3 is small: only 9, of which 5, in a traditional sense, could be considered typologically as "carinated tools". The refitting procedures showed, however, that the so-called "tools" in fact were bladelet and small flake cores. Further evidence for this was gained by a microwear study by Hugues Plisson. Even taking into account the small size of the sample, it is evident that the main desired end-products of the knapping operations at Anecrial were bladelets. These were produced either through prismatic technology, or through carinated/thick-nosed technology.

The flake cores show some variability (even considering that only three were found), both in reduction strategies and platform preparation. While the two prismatic flake cores have flat platforms, the only preparation being the creation of these by the removal of a cortical flake, the discoidal core shows evidence for platform faceting

platform rejuvenation after hinging), the carinated cores show generally no preparation, although in one case a crest was created to maintain the convexity of the debitage surface, and successively re-applied, during the process of bladelet production.

On all the bladelet cores the platforms were unfaceted. The use of faceting has only been recognized through the application of refitting to a series of bladelets and flakes that resulted from the exploitation of a thick-nosed core exported at abandonment (Figure 12). Abrasion is also a technique completely absent from the Anecrial bladelet cores, but it has been detected on part of the bladelet sample. The unfaceted platforms were created, on the prismatic core, by the removal of thick core tablets. On

Table 3
Anecrial Flint Core Types by Blank Produced

CORE TYPE	BLANK PRODUCED					
	Flakes		Bladelets		TOTAL	
	N	%	n	%	n	%
Discoidal	1	33.3			1	11.1
Double Opposed Platform Prismatic	1	33.3			1	11.1
Double Crossed Platform Prismatic	1	33.3	1	16.7	2	22.2
Carinated			4	66.7	4	44.4
Thick-Nosed			1	16.7	1	11.1
TOTAL	**3**		**6**		**9**	**100**
%	**33.3**		**66.7**		**100.0**	

during its exploitation. The refitting procedures showed how both this discoidal core and the one that at abandonment displayed two opposed platforms were produced from the same block of raw material. Such an association of different reduction strategies (in this case discoidal and prismatic), as well as a high core to cobble ratio is one of the main characteristics of the assemblage, independently of the raw material exploited, and of the desired end-products.

As with flake cores, the sample of bladelet cores is small: only 6, of which 5 come from a single block of raw material. This block, when totally refitted (Figures 7 and 8), documents how several maintenance products of a prismatic bladelet core (thick flakes or core tablets) were re-exploited, in order to continue with bladelet production, through a carinated/ thick-nosed technology. The majority of the bladelet flint cores from Anecrial are, thus, "cores on flake". The production of bladelets through carinated technology is one of the main characteristics of the assemblage, and resulted in cores that at their abandonment stages exhibit characteristics that would allow a traditional typologist to consider them as thick "scrapers" or "burins". The preparation of the bladelet cores is varied, according to the reduction strategy applied. While the prismatic core underwent several maintenance operations (exclusively related with

the carinated cores, all on flake, the platforms were the ventral surfaces of the original flakes, thus no platform creation was necessary. Most of the exploitation seems to have been performed with direct percussion, a pattern that becomes especially evident in the debitage analysis, where both platform abrasion and lipping are extremely rare.

While the bladelets produced through prismatic technology were more elongated than those resulting from carinated cores, the latter were more standardized, both in length and thickness. The application of a carinated technology seems, thus, not only to permit the knapper to maintain, in a easier way, the convexity of the debitage surface, but also to avoid, for a longer period, undesirable hinging which occurs mostly on prismatic cores. Furthermore, the carinated strategy, using either carinated or thick-nosed cores, allows the production of bladelets, which are naturally pointed. This pattern was clearly visible from the distal end analysis of the bladelet sample, where pointed cases even outnumbered the ones with feathered distal ends.

Bladelet production was clearly unidirectional, as seen in the dominance of parallel and convergent dorsal scar patterns, representing a combined 87.5 % of the total sample of flint bladelets. The cases of multiple platform cores represent, thus, a sequential and not alternate use of different platforms. These, independent of the reduction strategy applied, were essentially unprepared. Their reduction by abrasion was only detected on 13 bladelets (of a total of 66 where the attribute could be studied).

When compared with the core data, the blank attributes show that the vast majority of Anecrial flint bladelets recovered at the site resulted from the exploitation of carinated cores. The bladelet length, width and thickness averages parallel the dimensions of the bladelet scars on the carinated cores from Anecrial. The bladelets produced through prismatic technology, in fact, are underrepresented, as the refitting data have shown: several bladelets with straight profiles and parallel edges were surely exported. The sample that remained at the site is representative of how standardized bladelets can be when produced through a carinated technology: not only

The sample of quartz cores from Anecrial is composed of 14 artefacts, of which 9 are carinated or thick-nosed, that is, by artefacts that traditionally would be designated as "tools". Table 4 summarizes the frequencies of quartz cores by type and blank produced, at abandonment, and suggest a contrasting pattern: while most of the prismatic cores were exploited to produce bladelets (4 in 5), the carinated/thick-nosed cores show at abandonment exclusively flake (in some cases one could even say chip) scars. Although such a pattern could be interpreted as indicating different reduction strategies for different blank types, the refitting procedures clearly contradict such hypothesis. Some of the flake carinated cores, in fact, were exploited exclusively for the production of small flakes, but others, however, only produced flakes during their final stages, the bulk of their exploitation having been for bladelets. In sum, the reduction strategies represented in the quartz cores from Anecrial are identical

Table 4

Anecrial Quartz Core Types by Blank Produced

CORE TYPE	BLANK PRODUCED				TOTAL	
	Flakes		Bladelets			
	n	%	*n*	%	*n*	%
Single Platform Prismatic	1	10	1	25	2	14.3
Double Opposed Platform Prismatic			1	25	1	7.1
Multiple Platform Prismatic			2	50	2	14.3
Carinated	7	70			7	50
Thick-Nosed	2	20			2	14.3
TOTAL	**10**		**4**		**14**	**100**
%	**71.4**		**21.6**			

do they have naturally pointed distal ends, but also tend to have parallel or convergent edges. The presence of 10 bladelets with concave-convex lateral edges is also characteristic of the lateral exploitation of carinated cores. The "standardization" of Anecrial bladelets is further strengthened by the dominance of symmetrical artefacts (67) over asymmetrical ones (12).

One of the more striking characteristics of the lithic assemblage from Anecrial is that, in spite of usually being considered an inferior raw material, quartz was systematically exploited with reduction strategies identical to those applied to flint. The most common reduction strategies in quartz are also unidirectional prismatic and carinated/thick-nosed for bladelets or small flakes. In addition, the apparent contradiction, in the quartz materials, between bladelet cores (4 in 14, with some of the abandoned flake cores having undergone earlier bladelet production stages) and the relative absence of such blank type in the debitage (only 11 bladelets out of 121 debitage artefacts), suggests that the quartz bladelets might have been exported to a higher rate than those on flint.

to the ones already described for flint: that is, a generally high core to cobble ratio and the association of carinated and prismatic technology for bladelet production. There were, however, some differences that should be pointed out, namely, the condition under which the different blocks entered the cave. While, as aforementioned, most of the flint blocks were imported already decortified, the quartz cores underwent their decortification stage at the site. A total of 13 cores (out of 14) still showed cortical surfaces (rolled cobble surfaces, or neo-cortex). For the original blocks, the reconstructions have shown that a total of four original volumes were reduced, all of them small cobbles. In addition, the debitage study confirms that the process of decortification took place at the site, as seen by the presence of cortical and partially cortical elements.

As was the case for flint, most of the carinated and thick nosed cores on quartz are on flake, resulting from the exploitation of original prismatic cores. On the contrary, four out of five abandoned prismatic cores (most showing bladelet scars at abandonment) had cobble edges, indicating that they were the main and principal cores of the original blocks of exploitation. The main goal of the quartz debitage at Anecrial was the production of bladelets. This was, at the beginning, carried out through prismatic technology, which implied the decortification of the cobbles, and the creation of flat platforms. Such preparation stages created by-products that, afterwards, were considered still exploitable, in order to produce bladelets or small flakes, through prismatic, carinated or thick-nosed technology. The platforms in abandoned quartz cores were in the majority flat (unfaceted). One exception is a prismatic flake core with bad knapping qualities, whose platform remained unmodified. This core was abandoned shortly after its exploitation started. Abrasion was a technique completely absent, as was platform faceting.

The reduction strategies revealed by the flint cores were prismatic (unidirectional and in one case bi-directional), and carinated/thick-nosed. The refitting procedures showed that those different reduction strategies appear most of the time associated within single blocks of raw material. While the main reasons for abandonment of quartz prismatic bladelet cores were hinging and natural cleavages in the raw material, the carinated and thick-nosed cores seem to have been abandoned mainly due to their reduced sizes, and not as much to undesirable hinging.

The main goal of the knapping procedures in quartz was undoubtedly the production of bladelets. Contrary to flint, where many of the produced bladelets were recovered, the quartz bladelets are underrepresented in the collected sample. When comparing the relative proportions of bladelet cores and bladelets between flint and quartz such pattern is also emphasized: while the bladelet to bladelet core ratio in flint is of 13,3:1, the bladelet to bladelet core

in quartz is only 2,75:1. Although one could argue that such a difference relates to different knapping qualities of the two raw materials, the reconstructions permitted us to demonstrate that the lack of bladelets in the recovered quartz sample could only be attributed to blank curation.

The study of Profiles and Distal End attributes on the quartz bladelet sample, with the dominance of twisted and curved artefacts for the first, and of pointed and diffused tips for the second, indicates that, as with the flint, the quartz bladelets were produced through both carinated and prismatic reduction strategies. These were performed essentially in a unidirectional mode, as seen in the absence of bi-directional or crossed dorsal scar patterns. The aforementioned "standardization" of bladelets of Anecrial, as seen in the dominance of parallel and convergent edges, as well as on-axis artefacts, is as strong in the quartz bladelets as it was in the flint bladelet sample.

The tool sample from Lapa do Anecrial Layer 2 is very limited: only 29 retouched artefacts were recovered. In fact, if the carinated elements are considered cores and not tools, which at Anecrial was surely the case, the tool sample is even more limited: only 16 tools. For comparative purposes, however, it was considered useful, in Table 5, to maintain the carinated and thick-nosed elements in the "traditional" tool list of the site. It becomes extremely hard to bypass almost 50 years of typological tradition, especially when carinated and thick-nosed elements have been representative of Upper Palaeolithic complexes, such as the Aurignacian, and represent one of the main "tool types" of the French "Aurignacian V". The reader must, nevertheless, bear in mind that those lithic implements were not "tools" in a functional sense, but bladelet or small flake cores. Such a

Table 5

Lapa do Anecrial Typological Data: Tool Sample

Type Code	Tool Type Description	Flint	Quartz	TOTAL	Traditional typological %	Technologically weighted %
1b	Simple End Scraper on Flake	1		1	3.45	6.67
11	Carinated Scraper	2		2	6.90	
12	Atypical Carinated Scraper		7	7	24.14	
13	Thick-nosed Scraper	1	2	3	10.34	
17	Burin-Scraper	1		1	3.45	
29	Dihedral Burin (on angle)	1		1	3.45	6.67
32b	Carinated Burin	1		1	3.45	
74	Notch	4		4	13.79	26.67
77	Side-scraper	1		1	3.45	6.67
84	Truncated Bladelet	1		1	3.45	6.67
89	Notched Bladelet	1		1	3.45	6.67
90c	Bladelet with Marginal retouch	1		1	3.45	6.67
92a	Blade with atypical retouch	1		1	3.45	6.67
92b	Tool fragment	3		3	10.34	20.00
92d	Pointed Bladelet	1		1	3.45	6.67
	TOTAL	**20**	**9**	**29**	**100.00**	**100.00**

strong argument, although provocative, is not new (e.g. Sonneville-Bordes 1963b; Delporte 1968; Tixier & Inizan 1981; Ferring 1988; Rigaud 1993; Zilhão 1995, 1997; Zilhão *et al.* 1999; Lucas 1997; Almeida 1998, 1999, 2000) but at Anecrial has the strength of being grounded not only on the refitting results, but also on microwear data. The division between Traditional Typological Percentages and Technologically Weighted Typological Percentages in Table 5 was considered as a more insightful way to show the differences in tool lists when considering carinated elements as cores.

A traditional analysis of Table 5 shows how the tool sample from Lapa do Anecrial could easily be designated as "Aurignacian". The main represented types are carinated or thick-nosed elements ("scrapers" and one "burin"), both on flint and on quartz, which would contribute to an *Aurignacian Group Index* of 44.83. The best represented tool type after the thick "scrapers" are the notches, the presence of burins being insignificant. Actually, the reconstructions have shown that some, if not all, of the burins from Anecrial were also exploited as bladelet cores. The small degree of retouch on Anecrial bladelets (3 out of 80 in flint and none on quartz) can

quartz cobbles. Overall, the Anecrial lithic sample shows an intensive exploitation of prismatic cores, carinated cores and broken tools in order to produce bladelets. Curiously, the latter are the type of blank where retouch seems to have been extremely rare.

The adavantages of refitting to the technological study of Lapa do Anecrial

The detailed descriptions of each "major reconstruction" (Volkman 1989) from Lapa do Anecrial can be found elsewhere (Almeida 2000). Here, only a summary of the refitting data will be presented, having in mind essentially the technological and spatial patterning insights that the application of the method made possible.

The degree of refitting success at Anecrial is surely the highest for any archaeological assemblage in Portugal, and among the higher in Upper Palaeolithic European studies. Actually, it has been suggested that most of the sites where the method has been applied show an average refitting success of c. 20% in number of artefacts (Pigeot 1987). As shown in Table 6, the degree of refitting success in number of artefacts at Anecrial is over 50%,

Table 6

Lapa do Anecrial layer 2 (1992-1995) - Refitting success by raw material

	ARTEFACT TOTAL			REFITTED ARTEFACTS			
	n	Weight (g)	% of total sample	*n*	%	Weight (g)	%
Yellowish Orange Banded Flint (OBF)	3	8	0.50	2	67	3	38
Yellowish Pink Flint (YPF1,2,3,4)	37	119	6.20	24	65	100	84
Patinated Translucent flint (PTF)	12	36	2.00	10	83	35	97
Light Pink flint (LPF)	7	21	3.60	6	85	20	95
Grey Flint (GF,1,2,3)	257	310	52.40	141	55	290	94
Pink Flint (PF)	105	34	5.80	30	29	21	62
Indeterminate flint (F)	20	30	5.00	3	15	11	37
Quartzite (QZI)	10	113	1.70	9	90	113	100
Quartz (QZ,1,2,3,4)	140	524	23.70	76	54	504	96
TOTAL	**591**	**1194**	**100**	**301**	**51**	**1097**	**92**

have two main interpretations: either most of the retouched bladelets were exported (as blank kits or as lithic barbs already hafted), or their use as lithic barbs did not necessitate retouch.

In the relationship between blank selection and tool type, the tool sample from Lapa do Anecrial suggests an advantageous use of different blank types: while most of the thick flint flakes, resulting from the preparation and maintenance operations from prismatic cores, were exploited as carinated or thick-nosed cores (thus ending up as typological thick "scrapers" and "burins"), the quartz flakes had a similar pattern, but a parallel intensive use of cortical flakes, resulting from the decortification of

representing 92% in weight. In other words, the majority of non-refitted artefacts were either chips or small bladelets (Figure 4).

Such a high degree of refitting success establishes that the Layer 2 occupation of Anecrial was extremely well preserved, a pattern reinforced with the combined spatial data. In addition, it allowed an almost complete view of the reduction strategies applied to the lithic artefacts from the site: from raw material acquisition to tool discard.

The reconstructions show that at least fourteen different blocks of raw material were imported into the cave. Of these, nine were on flint, four on quartz, and one on

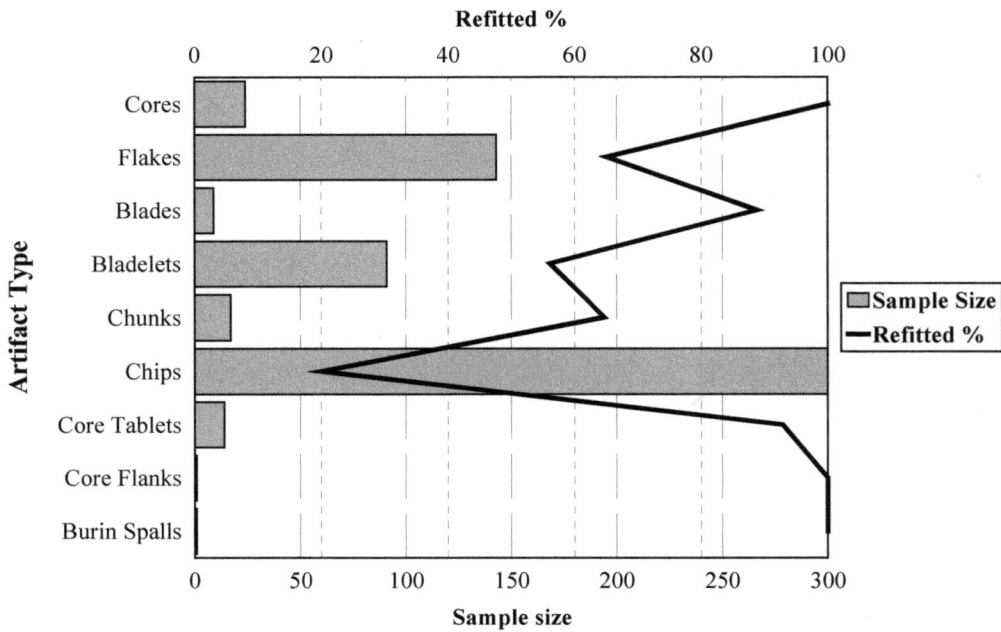

Figure 4. *Lapa do Anecrial. Refitting Success by Artefact Type*

quartzite. The application of refitting allowed us to clearly understand the states in which the different volumes entered the cave. There is a wide variability, which suggests a Terminal Gravettian extremely versatile travelling kit: it contained unknapped quartz cobbles and flint nodules, preformed cores, unretouched blanks, and finished tools. Also, the refitting results show that, at abandonment, several artefact types were curated; from bladelets to cores, both in flint and in quartz.

The flint reconstructions show that the nine original raw material volumes were composed of: a partially cortical

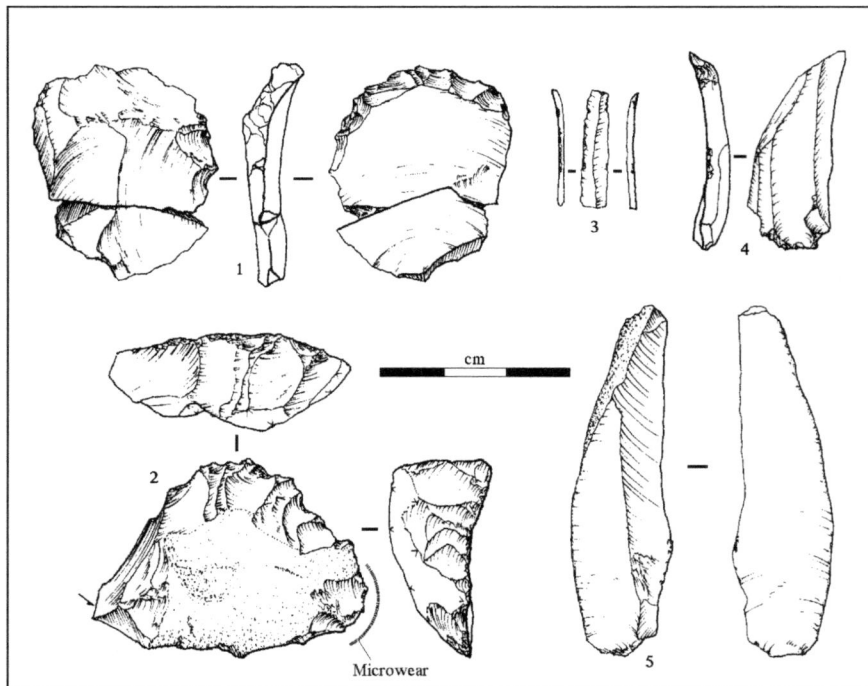

Figure 5. *Lapa do Anecrial Flint Tools. 1- Simple End-Scraper on Flake. 2- Composite Tool (Double scraper, and burin) with microwear traces on the thin scraper front. 3- Bladelet with Marginal Retouch. 4- Pointed Bladelet. 5- Blade with atypical retouch. Illustrations by Katherine Monigal.*

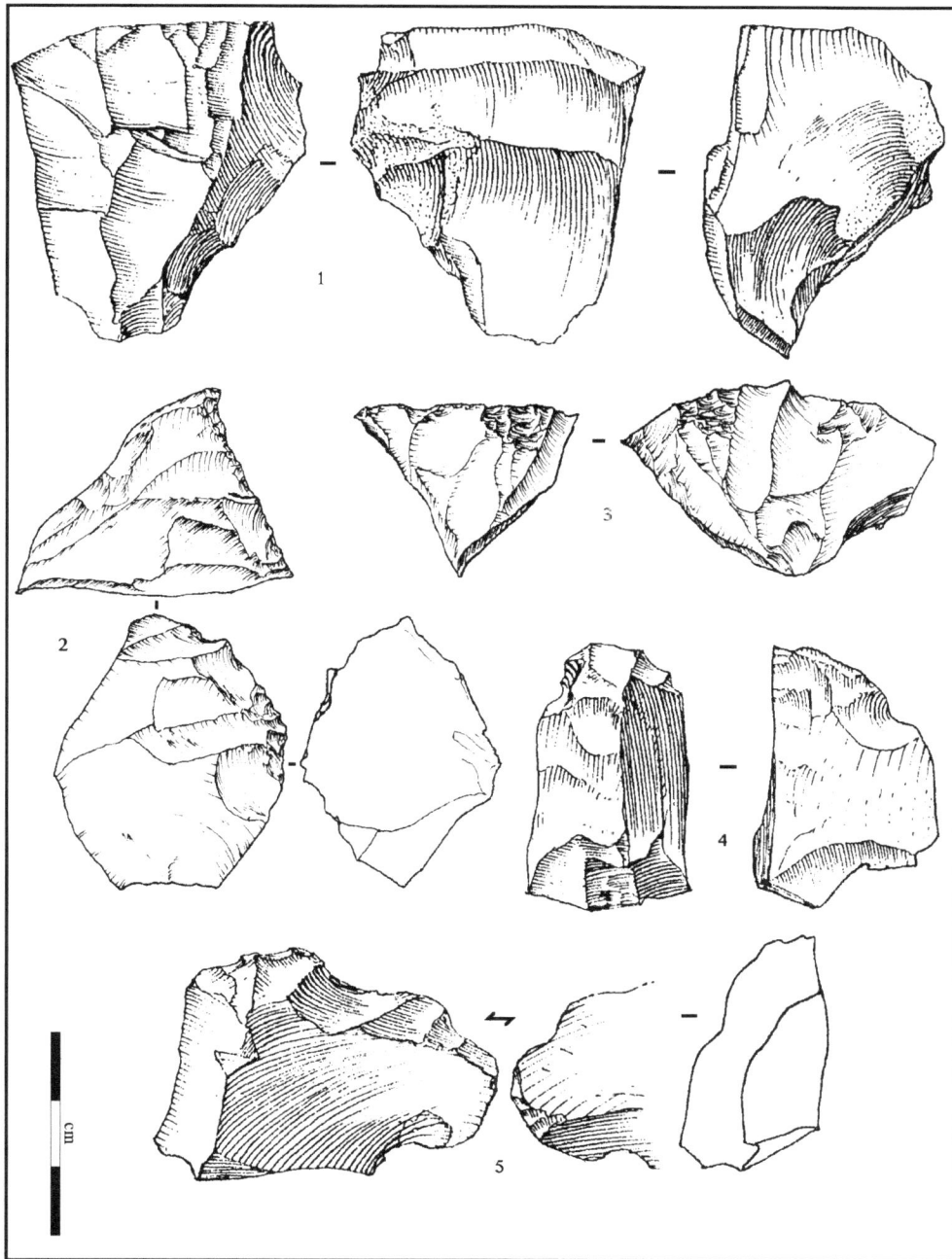

Figure 6. *Lapa Do Anecrial Abandonment Stage Of cores from Block GF 1. 1- Double Crossed Platform Prismatic Core. 2- Carinated/plain "Burin". In the platform view it is visible an unsuccessful bladelet production attempt. 3- Carinated "Scraper". 4- Carinated "Scraper". 5- Thick-nosed "Scraper". Illustrations by Thierry Aubry (1, 4, and 5) and by Katherine Monigal (2 and 3).*

cobble (block YPF), two core preforms already decortified (block GF1 – Figures 6 to 9 - and block PTF), two thick flakes which served as flake and bladelet cores (block GF2 and GF3 – Figure 12), one retouched side-scraper (block LPF – Figure 10). The other three volumes had either small sample sizes or small degrees of refitting success, thus not allowing the complete visualization of their original states. The sample of block OBF was

represented by only three artefacts, of which two were refitted. The absence of chips of this raw material suggests that the three blanks were imported, and not produced at Anecrial. The block of Pink Flint (PF), however, was surely knapped at Anecrial, as indicated not only by several partial reconstructions, but also by the dominance of chips. Although, due to the export of most of this raw material (either as cores, tools or blanks), it is

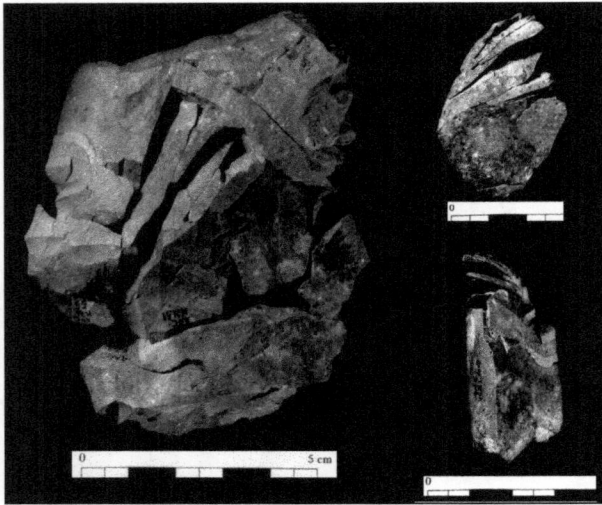

Figure 7. *Block GF 1 refit sets. On the left is the complete reconstruction of the original Prismatic core (number 1 in Figure 6). Note the missing bladelets on the central area. On the right are 2 of the 4 bladelet cores resulting from the re-exploitation of large by-products of the main core. The top right core was abandoned as a carinated-plain "burin" (number 2 in Figure 6), the bottom one as a carinated "scraper" (number 4 in Figure 6).*

difficult to reconstruct the way in which the original volume entered the site, it is certain that the Pink Flint initial volume was already decortified: no cortical

artefacts were recovered. Within the Indeterminate Flint class there were artefacts not possible to attribute to any of the other original blocks. Among them, only a retouched bladelet with marginal retouch deserves mention, since it is clear that it entered Anecrial already as a finished tool (Number 3 in Figure 5).

Independent of the state under which the various flint blocks entered the site, the main goal of the knappers was the production of bladelets. This production was carried out through an optimised exploitation of almost all the available blocks; from cores to broken "tools".

Block GF1, the most comprehensive reconstruction from Anecrial, shows a high core to cobble ratio: four by-products of an original bladelet prismatic core were re-exploited as bladelet cores, through carinated or thick-nosed technology. The association of a high core to cobble ratio and the combination of various reduction strategies in single blocks of raw material is perhaps the best defining characteristic of the Anecrial sample, and one that only through the reconstructions was possible to detect. The same pattern was visible in Block YPF, where prismatic and carinated reduction strategies are associated with a discoidal strategy, in order to produce both small flakes and bladelets.

The reconstruction of block LPF (Figure 10) shows how even some imported tools (in this case a side-scraper) were re-exploited as bladelet cores after breaking. This massive bladelet production can also be found on the quartz materials.

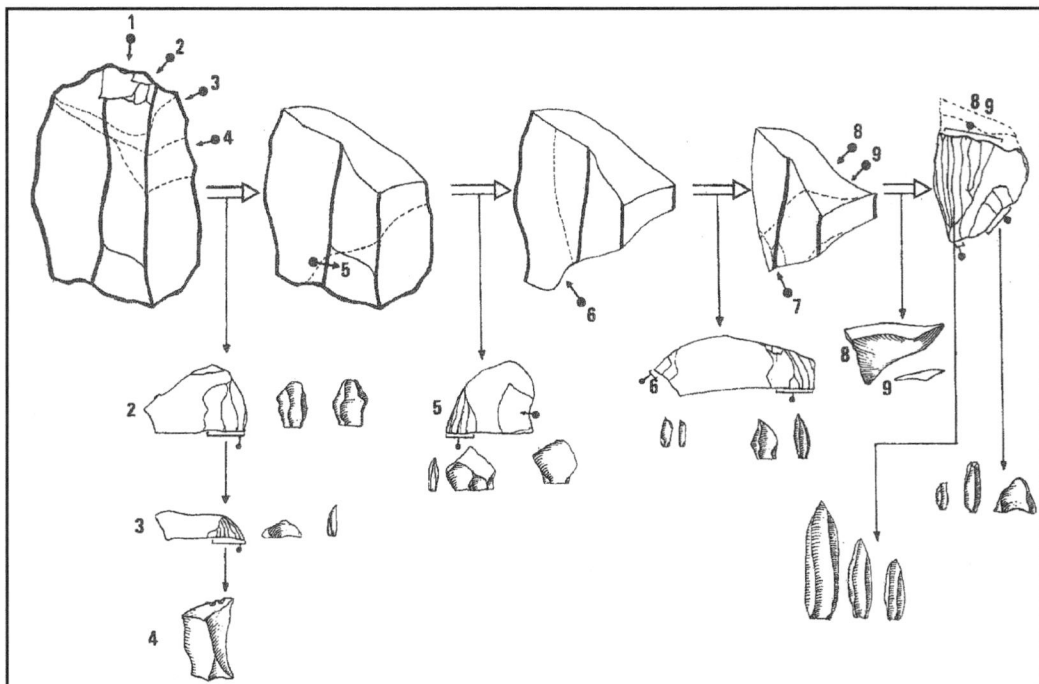

Figure 8. *Reduction Sequence of Block GF 1. Lapa do Anecrial Layer 2.(technological scheme by Thierry Aubry).*

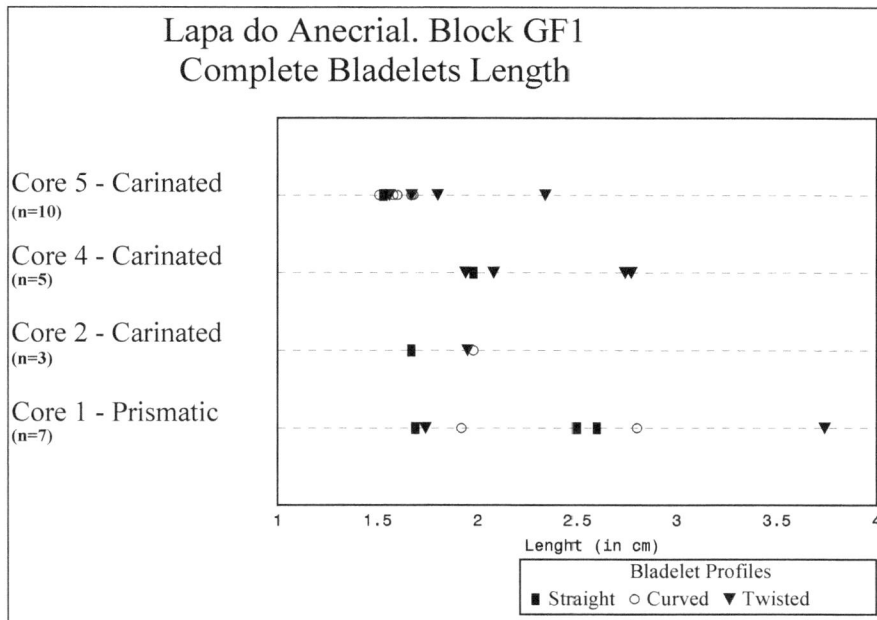

Figure 9. *Lapa do Anecrial. Bladelet attributes from block GF1; Length and Profiles*

The quartz reconstructions, here exemplified in Figure 11, show a pattern completely identical to the one seen in the flint. Although the four quartz blocks entered the site with cortex, after the first stage of decortification, they underwent an exploitation similar to that of the flint ones; that is, they show a high core to cobble ratio, and the association of prismatic and carinated/thick-nosed technology for bladelet and small flake production.

The reconstructions entirely confirm the hypothesis that carinated technology and thick-nosed technology were extremely efficient ways to produce bladelets (Zilhão 1995, 1997; Almeida 1998, 1999, 2000; Zilhão *et al.*1999). Also, the refitting shows that such technological reduction strategies allow an immediate way of maintaining the debitage surface convexity and, thus, avoiding, for a longer period, the problems of hinging which often afflict prismatic technologies. Last, but not least, as the reconstruction of Block GF1 perfectly exemplifies, bladelets produced through carinated/ thick-nosed strategy tend to be more standardized than those produced through prismatic technology: in general shape, in distal tips, in thickness, and in length (Figure 9).

Although the refitting results from Lapa do Anecrial were successful in showing that the carinated elements were bladelet cores, it was necessary to demonstrate that those elements were never used as tools. A use wear study became, as a consequence, important. Hugues Plisson undertook this analysis, and its results are consistent with the interpretation of the carinated "scrapers" as cores and not as tools. Of the 36 artefacts analysed only one showed use wear traces: a composite "tool" which consisted of a double scraper - burin. The two "scraper fronts" of this

particular piece had different characteristics: while one was clearly carinated and was possible to refit bladelets onto this part, the other front was clearly a typical thin scraper (Figure 12 and number 2 in Figure 5). Of course,

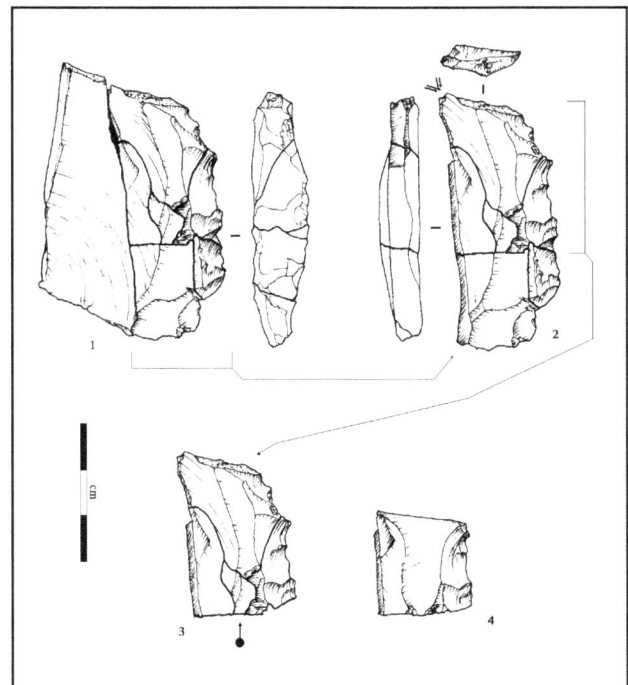

Figure 10. *Illustrated is the re-exploitation of a side-scraper as a bladelet core. (Block LPF). After fracture (1), bladelets were produced through a burin technique. After a second fracture, bladelet production was still attempted in one of the fragments (3). 4- Abandoned "core"*

Francisco Almeida

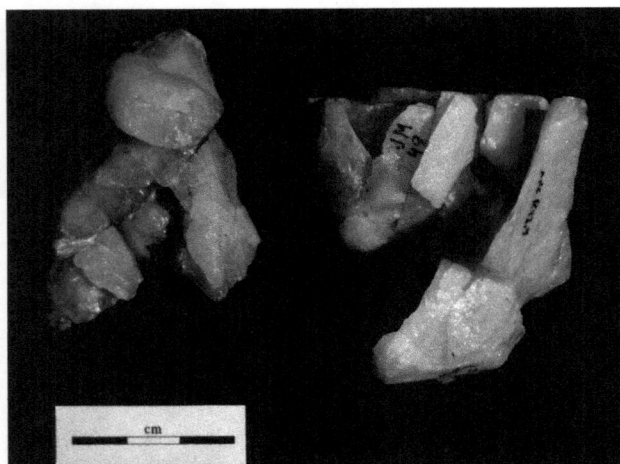

Figure 11. *Two reconstruction sets from Block QZ4 (Quartz). While the one on the left shows the re-exploitation of several thick flakes (some of them resulting from decortification) as carinated bladelet cores, the reconstruction from the right shows the bi-directional reduction of a prismatic bladelet core, with several of the produced blanks missing (probably exported). Some of the larger blanks removed from this core were also re-exploited as bladelet and small flake carinated cores.*

and as expected, only the thin scraper front showed use wear, probably related to hide scraping.

The absence of use wear traces on most of the flint carinated materials from Anecrial could be questioned, however, because a major part of the sample presented some sort of chemical alteration that, according to Hughes Plisson, could have erased original use wear traces. The analysis of the quartz materials with no chemical alteration, however, presented no such doubts: according to Plisson "the edges of the quartz carinated cores were as fresh as if they have been knapped in this precise moment: no use wear at all." (Plisson, pers. comm.). Other independent data show that the Anecrial carinated flint elements could not have been used as scraping tools: in at least two cases, two bladelets were not removed successfully from the carinated cores, which, however, showed hammering traces. If the "fronts" of such pieces were used after such unsuccessful removals, the scraping motion would have removed those bladelets.

The Advantages of the Application of Refitting to the Spatial Analysis of Lapa do Anecrial

The detailed spatial analysis of Lapa do Anecrial layer 2 occupation is still under process. It is possible, however, to present here some preliminary results that undoubtedly demonstrate the multiple advantages of a combined use of lithic refitting and spatial data. The reading of Figures

13, 14, 15 and 16 is perhaps the best way to understand some of the results already obtained during our spatial study of the site. Although a simpler "Minimal Nodule Analysis" (Larson & Ingbar 1992) would have obtained as efficiently some of the results here shown, the application of refitting permitted and will permit a much more detailed and dynamic view of the spatial organization of the Anecrial habitat.

To date, the reconstructions have enriched the ongoing study of the spatial organization of Lapa do Anecrial layer 2 by providing quite interesting patterns which mainly relate to:

- The identification of drop and toss zones around the hearth;

- The identification of how many knappers were responsible for the various clusters of different raw materials;

- In the cases of similar raw material artefacts (as the grey flint – Figure 14 – and the quartz), the identification of how many blocks were in fact exploited;

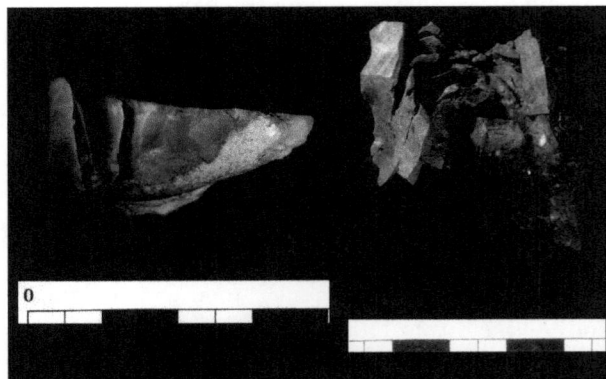

Figure 12. *On the left, Block YPF 1: a composite "tool", with two "scraper fronts" – a carinated front on the left (where several bladelets were refitted), and a thin front on the right, where scraping microwear was detected. On the right, Block GF 3, a reconstruction of a set of 30 artefacts (small flakes, chips and bladelets), which constitute what originally was a thick-nosed core "front". The original core was not found in the excavation, and seemingly left the cave still in a workable state.*

- The identification of the different goals of each individual's knapping procedures, as well as their respective technical capacity;

- The quite possible identification of "specialization" (Figure 16) in an Upper Palaeolithic context;

68

- The identification of specific artefact clusters (Figure 16), probably related to blank curation activities, just before abandonment.

DISCUSSION

In this paper, we tried to present the main characteristics of the Terminal Gravettian occupation from Lapa do Anecrial, especially the technological and spatial patterns

that were recognized through the application of the refitting method. Although the multivariate advantages of the method have been systematically advocated in the last three decades, it is always useful to enlarge the database of archaeological assemblages and sites where reconstructions have been applied. This was the main goal of this paper: to show how refitting allowed a more detailed archaeological pattern recognition endeavour, and thus detect technological and spatial organizational

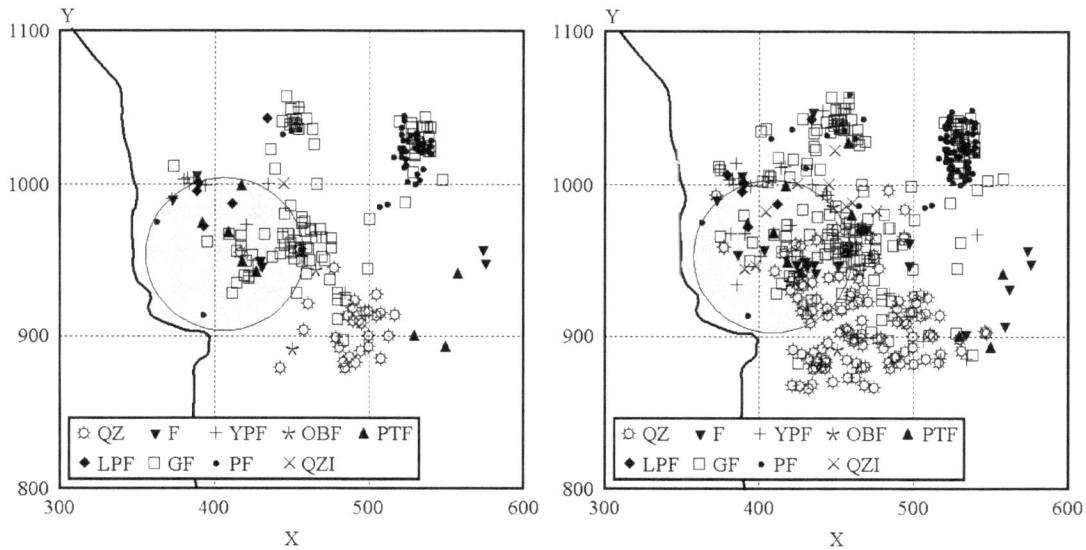

Figure 13. *Spatial Distribution of Artefacts by Raw Material Block (QZ – Quartz. F-Indeterminate Flint. YPF-Yellowish Pink Flint. OBF- Orange Banded Flint. PTF-Patinated Translucent Flint. LPF – Light Pink Flint. GF-Gray Flint. PF-Pink Flint. QZI-Quartzite - see Table 6). On the left, the artefacts that were actually piece-plotted. On the right, we added randomly the artefacts collected during the screening procedures. Since the excavation was undertaken by four quadrants of 50 cm² for each unit, the original spatial positioning of artefacts could in this way be partially estimated.*

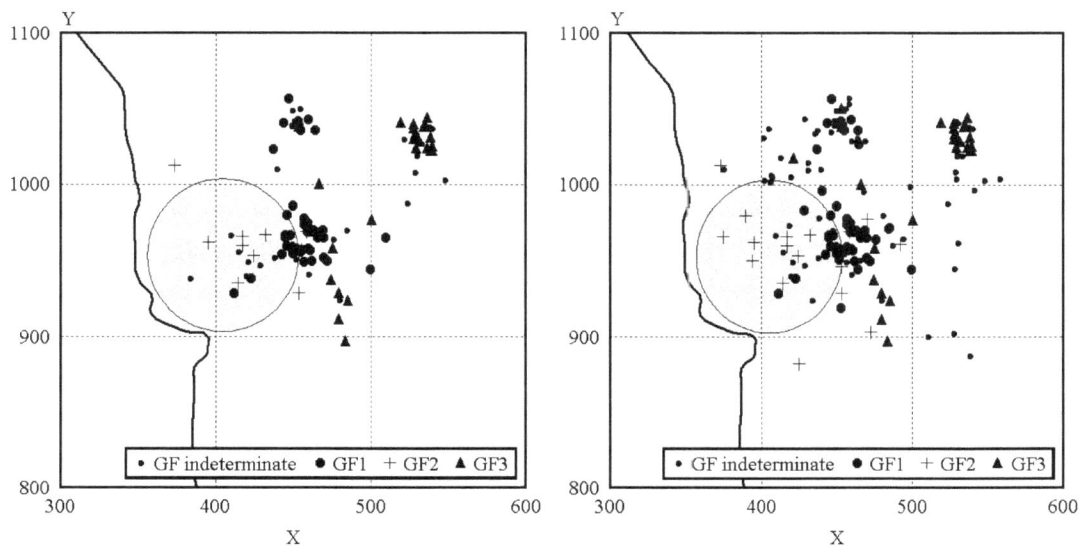

Figure 14. *Spatial Distribution of the Artefacts in Grey Flint. (Left: Piece-plotted artefacts. Right: Piece-plotted artefacts and screened artefacts). Note the difference in the clustering between block GF 2 and blocks GF 1 and GF 3.*

69

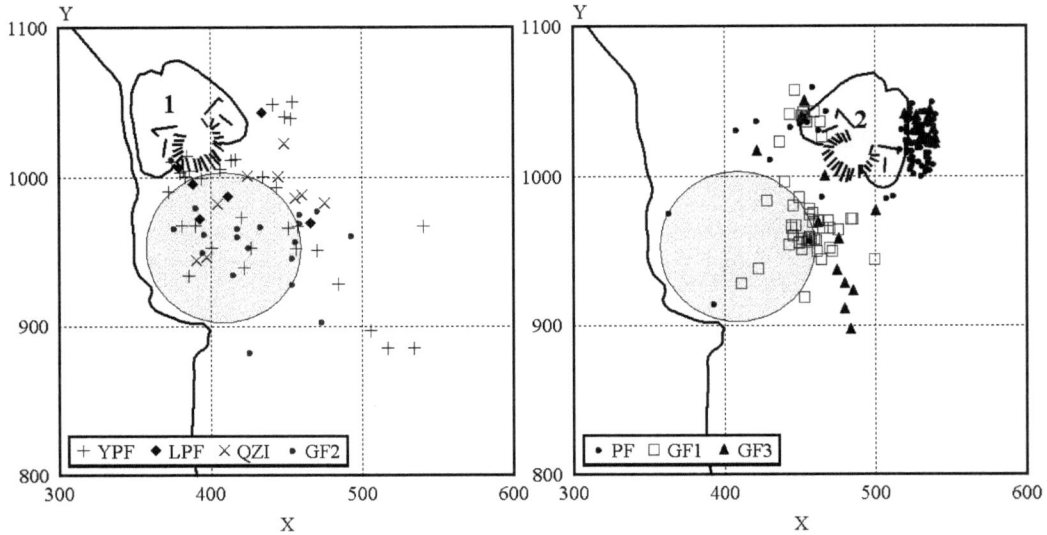

Figure 15. *Finding the Knapper' spots . On the left, the spatial distribution (by block) of the artefacts knapped by individual # 1. This individual seemingly exploited at least 5 blocks of raw material, including the recycled side scraper illustrated in Figure 10. Most of the obtained end products were small flakes (in flint and in quartzite), obtained in an expedient way. On the right, the artefacts supposedly knapped by individual # 2. Contrary to individual #1, most of the produced end products were flint bladelets, obtained either through prismatic or essentially through carinated reduction, in a very efficient way. On the left side of the knapper, a dense cluster of bladelets and chips was found, corresponding probably to his main production area. On its front, a toss zone, close to the hearth, where most of the cores were collected. On its right another cluster was detected, almost exclusively composed of bladelets from several blocks, including some produced by individual #1.*

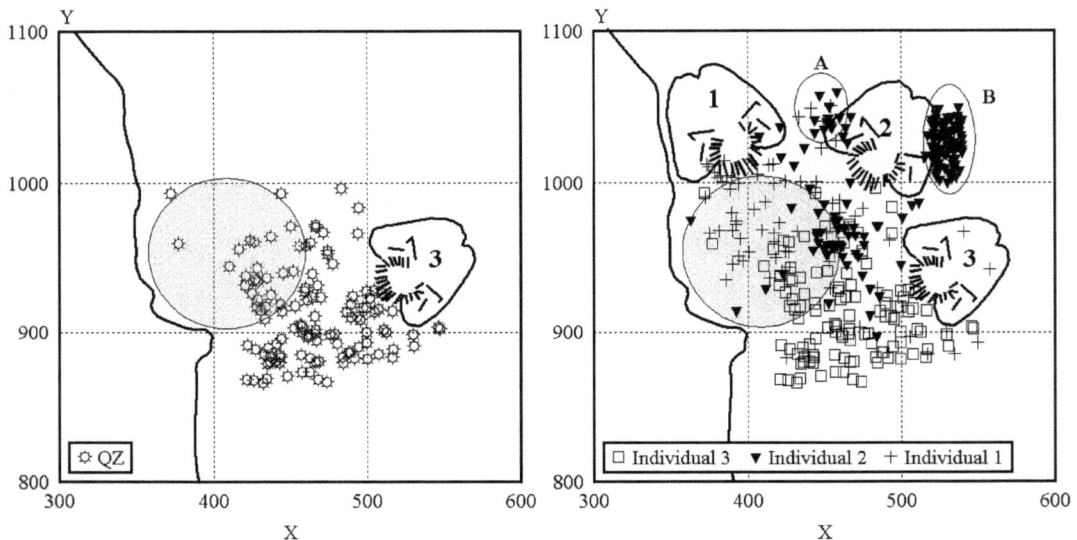

Figure 16. *Detecting "Specialization" and Reconstructing Drop and Toss Zones through Refitting.*
On the left, the spatial distribution of artefacts knapped by Individual # 3. The reconstructions have shown that this individual knapped at least 4 different quartz blocks, in order to produce essentially bladelets. The reduction sequences of the good quality quartz blocks show undoubtedly that individual # 3 was an experienced quartz knapper. Most of the bladelets produced in quartz seem actually to have been exported at abandonment. The cluster of quartz artefacts shows almost no overlap with the clusters from the other two individuals. On the right, the general interpretation of Lapa do Anecrial Layer 2 lithic scatters, after combining the spatial data with the refitting results. The most parsimonious interpretation of the lithic scatters from layer 2 is that at least three individuals performed knapping operations around a hearth. The fact that most of the cores were found on the proximity or even inside it seems to suggest that the hearth served as a common toss zone. The ongoing detailed study of clusters enable us to detect a drop zone of individual # 2 (B), composed essentially of flint chips and small bladelets. It also permitted the detection of one other interesting concentration, located between individuals # 1 and # 2, very rich in bladelets not only produced by individual # 2, but also by individual # 1. It seems as though both knappers, after choosing which bladelets were good enough to be exported, abandoned the remaining bladelets in a single concentration. Individual # 3, on the other hand, as the reconstructions have shown, produced several quartz bladelets from which the vast majority was exported at abandonment, leaving behind only the respective cores and flake debitage.

behaviours that would otherwise be hard to successfully identify.

The study of the lithic assemblage from Lapa do Anecrial, through a combined use of attribute analysis and refitting, provided exceptional data on the lithic reduction strategies of the Estremaduran Terminal Gravettian. The fact that the lithic sample seemingly represents activities that took place during a very short period of time had two main consequences. The first is that the artefact sample is relatively small and, thus, the results of the attribute analysis are not completely adequate for statistical comparisons with other contexts. On the other hand, being a short-term occupation and extremely well preserved spatially and stratigraphically, it allowed, through a refitting success of over 92% in weight, the complete modelling of the reduction strategies applied to both flint and quartz.

For raw material acquisition and transport strategies, the study of Anecrial lithic assemblage leads to the conclusion that there were differences in how the different materials were curated. While flint entered the cave, for the most part, already decortified (either as core preforms, blanks, or finished tools), quartz was transported essentially unmodified (with the exception of thin removals for raw material testing at the source). The difference between the two main raw materials exploited at Anecrial, however, was exclusively related to the conditions under which they entered the site.

The platform preparation strategies were identical for both quartz and flint, with an almost exclusive use of flat (unfaceted) platforms. The maintenance of cores of both materials (required mainly due to hinging) was carried out through the renewal of the platforms by core tablet removals.

The main technological characteristics of the Anecrial sample, as seen through refitting, are: a high core to cobble ratio, that is, for each block of raw material more than one core was exploited; and the association of different reduction strategies. Of these, the dominant were Unidirectional Prismatic, Carinated, and Thick-Nosed for Bladelets. The resulting abandoned cores show characteristics that could be easily misleading, if a traditional typological study had been done on the assemblage. Such a study would have classified the Anecrial assemblage as "Aurignacian", because of the dominance of thick "scrapers". These scrapers, as the reconstructions have clearly demonstrated, were instead bladelet cores and, as the microwear study has shown, were never used as real "tools".

The main end-products from Anecrial, thus, were bladelets. The differences in the presence of quartz and flint bladelets in the studied sample relates mostly to the fact that the former were exported to a higher degree than

were the latter. In addition, the refitting data show that, although the main exported artefacts were bladelets, the Terminal Gravettian people took also some cores (prismatic and thick-nosed) when they left the site. The almost complete absence of retouched bladelets indicates that this type of blank was probably never retouched, or, when it was, only through marginal retouch, real backing being extremely rare (which was a characteristic of the earlier stages of the Gravettian complex).

In summary, Lapa do Anecrial lithic sample is coherent with a rational and optimised exploitation of the available raw materials, in order to produce bladelets. The high core to cobble ratios both in flint and quartz indicate an intensive use of almost all the thick flakes (resulting from preparation and maintenance operations from prismatic cores) as bladelet cores. The similarity between flint and quartz reduction strategies (dominated by the exploitation carinated/thick-nosed cores and prismatic cores) is one of the main characteristics of the Portuguese Terminal Gravettian and Anecrial is surely its best example, mainly because of the excellent characteristics of the available quartz.

As to what concerns the spatial analysis, the data from the reconstructions, although still under processing, has provided interesting insights into the micro-scale past organization of a small hunter-gatherer group. The combining of the reconstructions with the clustering of the abandoned artefacts made possible the attribution of the various blocks of raw material to at least three knappers, supposedly located in different areas around a hearth, which served as a common toss zone. The following stage of the spatial study from Anecrial is going to be the detailed analysis of each reconstruction "chronology" and spatial distribution. The main goal of this process is to identify more precisely the eventual movements of artefacts between the various stages of exploitation, and between the three individuals.

BIBLIOGRAPHY

ALMEIDA, F. 1998 O método das remontagens líticas: enquadramento teórico e aplicações. *Trabalhos de Arqueologia da EAM* 3: 1-40.

ALMEIDA, F. 1999 Cores, tools, or both? Methodological contribution for the study of carinated lithic elements: the Portuguese case. Paper presented at the Society for American Archaeology 64th Annual Meeting

ALMEIDA, F. 2000 *The Terminal Gravettian of Portuguese Estremadura*, Unpublished Ph.D. Dissertation, Southern Methodist University.

ARTS, N. & E. CZIELA 1990 Bibliography (1880-1988) on the subject of refitting stone artefacts. In *The Big Puzzle. Internation Symposium on Refitting Stone Artefacts*, edited by E. CZIESLA, S. EICKHOFF, N. ARTS & D. WINTER,. Studies in Modern Archaeology, Vol 1. Holos, Bonn, pp. 652-683.

AUBRY, T., L. DETRAIN & B. KERVAZO 1995 Les niveaux intermédiaires entre le Gravettien et le Solutréen de L'Abri Casserole (Les Eyzies de Tayac): mise en evidence d'un mode de production original de microlithes et implications. *Bulletin de la Société Préhistorique Française*, 92: 296-301.

AUBRY, T., J. ZILHÃO, F. ALMEIDA & M. FONTUGNE 1997 Production d'armatures microlithiques pendant le Paléolithique supérieur et le Mésolithique du Portugal. In (R. Balbín & P. Bueno, Eds.), *II Congreso de Arqueología Peninsular. Paleolítico y Epipaleolítico*. Fundación Rei Afonso Henriques, Zamora pp.259-272.

BINFORD, L. 1973 Interassemblage variability: the Mousterian and the Functional argument. In *The Explanation of Cultural change: Models in Prehistory*, edited by C. Renfrew, Duckworth, London, pp. 227-254.

BINFORD, L. 1983a *In Pursuit of the Past. Decoding the Archaeological Record*. Thames and Hudson, London.

BINFORD, L. 1983b *Working at Archaeology*. Academic Press, New York

BORDES, F. 1968 *Le Paléolithique dans le Monde*, Collection L' Univers des Conaissances, Hachette, Paris.

BORDES, F. 1980a Question de Contemporanéité: L'Illusion des Remontages. *Bulletin de la Société Préhistorique Française* 77(5): 132-133.

BORDES, F. 1980b Savez-vous Remonter les Cailloux a la Mode de Chez Nous? *Bulletin de la Société Préhistorique Française* 77(8): 232-234.

CAHEN, D. 1980 Question de contemporanéité: L'apport des remontages. *Bulletin de la Société Préhistorique Française* 77 (8): 230-232.

CAHEN, D. 1981 Premiers Resultats de l'Étude par Remontage. *Gallia Prehistoire* 24(1): 123-137.

CAHEN, D. & L.H. KEELEY 1980 Not less than two, not more than three. *World Archaeology* 12(2): 166-180.

CAHEN, D., L.H. KEELEY & F. VAN NOTEN 1979 Stone tools, Toolkits, and Human Behavior in Prehistory. *Current Anthropology* 20: 661-672.

CZIELA, E. 1990 On Refitting of Stone Artefacts. In *The Big Puzzle. Internation Symposium on Refitting Stone Artefacts*, edited by E. CZIESLA, S. EICKHOFF, N. ARTS & D. WINTER,. Studies in Modern Archaeology, Vol 1. Holos, Bonn, pp. 9-44.

DELPORTE, H. 1968 L' Abri du Facteur à Tursac. *Gallia Préhistoire* XI (1): 1-112.

FERRING, C.R. 1980 *Technological variability and change in the Late Palaeolithic of the Negev*. Unpublished PhD Dissertation, Southern Methodist University. Ann Arbor: University Microfilms.

FERRING, C.R. 1988 Technological Change in the Upper Palaeolithic of the Negev. In *Upper Pleistocene Prehistory of Western Eurasia*, edited by H. Dibble & A. Montet-White, University of Pennsylvania Museum, Philadelphia, pp. 333-348.

GRIMM, L.T. & T.A. KOETJE 1992 Spatial patterns in the Upper Perigordian at Solvieux: implications for activity reconstruction. In *Piecing Together the Past: Applications of Reffiting Studies in Archaeology*, edited by J. Hofman & J. Enloe. BAR International series 578, Oxford, pp. 264-286.

HOFMAN, J.L. 1981 The Refitting of Chipped Stone Artefacts as an Analytical and Interpretive Tool. *Current Anthropology* 22 (6): 691-693.

HOFMAN, J.L. 1986 Vertical movement of artefacts in alluvial and stratified deposits. *Current Anthropology* 27(2): 163-171.

HOFMAN, J.L. 1992 Putting the pieces together: An Introduction to Refitting. In *Piecing Together the Past: Applications of Reffiting Studies in Archaeology*, edited by J. Hofman & J. Enloe. BAR International series 578, Oxford, pp. 1-20.

HOFMAN, J.L. & J.G. ENLOE, J.G. (editors) 1992 *Piecing Together the Past: Applications of Reffiting Studies in Archaeology*. Oxford , BAR International series 578.

JULIEN, M., C. KARLIN & B. VALENTIN 1992 Déchets de silex, déchets de pierres chauffées de l'intéret des remontages à Pincevent (France). In *Piecing Together the Past: Applications of Reffiting Studies in Archaeology*, edited by J. Hofman & J. Enloe. BAR International series 578, Oxford, pp. 287-295.

LARSON, M.L. & E.E. INGBAR 1992 Perspectives on refitting: Critique and a Complementary approach. In *Piecing Together the Past: Applications of Reffiting Studies in Archaeology*, edited by J. Hofman & J. Enloe. BAR International series 578, Oxford, pp. 151-162.

LEROI-GOURHAN, A. & M. BREZILLON 1972 *Fouilles de Pincevent. Essai d'analyse ethnographique d'un habitat magdalénien(La section 36)*. VII supplement a "Gallia Prehistorique". CNRS, Paris.

LUCAS, G. 1997 Les Lamelles Dufour du Flageolet I (Bézenac, Dordogne) dans le contexte Aurignacien. *Paleo* 9: 191-219.

LUCAS, G. 1999 Production expérimentale de lamelles torses: approche préliminaire. *Bulletin de la Société Préhistorique Française* 96 (2): 145-151.

MARKS, A. (Ed.) 1983 *Prehistory and Paleo-environments of the Central Negev, Israel*.(3 vols.). SMU Press, Dallas.

MARKS, A. & VOLKMAN, P. 1983 Changing core reduction strategies: a technological shift from the Middle to the Upper Palaeolithic in the Southern Levant. In *The Mousterian legacy: Human biocultural change in the Upper Pleistocene,* edited by E. Trinkaus. BAR International series, 164, Oxford, pp. 13-34.

MARKS, A. & F. ALMEIDA 1996 The late Aurignacian and "Aurignacian" Elements in the Upper Palaeolithic of the Portuguese Estremadura, Portugal. In *XIII International Congress of Prehistoric and Protohistoric Sciences: The Upper Palaeolithic, The Late Aurignacian.* Forlí: ABACO Edizioni, pp.11-21.

PIGEOT, N. 1987 *Les Magdaléniens de l'Unité U5 d'Étiolles. Étude technique, économique, sociale, par la dynamique du débitage.* XXVe supplément à Gallia Préhistoire.

RIGAUD, J.-Ph. 1993 L'Aurignacien dans le Sud-Ouest de la France. Bilan et perspectives. *Actes du XIIe Congrès International des Sciences Préhistoriques et Protohistoriques. Bratislava, 1-7 septembre 1991.Aurignacien en Europe et au Proche Orient.* Vol.2. Bratislava, UISPP: pp. 181-186.

RIGAUD, J.-P. & J. SIMEK 1991 Interpreting Spatial Patterns at the Grotte XV: A Multiple-Method Approach. *In The Interpretation of Archaeological Spatial Patterning,* edited by E. Kroll and T. Price, Plenum Press, New York and London, pp. 199-220.

ROEBROEKS, W. & P. HENNEKENS 1990 Transport of lithics in the Middle Palaeolithic: conjoining evidence from Maastricht-Belvedere (NL). In *The Big Puzzle. Internation Symposium on Refitting Stone Artefacts,* edited by E. CZIESLA, S. EICKHOFF, N. ARTS & D. WINTER,. Studies in Modern Archaeology, Vol 1. Holos, Bonn, pp. 283-296.

SACCHI, D., I. SOLER, N. MASFERRER, I. MAROTO, J. GENOVER & E. DOMENECH FAUS 1996 La question de l' Aurignacien tardif dans le domaine méditerranée nord-occidental. In *XIII International Congress of Prehistoric and Protohistoric Science: The Upper Palaeolithic, The Late Aurignacian.* ABACO Edizioni, Forlí, pp. 23-40.

SONNEVILLE-BORDES, D. 1963 Aurignacien et Périgordien entre Loire et Garonne. In Aurignac et l' Aurignacien, Centenaire de Fouilles d' E. Lartet. *Bulletin de la Société Méridionnale de Spéléologie et de Préhistoire* 6-9: 51-62.

THACKER, P. (1996). *A Landscape Perspective on Upper Paleolthic Settlement in Portuguese Estremadura.* Unpublished Ph.D. Dissertation. Southern Methodist University.

TIXIER, J. & M.-L. INIZAN 1981 Ksar'Aquil, stratigraphie et ensembles lithiques dans le Paléolithique Supérieur:fouilles 1971-1975. *In Préhistoire du Levant. Chronologie et organisation de l' Espace depuis les origines jusqu' au VIème millénaire. Colloques Internationaux du CNRS, 10-14 juin Lyon, Maison de l' Orient.* CNRS, Paris, pp. 353-367.

USIK, V. 1989 Korolevo - Transition from Lower to Upper Palaeolithic According to Reconstruction Data. *Anthropologie* 27(2-3): 179-212.

VAN NOTEN, F. & D. CAHEN 1978 *Les Chasseurs de Meer* (2 vols.). Dissertationes archaeologicae gandenses. Brugges, De Tempel.

VOLKMAN, P. 1983 Boker tachtit: the core reconstructions. *In Prehistory and Paleo-environments of the Central Negev, Israel.III* , edited by A. Marks, SMU Press, Dallas, pp. 127-190.

VOLKMAN, P. 1989 *Boker tachtit: The Technological Shift from the Middle to the Upper Palaeolithic in the Central Negev, Israel.* Unpublished Ph.D. Dissertation. Southern Methodist University.

WYCKOFF, D.G. 1992 Refittting and protohistoric knapping behaviour. In *Piecing Together the Past: Applications of Reffiting Studies in Archaeology,* edited by J. Hofman & J. Enloe. BAR International series 578, Oxford, pp. 83-127.

ZILHÃO, J. 1994 La séquence chrono-stratigraphique du Solutréen portugais. *Férvedes*, 1: 119-129.

ZILHÃO, J. 1995 *O Paleolítico Superior da Estremadura Portuguesa.* Unpublished Ph.D. Dissertation, Lisbon: Faculdade de Letras da Universidade de Lisboa.

ZILHÃO, J. 1997 *O Paleolitico Superior da Estremadura Portuguesa*. Edições Colibri, Lisbon.

ZILHÃO, J. 2000 Nature and culture in Portugal from 30,000 to 20,000 bp. In *Hunters of the Golden Age: The Mid Upper Palaeolithic of Eurasia 30,000-20,000 BP*, edited by W. Roebroeks, M. Mussi, J. Svoboda & K. Fennema. University of Leiden, Leiden, pp.337-354.

ZILHÃO, J. & T. AUBRY 1995 La pointe de Vale Comprido et les origines du Solutréen, *L'Antropologie*, 99: 125-142.

ZILHÃO, J., A.E. MARKS, C.R. FERRING, N.F. BICHO & I. FIGUEIRAL 1995b The Upper Palaeolithic of the Rio Maior basin (Portugal). Preliminary results of a 1987--1993 Portuguese-American research project. *Trabalhos de Antropologia e Etnologia*. 35: 69-88.

ZILHÃO, J., T. AUBRY & F. ALMEIDA 1997 L'utilisation du quartz pendant la transition Gravettien-Solutréen au Portugal, *Préhistoire Anthropologie Méditerranéennes*. 6: 289-303.

ZILHÃO, J., T. AUBRY & F. ALMEIDA 1999 Un modèle technologique pour le passage du Gravettien au Solutréen dans le sud-ouest de l'Europe. In *XXIV Congrès Préhistorique de France : Les Faciès leptolithiques du Nord-Ouest méditerranéen: milieux naturels et culturels*, pp. 165-183.

Address of author:

Francisco ALMEIDA
Centro de Investigação em Paleoecologia Humana e Arqueociências. Instituto Português de Arqueologia
Av. da Índia, 136
1300-300 Lisboa, Portugal

falmeida@ipa.min-cultura.pt

THE INTERPRETIVE POTENTIAL OF LITHIC REFITS IN A MIDDLE PALEOLITHIC SITE: THE ABRIC ROMANÍ (CAPELLADES, SPAIN)

Manuel VAQUERO, Gema CHACÓN & José M. RANDO

Abstract

The Abric Romaní (Romaní rockshelter) has provided a thick stratigraphic sequence including several Middle Palaeolithic archaeological levels dated between 40 and 70 ka BP. These levels have been exposed over large surfaces and are characterised by a high temporal resolution. Moreover, many structures, including hearths, have been documented. This allows spatial analysis to be developed. Refitting of lithic artefacts forms a substantial part of this analysis. The refits obtained from a series of levels excavated in recent years, dated between 45 and 52 ka BP, have provided interesting results concerning three main issues: a) the definition of spatial units, especially in hearth-related assemblages, b) the organisation of campsites and the connection between activity areas, and c) the temporal relationships between the artefacts and spatial units.

Résumé

Au gisement de l'Abric Romaní on a mis en évidence une puissante séquence archéologique renfermant plusieurs niveaux du Paléolithique moyen datés entre 40 et 70 ka BP. Ces niveaux ont été fouillés sur des grandes surfaces et sont caractérisés par une haute résolution temporelle. D'autre part, on a trouvé plusieurs structures anthropiques, parmi lesquelles il faut souligner les foyers. Ces caractéristiques favorisent le dévelopement des analyses spatiales. Les rémontages de témoins litiques forment une partie fondamentalle de cette analyse. Les remontages obtenus aux niveux archéologiques fouillés pendant ces dernières années, datés entre 45 et 52 ka BP, ont permis d'avoir des données intéresantes sur trois sujets principaux : a) la définition des unités spatiales, spécialement aux assemblages associés aux foyers ; b) l'organisation des campements et la connexion entre des aires d'activité ; et c) les rélations temporelles entre les témoins et les unités spatiales.

INTRODUCTION

The aim of this paper is to present a synthesis of the contributions that lithic refits have provided on the Neanderthal behavioural strategies in the Middle Palaeolithic site of the Abric Romaní (Capellades, Spain). Two domains have been traditionally recognised in refitting analysis: the study of reduction strategies and the

spatial analysis of sites. This paper will be focused on the spatial dimension of refits, since the sedimentary characteristics of the Abric Romaní and the large surface excavated are well suited for reconstructing the occupation strategies. We have obtained less information about reduction methods, due to the fragmentary character of the *chaînes opératoires* at the site. Few reduction sequences were entirely carried out at the rockshelter and only some stages of the knapping processes are represented. However, these refits have provided significant data with regard to technical behaviours in a discoidal context. In addition, some technical procedures for maximising raw material exploitation have been well documented by refits.

Refitting provides essential data to reconstruct spatial organisation strategies, although its systematic use in Middle Palaeolithic sites has not been very common. This is due in part to the small scale of excavation at many sites, especially in caves and rockshelters. Nevertheless, the results obtained at some locales (Locht 2001; Roebroeks 1988) indicate the relevance of refits in the analysis the spatial behaviour of Neanderthal groups. However, most studies focus on open air sites, so the spatial patterns of cave and rockshelters occupations remain poorly known. This issue is especially significant, since spatial arguments have been used in recent years to compare the behavioural capabilities of Neanderthals and anatomically modern humans. In this context, some scholars consider Neanderthal spatial patterns as structurally different, that is, simpler than those from anatomically modern humans (e.g. Farizy 1994; Mellars 1996; Pettitt 1997). A marked contrast in their respective cultural, and especially communicative capabilities, would explain these differences. These conclusions were drawn from the few Middle Palaeolithic sites that have been extensively and systematically studied from a spatial point of view. In addition, Upper Palaeolithic spatial patterning was mainly defined using some well-studied open air sites, like sites in the Paris basin (Pincevent, Etiolles or Marsagny), where the occupational strategies were in large part reconstructed through intensive refitting analyses (e.g. Julien et al. 1988; Olive 1988; Schmider and Croisset 1990). It remains to be ascertained if the cave and rockshelter occupations of Neanderthals and anatomically modern humans are really so different.

The Abric Romaní is located in the northeastern corner of the Iberian Peninsula, 50 km Northwest of Barcelona. It is a wide rockshelter opened in a travertine cliff formed at the right margin of the Anoia river. Amador Romaní, who almost entirely excavated the uppermost layers, discovered the site at the beginning of the 20th century. The current archaeological project started at 1983 and was directed to the reconstruction of spatial organisation strategies. The archaeological levels are excavated over large surfaces, up to 250 m², in some cases, and the spatial location of archaeological remains is carefully recorded. The stratigraphic sequence is almost 20 m thick and has been dated by uranium-series to between 40 and 70 ka BP (Bischoff et al. 1988). Except the uppermost one, all the archaeological levels correspond to the Middle Palaeolithic (Carbonell et al. 1996). Palynological analyses indicate the succession of five climatic phases, between the final moments of OIS 5 and the Hengelo Interstadial (Burjachs and Julià, 1994). Faunal assemblages are dominated by red deer and horse remains. Taphonomic and zooarchaeological analyses clearly indicate that humans formed these assemblages (see Cáceres et al. 1998).

Most of the sequence is formed by the precipitation of carbonates, usually in the form of well-bedded travertine layers (Carbonell et al. 1994). This formation process is characterised by a high rate of deposition. The archaeological levels occur as thin strata embedded between the travertine layers (Figure 1). They are therefore vertically well-defined and the formation of palimpsests is limited, especially compared to other Middle Palaeolithic sites. In addition, the conservation of some archaeological evidence, like hearths and wood implements, is good in this sedimentary context. Fire damage is well-recorded on the travertine surfaces allowing easy identificaton and delimitation of combustion structures (Pastó et al. 2001). A large number of hearths has been discovered in each archaeological horizon (i.e. over 50 in level Ja) making a thorough analysis of the role of these structures in occupation strategies possible. The upper levels (A to F-G) were seriously damaged by previous excavations therefore the spatial analyses focused on the archaeological layers excavated since 1989 (levels H to L).

Our main concern here are the lithic refits. Refitting of bone remains have provided some interesting results (Bravo, 2001), but so far they are limited to one of the archaeological levels (Ja) and will not be treated here. It seems clear, however, that this will be a promising domain for future research. Flint is the dominant raw material in all the archaeological horizons, although other materials, like quartz and limestone, were also knapped and reach significant percentages in some levels. Flint mainly comes from Paleogen formations west of the site and shows a high macroscopic variability, as far as colour and texture are concerned. This makes the segregation of remains according to raw material characteristics prior to refitting easy. Limestone remains are also highly variable, whereas quartz is fairly homogeneous. As should be expected then, flint and limestone have higher refitting rates than quartz. The deficient knapping qualities of the latter as well as the well-known difficulties to discern technical features on quartz artefacts contribute to their low refitting rate. Flint and limestone were collected as cobbles in the fluvial formations of the Anoia river, while quartz comes from the outcrops located close to the site. Lithic assemblages are essentially formed by knapping debris. Flakes and flake fragments are clearly dominant in all the archaeological levels and their size distribution is in agreement with knapping in the shelter. Small flakes and chips constitute the bulk of the assemblages. Cores and retouched artefacts are scarce (less than 4% of lithic remains in most archaeological horizons) (Vaquero 1999b). Limestone fragments derived from the use of unworked cobbles are common, especially in some archaeological horizons, like levels H and Ja. Most of these cobbles were utilised as hammerstones, but some show thermal damage suggesting their use in activities related to hearths.

The spatial interpretation of archaeological sites depends on the geological formation processes. The first step of spatial analysis should be to ascertain if post-depositional movements have significantly altered the location of remains. Lithic refits can provide some clues on this subject. At the Abric Romaní, the mean length of connection lines (Table 1) is in agreement with the values provided by the experimental reproduction of reduction sequences (Barton and Bergman 1982; Boëda and Pelegrin, 1985; Newcomer and Sieveking 1989). This suggests that the post-depositional alteration of the archaeological remains has been weak. Connection lines shorter than one meter are dominant in all the archaeological levels and

Table 1

Distribution of refit lines in distance intervals for each archaeological level and mean refit distance.

Level	0-1 m	1-2 m	2-4 m	4-8 m	> 8 m	Total	Mean (cm)
H	25	1	1		1	28	87,1
I	17	5	8	1		31	119,5
Ja	66	38	36	13	5	158	194,3
Jb	47	17	3	2		69	81,4
K	48	18	6	2	1	75	69,1
Total	203	79	54	18	7	361	110,2

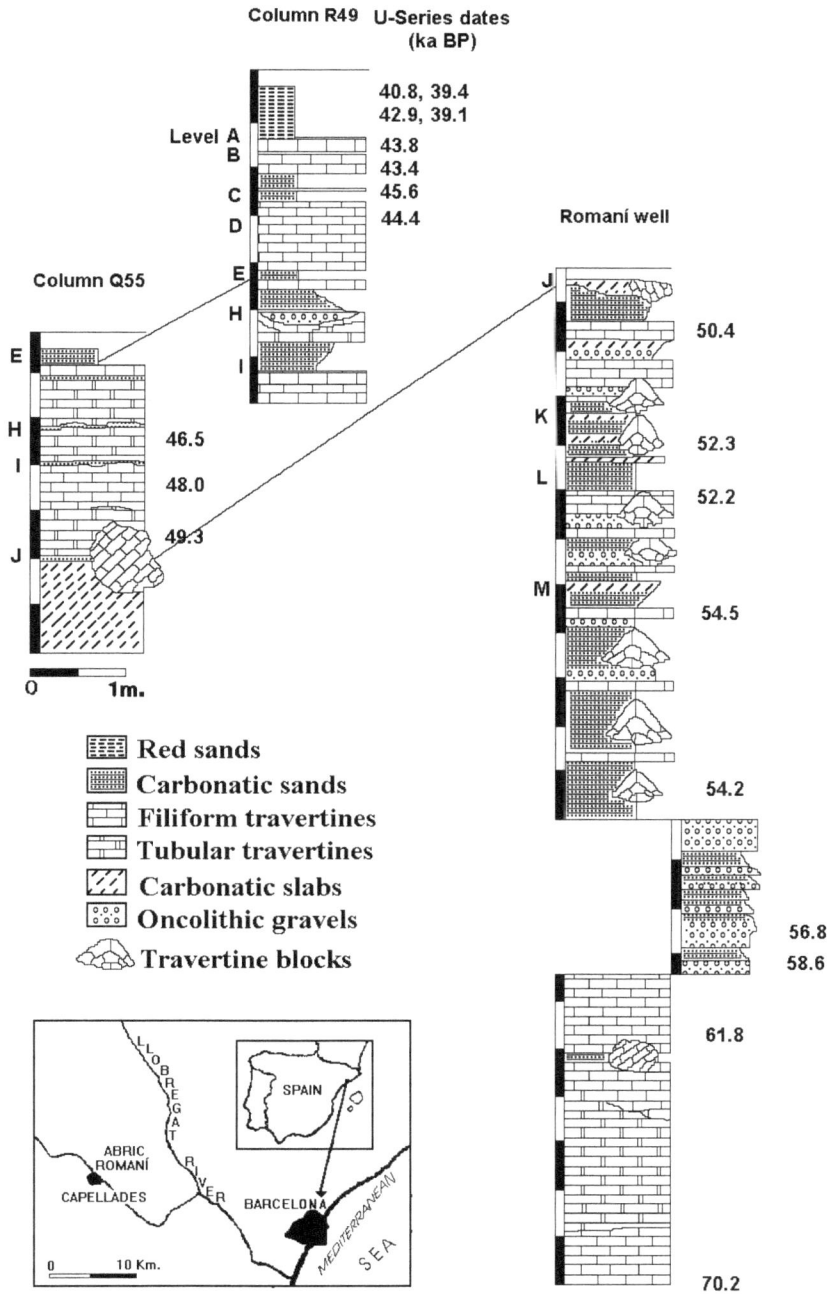

Figure 1 *Location of the Abric Romaní and schematic lithostratigraphy of the Abric Romaní sequence. The archaeological levels so far excavated and the U-Series dates are indicated.*

the mean distances are generally between 70 and 120 cm, except in level Ja, where it reaches almost 2 m. However, this increase of the mean length in level Ja is produced, as we will see below, by some long connections corresponding to the intentional transport of lithic artefacts. Because of the reduced thickness of the archaeological layers, vertical movements are also not significant. Refitting indicates therefore that the Abric Romaní levels are well suited for spatial analyses.

All types of refits have been recorded, but those corresponding to core reduction sequences are dominant (Table 2). It may be said, however, that determining the type of refit is not always an easy task, especially when few artefacts are connected. This uncertainty increases when small flakes are the ones being refitted. This is especially true at level H, where the lithic assemblage is mainly composed of small flakes. No cores were found in this level and the reduction sequences are poorly

Table 2
Distribution of connection lines by types of refit at each archaeological level.

	Core reduction	Retouch	Breakage	Total
H	10	7	13	30
I	14	2	15	31
Ja	102	2	54	158
Jb	54	0	15	69
K	55	3	17	75
Total	235	14	114	363

represented. Transport of cores from the site may account for this pattern. Nevertheless, the attribution of connection lines to core reduction sequences remains problematical in this level as they could correspond to retouch sequences. This uncertainty is reduced at the other levels, since the core reduction character of most connection lines are clear. At these levels, core reduction lines tend to be dominant, although connections between broken pieces are also well represented. Retouch refits are uncommon, except in level H. This could be explained in part by the small size of the retouch flakes, as refitting small artefacts is more difficult. Nonetheless, it seems that the introduction of previously retouched artefacts into the site was a common practice. Most break refits correspond to flakes broken by knapping accidents or post-depositional factors, like burning. Others result from the fragmentation of limestone cobbles used as

hammers. Some refits prove that broken limestone cobbles previously used as hammerstones were reused as cores.

The refitting studies carried out at the Abric Romaní have provided valuable data on different issues linked to the spatial organisation of campsites, the spatial and temporal scheduling of the *chaînes opératoires*, and the transportation strategies for lithic resources. This information will be presented in three main headings. These represent three analytical levels of increasing complexity, corresponding both to intra- site and inter-site perspectives: 1) the archaeological accumulations within an occupation level, 2) the occupation level and the relationships between different activity areas, and 3) the settlement strategies and the relationships between different sites.

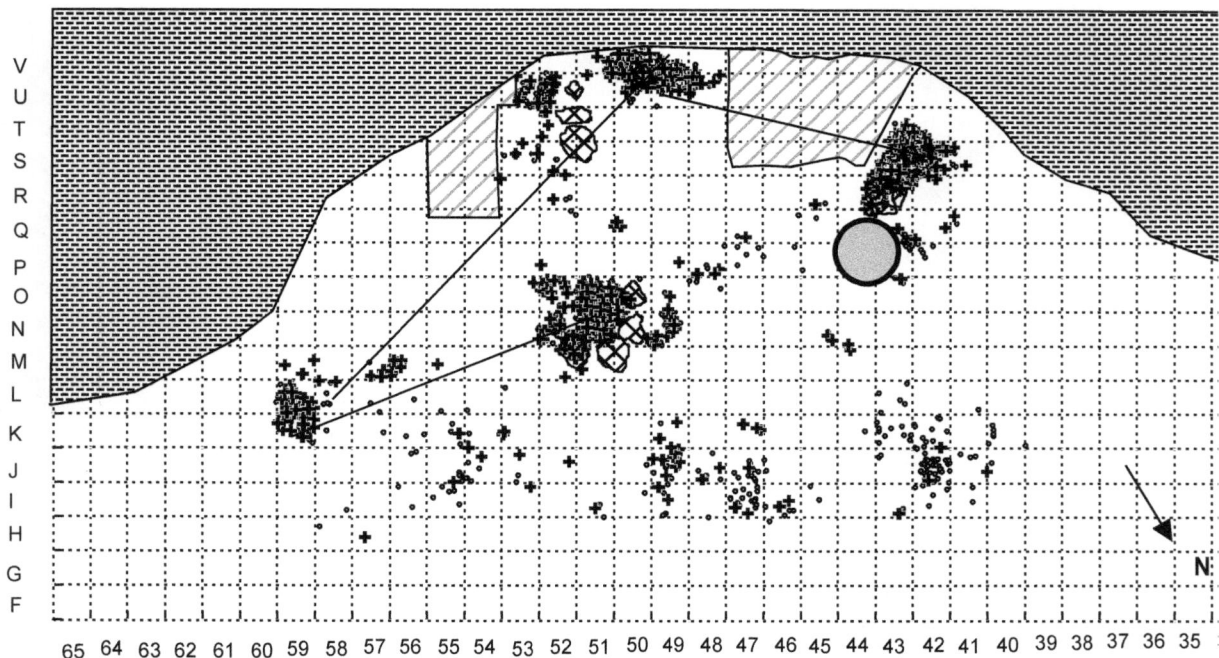

Figure 2 *General distribution of the archaeological remains from level L: lithic artefacts (cross), bone remains (white circle), retouched artefacts (black box), hearths (crossed area). Note the different accumulation areas and the refitting lines connecting them.*

Manuel Vaquero, Gema Chacón & José Rando

Table 3
Distribution of connection lines from accumulation L3 by length.

	0-25 cm	25-50 cm	50-75 cm	75-100 cm	>100 cm	Total
Breakage	15					15
Reduction	65	5	3		2	75
Total	80	5	3		2	90

THE ANALYSIS OF ARCHAEOLOGICAL ACCUMULATIONS AND THE DEFINITION OF ACTIVITY AREAS

The study of the spatial distribution of archaeological remains has allowed the definition of different spatial units. Refits are essential to characterise these units. At the Abric Romaní, the most common spatial unit is the hearth-related accumulation (Vaquero and Pastó 2001). Activities were focused around hearths at all the archaeological levels and this produced a clustered distribution of remains, especially lithics (Vaquero et al. 2001). Distribution of bone remains is more homogeneous, although concentrations around hearths are also visible. This spatial unit shows characteristics similar to those described for household areas among contemporary hunter-gatherer groups. They can be described as a drop zone where small lithic and bone remains are dominant (Binford 1978). It should be stressed that household areas are not simply a functional area linked to fire, but they are essentially a socialising space, where face-to-face interactions take place. Archaeologically identifying these household areas is fundamental to ascertain when a social structure similar to that described among current hunter-gatherers may be present. The cognitive implications of this finding are clear: the social processes developed in household areas need fully modern communicational capabilities. Lithic refits are essential to characterise the technical activities carried out at these domestic areas. Refitting has allowed to identify the focus of activity at these spatial units and to ascertain the temporal relationships among different reduction sequences. As Stevenson has pointed out (Stevenson 1991), the succession of different knapping episodes in the same area can be identified by the differential dispersion of the lithic remains corresponding to different reduction sequences.

As an example of the contribution of lithic refits to the study of hearth-related assemblages we will present one of the hearth related accumulations identified at level L. This level showed a spatial structure characterised by four main accumulations, three of them clearly associated with multi-focused hearths. These accumulations, well-defined horizontally and vertically, are connected by refits (Figure 2). The accumulation L3 is located near the shelter wall (squares R-T/42-44) and includes an assemblage of 791 artefacts (only items recorded in three dimensions are considered). Most of the remains (68,5%)

are lithics, which suggests the significance of knapping among the activities carried out in this zone. It is a 200 x 100 cm oval accumulation associated with a combustion area where three different combustion centres have been recognised (Figure 3A). Although some remains rested directly atop the combustion area, most of them were located outside of it. The accumulation is vertically well-delimited and the archaeological remains are clustered within a 5-10 cm thick band. The lithic assemblage is

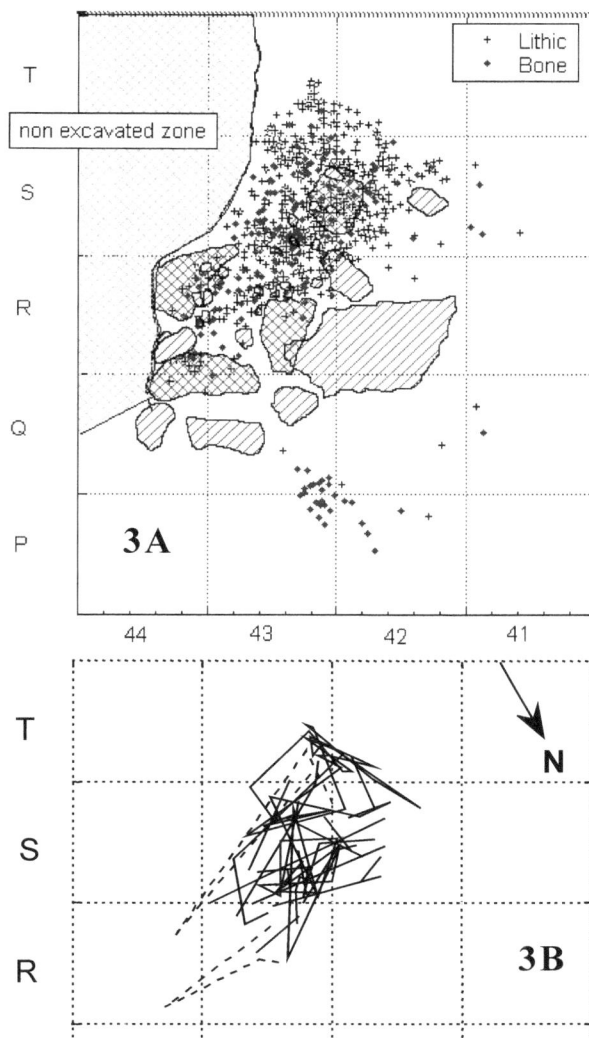

Figure 3 *A) Distribution of archaeological remains in the accumulation area L3. B) Spatial distribution of the lithic refits in accumulation area L3.*

79

Manuel Vaquero, Gema Chacón & José Rando

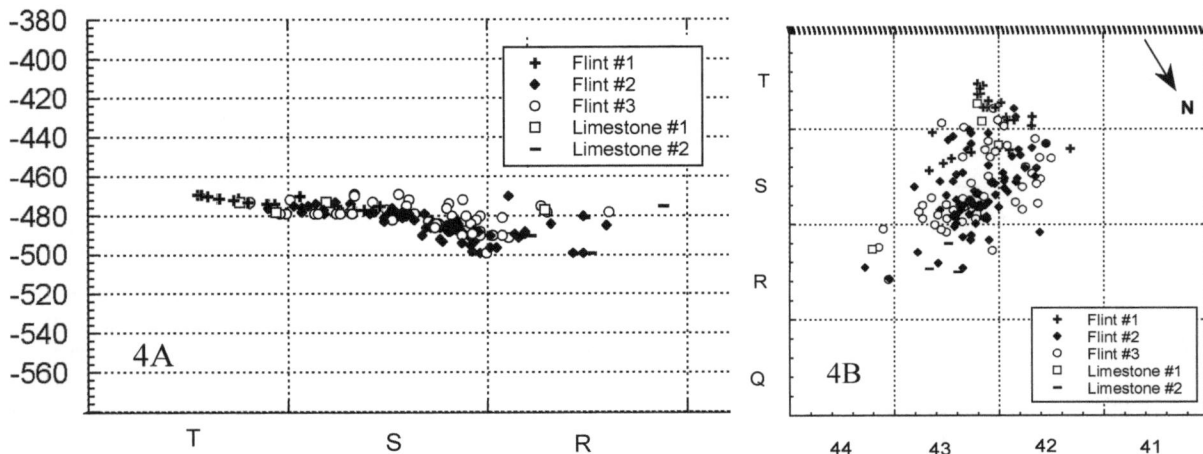

Figure 4 *Raw material units identified in accumulation area L3. A) Vertical plot of the same lithic groups. B) Horizontal distribution of the main units.*

composed of flint, limestone and quartz objects. Flint is dominant. Most of the lithics are unretouched flakes and flake fragments. Cores and retouched artefacts are present in very low percentages. As at most of the hearth-related accumulations documented at the Abric Romaní, small items dominate the assemblage (Vaquero and Pastó 2001).

Twenty-one percent of all lithics have been refitted, reaching up to 90 connection lines. Most refits correspond to reduction sequences, and retouch refits have not been documented. Although some connections

link this accumulation to other hearth-related areas, most of the refits are within L3 (Figure 3B). The main length of connection lines is 49 cm and the majority of them are less than 25 cm (Table 3). These values indicate that the archaeological record has been little affected by post-depositional movements. Connection lines are clustered, defining well-delimited knapping areas (Figure 4B). This clustering is also documented on the vertical plot, which does not show different accumulation boundaries that could indicate temporal gaps between knapping episodes (Figure 4A.). The refitted raw material units exhibit different paths of introduction into the rockshelter. Most

Figure 5 *Refitted reduction sequence from accumulation L3. A) Reconstructed nodule. B) Artefacts from the refitted sequence. They are placed in order, starting at the bottom right. The core is in the upper left corner.*

80

Manuel Vaquero, Gema Chacón & José Rando

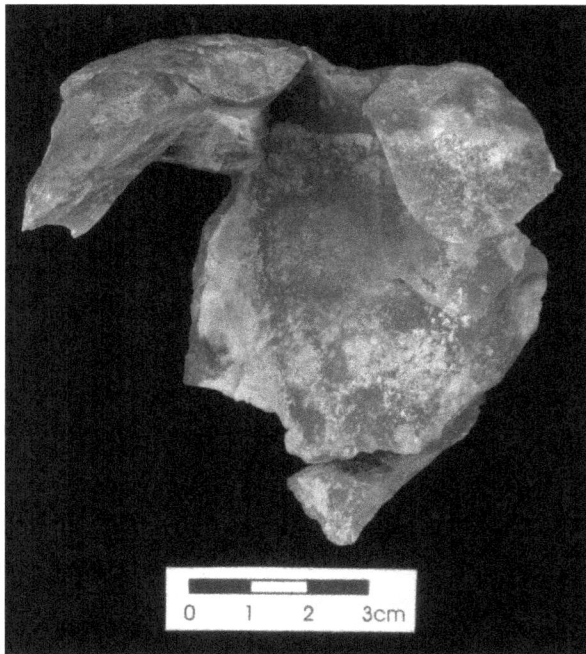

Figure 6 *Refitting assemblage from accumulation L3 corresponding to the initial stage of the core reduction sequence.*

of them present only a segment of the *chaîne opératoire* and only two units (Flint-1 and Flint-3) show a nearly complete reduction sequence. Figure 5 shows the almost

complete refitting of the reduction sequence of a small flint cobble. All the products of this sequence have been found in the accumulation area, except for a large flake that was detached in the last reduction stage. The refitting showed in Figure 6 correspond to the initial stages of the reduction sequence and is characterised by a high percentage of large cortical flakes. The initial phase of cortex removal of the original nodule has been almost completely reconstructed through refitting. The core and products obtained in the last phases of the knapping process have not been found.

Fifteen raw material units (RMU) have been identified through refits in the accumulation L3. The spatial distribution of the RMU with the highest number of items shows the spatial clustering of the remains corresponding to the same reduction sequence. Two of the flint RMU (Flint-2 and Flint-3) present a similar distribution, focused on the northern part of square S43. They show a preferential scatter of remains towards the southwest (Figure 4B). Flint-1, however, is concentrated on the northern corner of square T43 and shows a preferential scatter to the east. Overall, two different knapping spots may be discerned in this accumulation area, one close to the hearth including Flint-2 and Flint-3, and a more distant one where the reduction sequence of Flint-1 took place. In addition, the scatter of remains suggests that the knapping direction was also different. The vertical plot of the lithic remains corresponding to these units does not show significant differences in the vertical distribution of these items.

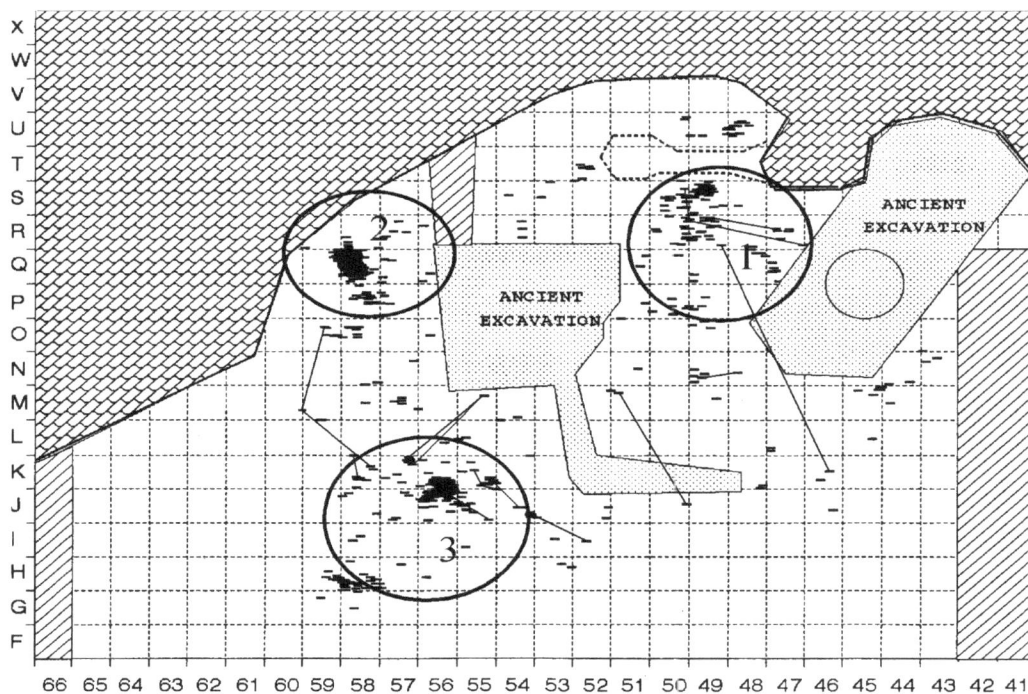

Figure 7 *Spatial distribution of lithic remains and refitting pattern at level I.*

81

Manuel Vaquero, Gema Chacón & José Rando

THE SPATIAL ORGANISATION OF CAMPSITES

The second level of spatial analysis is related to the connections between activity areas defined at the first level. This is fundamental for reconstructing the spatial organisation of the occupied surface as a whole, including the differential distribution of activities across the site and the contemporaneity of different activity areas. In addition, the refitting data can show differences in the degree of spatial connection due to occupation length and/or group size. From this point of view, refits are essential to define types of occupation. The differences between the Abric Romaní levels as far as the activity area relationships are concerned have been described elsewhere (Vaquero, 1999a) and we will only present a brief synthesis here. Some archaeological horizons, like levels H and I, with clearly defined activity areas associated with hearths, do not show connections between them. Figure 7 shows the spatial distribution of lithic remains and the refitting pattern of level I. Three main lithic clusters can be easily recognised. These clusters are associated with hearths and their characteristics suggest that they can be interpreted as household areas. Core reduction sequences are dominant among the lithic activities carried out in these areas. No connections have been recorded between the main accumulation areas. Raw material units are exclusive to specific activity areas. It seems that these areas correspond to different occupational events confined to a relatively restricted area of the site.

Other layers, particularly level Ja, are characterised by a high connectivity between household areas. As can be seen in Figure 8, most of the occupied surface in level Ja is connected by refits. Distribution of remains in this level is not so strongly clustered as in level I, but some areas of higher density can be identified. The archaeological record of these high-density areas indicates that they are hearth-related household areas. Refits between these areas are especially numerous. Most long connection lines are the result of the intentional transport of artefacts. Cores and retouched items, artefacts with long technical histories, are the most mobile categories. These patterns of inter-area connections are correlated with other differences in the distribution of lithic remains, especially these related to size sorting. Such size sorting can be attributed to secondary refuse. Ethnoarchaeological studies indicate that size sorting is linked to occupation length. According to these refitting and distributional data, the archaeological record of level I has been attributed to short occupations by small groups, while level Ja suggests more permanent occupations and larger groups. The variability of occupation types documented at the Abric Romaní indicates therefore that occupation length and group size is a main factor in Middle Palaeolithic settlement strategies.

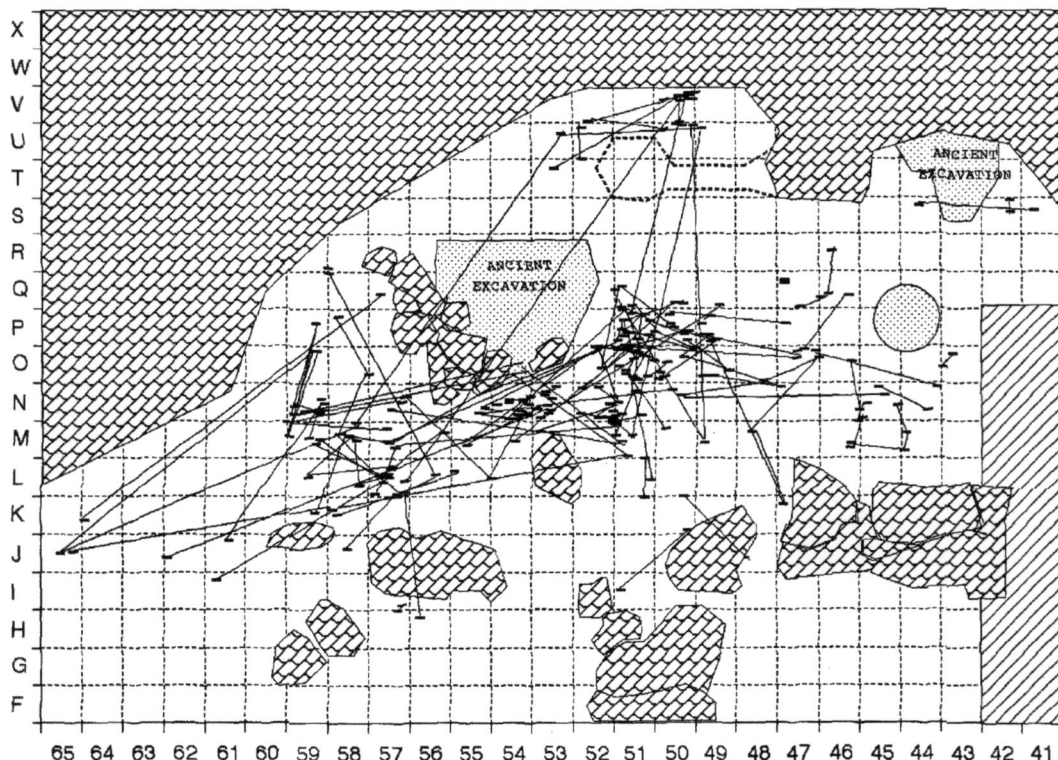

Figure 8 *Refitting pattern in level Ja*

Manuel Vaquero, Gema Chacón & José Rando

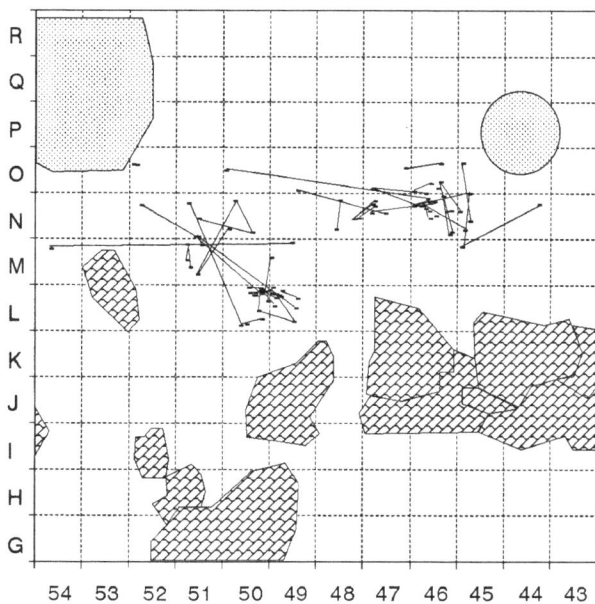

Figure 9.- Refitting pattern of level Jb.

Although most refit connections are short, there are some examples of transport over long distances documenting the mobility of certain items throughout the occupied surface. The best examples are some cores knapped successively in different locations, like the reduction sequence of a limestone cobble found at level Ja. This sequence shows at least three different knapping episodes (Vaquero et al. 1998, 2001). Use-wear analysis suggests that each movement is related to episodes of artefact use. The nucleus is conceived as a mobile raw material resource that can be transported several times and is subject to deferred reduction according to immediate requirements. The intrasite transport of cores has been already documented at other Palaeolithic sites (Boëda & Pelegrin, 1985b; Cahen & Keeley, 1980; Roebroeks, 1988). As we will see below, the Abric Romaní data indicates that the artefact classes generally transported between sites (cores, retouched artefacts and large flakes) are also the items most commonly moved between sites.

In some instances, the core has been found some meters away from the main scatter of flakes detached at the final stages of the reduction sequence. This may indicate that exhausted cores tended to be tossed out of the activity area when the reduction sequence was finished. The spatial segregation of different stages of the reduction sequences is sometimes correlated with a differential dispersion of the remains corresponding to each stage. A good example is provided by level Jb, where a reduction sequence almost entirely developed at the rockshelter shows two different distribution patterns. The refitting pattern of this level is characterised by two well-defined activity areas, as can be seen in Figure 9. At the first one, on the right of Figure 9, refits correspond to several core reduction sequences, but at the second one, on the left,

most connections come from the same *chaîne opératoire*. The remains from the first phases of this knapping sequence are widely scattered over a large area defined by squares M51 and N50-52. The remains of the last reduction stage, however, defined by the recurrent detachment of small flakes shorter than 2 cm, are extremely clustered between squares L49 and L50. 28 small flakes from this final episode have been conjoined (Figure 10).

Such spatial segregation and stronger clustering of the last phase of the reduction sequence have also been documented in the refitted assemblage from level Ja. Various explanations can account for this double pattern. On the one hand, the differential scattering according to the knapping stage may indicate that there was a temporal gap between the initial and the last phases of the reduction sequence. The widest distribution of the firsts stages would be in agreement with Stevenson's model on the formation processes of hearth-related assemblages (Stevenson, 1991). Remains produced during the first

Figure 10 *Refitted assemblage from level Jb. This last stage of the core reduction sequence is characterised by the systematic detachment of small flakes.*

83

moments of an occupation would be more subjected to post-depositional movements by trampling. In this context, the recycling of a core discarded by previous occupants of the site cannot be excluded and the two spatially segregated reduction stages could correspond to different occupational events. On the other hand, this change in the spatial pattern could be related to differences in the goals of each stage of the reduction sequence. The final stage seems clearly directed to the systematic production of small flakes. Although use-wear analyses have proven that these small artefacts were used at other levels of the Abric Romaní (Martínez Molina and Rando 2000), they were not necessarily used. In this context, the use of these small cores in learning processes, although difficult to test, could be an exciting hypothesis.

The connection through refits of different activity areas allows the temporal relationships between accumulations of artefacts to be evaluated. Refits are not enough to prove that two activity areas were contemporaneous (Larson & Ingbar, 1992), since remains discarded during an occupational event can be recycled by later occupants and transported to another area of the site. Nevertheless, they may be used as an heuristic device to establish what relationships should be investigated. It must be stressed that the technical processes documented at the Abric Romaní are characterised by an economising behaviour. Cores are discarded only when they are almost completely exhausted. This considerably reduces the possibility of recycling cores abandoned by previous occupants of the site. Nevertheless, some recycling episodes seem to be present at levels Jb and L, where an intrasite transport of very exhausted cores has been documented.

In some instances connections between activity areas present similar characteristics. Refitting between different hearth-related domestic areas are the most common example of this type of connection. It has been documented at levels Ja, K and L. This pattern can be seen in Figure 2, corresponding to the spatial distribution of remains in level L. The four archaeological accumulations clustering most of the lithic and bone remains are connected by refits. These connections are very suggestive from the point of view of the social structure of the human groups occupying the shelter. As we have seen above, ethnoarchaeological research indicates that the household areas are the spatial hallmark of domestic units, the basic component of hunter-gatherer groups (O'Connell 1987; Yellen 1977). The connection between household areas can indicate that different domestic units occupied the site at the same time, creating a modular structure considered by some authors (Binford 1998) as a diagnostic trait of modern human behaviour. Contemporaneous domestic units have been proposed for Upper Palaeolithic sites, like the magdalenian locations of the Paris basin (e.g. Enloe et al. 1994). The Abric Romaní evidence suggest that these spatial pattern would be already present in the Middle Palaeolithic, suggesting therefore a social structure analogous to that exhibited by current hunter-gatherers. However, the recycling episodes found at level L suggest that some of the household areas identified in this level were not contemporaneous, although they are connected by refits.

Other connections link activity areas with different functions. These relationships have been established in levels I and K between domestic hearth-related assemblages and exterior areas characterised by a

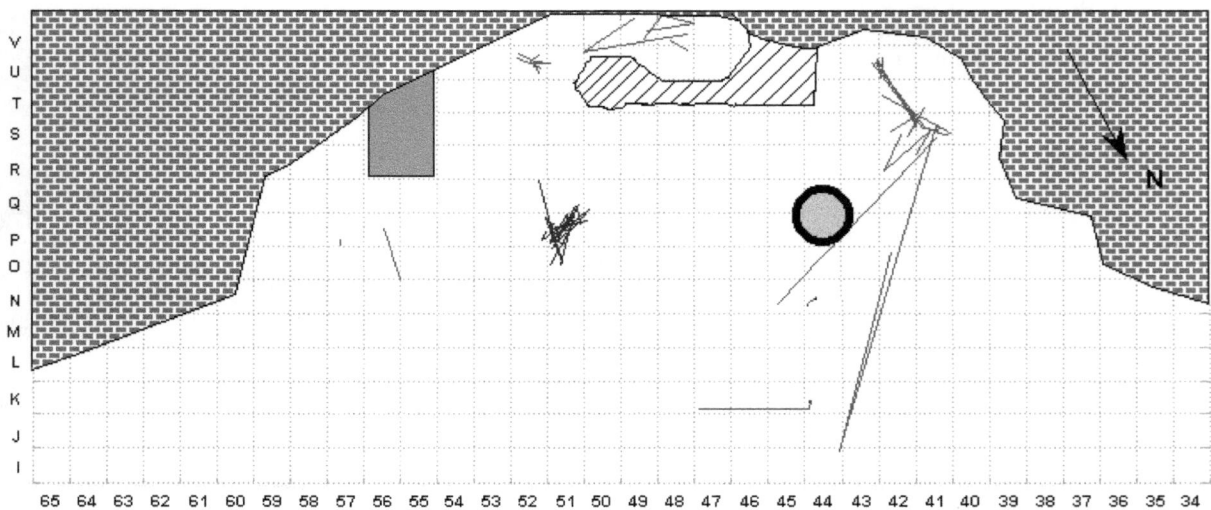

Figure 11 *Refitting pattern at level K. The connections linking the household area and the faunal processing area are at the right.*

dominance of faunal remains. Figure 11 shows the distribution of refit lines from level K. The refits connecting the inner domestic area and the outer faunal processing area can be seen on the right of the figure. They correspond to eight artefacts, which include the core. The reduction sequence was carried out at the domestic area and two flakes were transported toward the faunal processing area. A maximum connection length of 975 cm has been recorded. In this outer zone, large bone fragments are more common than in the rest of the site and taphonomic analysis has identified cut-marks and evidence of intentional bone breakage. This evidence suggests that activities of processing animal carcasses took place in this area of the shelter. Lithic remains are scarce in this zone, suggesting that knapping processes were not common. Nevertheless, some small and well-defined clusters composed by a few remains from singular raw material units have been noted, indicating that isolated and short knapping sequences were developed. One of these sequences seems to correspond to artefact retouching. The faunal and lithic assemblages documented at the inner area are fairly different. Small bone remains are clearly dominant and many of them show burning damage, consumption seems to be the main activity. Lithic remains are abundant and most of them come from reduction sequences carried out on the spot. The use-wear analysis of the refitted artefacts indicates that the flakes produced in this reduction sequence were only used in faunal processing activities. All the activities involved in the sequence of faunal processing have been documented. The analysis of faunal and lithic remains and the refitting pattern suggest therefore that these two zones were complementary. In the exterior area, intense activities of initial carcass processing took place. Resources obtained by this processing would be transported to the household area for consumption. The lithic remains show the opposite pattern. Cores were reduced in the household area, and flakes were moved to the exterior area to be used.

ARTEFACT TRANSPORT AND RAW MATERIAL PROVISIONING

The third level of spatial analysis is focused on the role of the site in a regional settlement pattern. The relationships with the environment and other sites can be analysed through the inputs and outputs of lithic resources. Refitting is the best way for reconstructing these movements (Close, 2000). Transport strategies are documented by the absence of certain artefacts from reduction sequences almost entirely refitted. One example comes from the accumulation L3 of level L, where it has been possible to reconstruct the reduction sequence of a small flint cobble (Figure 5). All the artefacts from this sequence were clustered forming a small scatter, except one large flake produced at the final stage of reduction. The absence of this flake suggests that

it was transported into another activity area or site. As we have seen earlier, another refitted assemblage from this same accumulation corresponds to the initial stage of reduction. However, the core and the products from the following stages are absent, suggesting the transport of the partially reduced core. This core and the last flakes were found in another activity area of the same level. The transport of partially reduced cores seems to have been a common provisioning strategy. As pointed out above, a low percentage of the reduction sequences documented at the Abric Romaní were carried out in the rockshelter. Rather, spatial fragmentation of the *chaînes operatoires* is the rule. From the nine RMU documented in scatter L3, only two were introduced as unworked nodules and totally reduced at the site. The rest of the RMU reflect only partial reductions.. This emphasises the mobile character of cores, well documented at other Middle Palaeolithic sites (Conard & Adler, 1997; De Loecker, 1994; Deloze et al, 1994; Roebroeks, 1988; Roebroeks & Hennekens, 1990).

The proportions of items refitted for each artefact class provide some clues of transport strategies. This percentage has been calculated for level Ja, the level with the highest number of refitted artefacts. It should be stressed that retouched artefacts are the lithic category with the lowest percentage of items included in refits. Only four tools (2,6% of the retouched artefacts found in this level) are involved in refits. This is especially striking if we take into account that retouched artefacts are generally large objects with many scars and they have therefore a higher probability of being connected with other items. In addition, only two of these four retouched artefacts have been refitted with their core reduction sequence. These data suggest that most retouched artefacts are not related with the core reduction processes developed at the Abric Romaní and were therefore introduced into the shelter either as tools or unmodified flakes. This reinforces the mobile character of retouched artefacts, which tend to be carried out during movements between sites. In addition, retouch intensity seems to be also related with transport. Retouched artefacts from reduction sequences developed at the site are generally less modified than those introduced from the outside. The introduction of retouched artefacts into sites has also been established at other Middle Palaeolithic sites where the proveniencing of the raw materials has been studied (Geneste 1988; Meignen 1988). Nevertheless, there are some differences between the Abric Romaní and those sites as far as the types of retouched artefacts are concerned. According to Geneste and Meignen, sidescrapers and bifaces were the most mobile artefacts, whereas denticulates, predominantly made on local raw materials, were characterised by low levels of mobility. At the Abric Romaní, denticulates and notches are the dominant types in all the archaeological levels, sometimes reaching values over 90%. Refitting data indicate that these were also mobile artefacts, suggesting the importance of transport in the formation of Middle Palaeolithic tool assemblages.

An example of such artefact import is a refit from level H (Figure 12). It is composed of seven items derived from the retouching of a denticulate: six retouch flakes and the tool. No other remains from this raw material unit have been recovered in this archaeological level excavated over 200 m². Besides the information on transport strategies, this refit is also significant to interpret the retouch sequences in general and the production of denticulates in particular. This refit suggests that a large flake was introduced into the site, where the retouching took place. Most remains are spatially clustered, as can be seen in Figure 12. The four flakes corresponding to the

that the final morphology of this denticulate was the intentional product of a single technical episode.

CONCLUDING REMARKS

The refitting studies carried out at the Abric Romaní have provided valuable information about the settlement strategies of Middle Palaeolithic groups. This information is relevant in several areas of research such as: definition of spatial units with behavioural significance, social background of spatial patterns, lithic provisioning strategies, spatial segregation of different activities, patterns of mobility, and types of occupation. The global picture emerging from the refitting data is that Neanderthal spatial patterns are more complex than

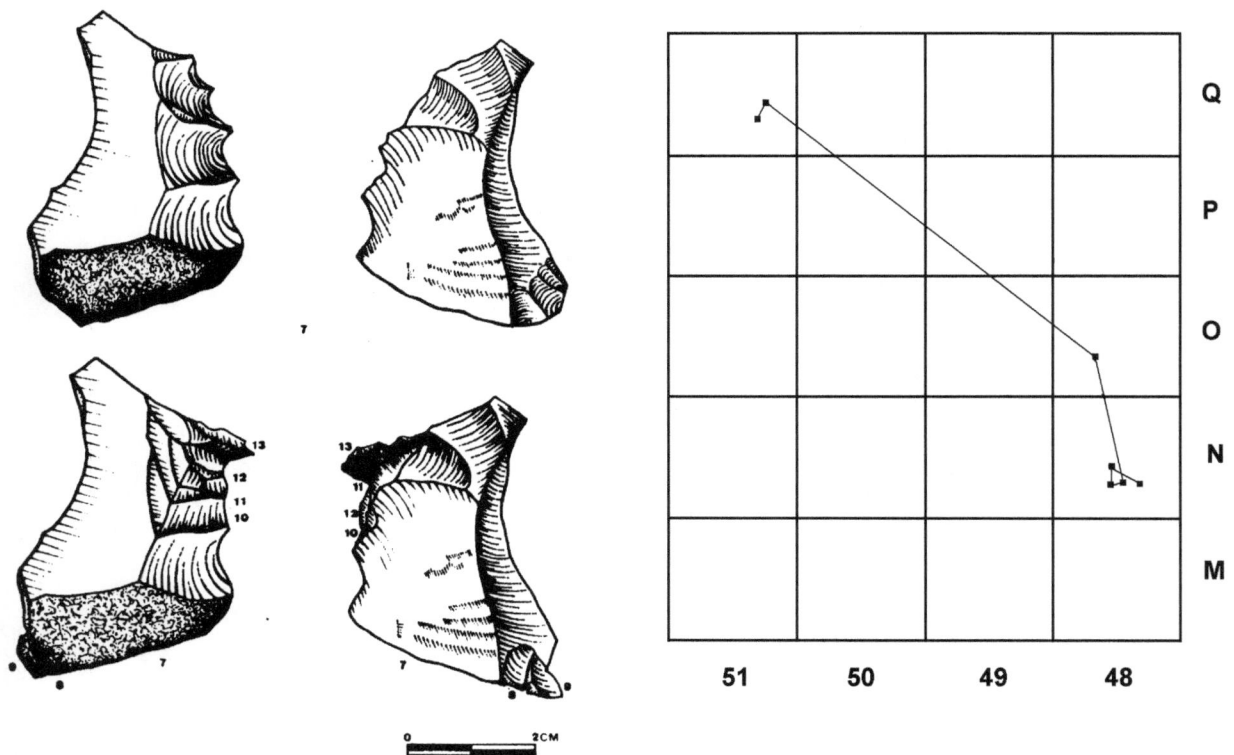

Figure 12 *Drawing and spatial distribution of a retouch sequence from level H (from Carbonell 1992)*

denticulate edge are concentrated in square N48, while the retouched artefact was found 108 cm away in square O48. Two flakes are located in square P51, 342 cm from the first group. They were removed from the basal part of the retouched artefact and do not correspond to the construction of the denticulate edge. According to these data, two spatially separated retouching events can be envisaged, although it seems clear that the denticulate edge was produced during a single episode. This indicates that denticulates, or at least some denticulates, are not the result of the overlapping of notches throughout several resharpening episodes, as suggested by Dibble (1995). The sequence refitted at level H shows

previously stated by some scholars. Firstly, it seems clear that, although all Palaeolithic sites may be considered palimpsests by nature, a synchronous interpretation is possible when sedimentary contexts of high resolution are present. Maybe the main feature of spatial patterns at the Abric Romaní is that activities, particularly technical activities, are strongly focused around hearths. Refitting has clearly shown that reduction sequences were preferentially carried out in hearth-related areas, where consumption of animal resources was also common. The Neanderthal space is organized by combustion structures. Identifying hearth-related household areas is especially important, since the formation of domestic spaces is the principal characteristic of the residential campsites of the hunter-gatherer communities documented by ethnoarchaeological studies. The social implications of these structures have been pointed out earlier; the hearths are the focus of social practices needing fully developed communication abilities.

Neanderthal and modern hunter-gatherer spatial patterns also share other characteristics, for example the weak functional differentiation of campsites. Few activities are developed outside of household areas and, particularly, zones specialised in knapping activities have not been documented. Only faunal processing activities are sometimes segregated towards outer parts of the shelter. According to the wide distribution of remains in these areas, it seems that they were extensive activities, demanding large surfaces. Anyway, the removal of messy or extensive activities from the preferentially occupied household zones has also been well documented among hunter-gatherer groups (see Yellen 1977). Lithic refits strongly suggest that faunal-processing areas and some household areas were contemporaneous, although it should be remembered that refitting evidence is not enough to prove these temporal relationships. In the same context, the connections between different household areas also suggest that different social units lived together during the same occupational events. What is more important is that the presence of household areas is the best criterion to identify residential sites archaeologically.

The identification of specific activity episodes through refitting provides information on the contextual nature of archaeological variability. It is therefore possible to analyse how the contextual factors affecting technical activities are responsible for some trends of inter-assemblage variability. Since these factors operate on single episodes of activity, these episodes, defined through refits, should be the main unit of analysis when studying cultural formation processes. The Abric Romaní provides a good example of this. As we have seen, the *chaînes opératoires* tend to be spatially and temporally discontinuous. Few reduction sequences were carried out entirely in the shelter. Mobility and transport are therefore fundamental to explain the range of lithic items represented in each archaeological level. Nevertheless, this conclusion is only evident when specific raw material units are taken into account. The reduction sequences are differentially segmented. Some of them are represented by the initial stages, others by the last ones. If the whole lithic assemblage, without discriminating the different RMU would have been the unit of analysis, it would have given the impression a complete reduction sequence is present.

Artefacts are transported across the landscape only in anticipation of future needs. It seems clear therefore that planning played an active role in the behavioural strategies of these Neanderthal groups. The temporal

depth of this planning could be discussed and some authors have pointed out that only short-term planning can be proven before the Upper Palaeolithic (see Binford 1989), especially when mobile artefacts are the personal gear commonly transported by individuals during their displacements (Kuhn 1995). However, the planning depth of Neanderthals is only one dimension of the problem. What is more important for us is that, regardless of the temporal depth of the anticipatory behaviour, provisioning for future needs was fully integrated in the daily live of Neanderthal communities, since, as we have discussed earlier, transport of partially reduced cores, large flakes and retouched artefacts are most common at Abric Romaní.

All these are complex issues and cannot be thoroughly discussed here. We have simply pointed to them to show the wide range of questions that can be solved through the spatial use of refitting data. Since many behavioural issues concerning the cultural capabilities of archaic humans are rooted in the contextual world of daily life, they can only be approached through the singular events reconstructed by refits. Therefore, when the geological and archaeological formations processes make it possible, the systematic search of refits should be an essential step in the study and interpretation of Middle Palaeolithic sites.

ACKNOWLEDGEMENTS

Fieldwork in the Abric Romaní and the "Abric Romaní-Cingles del Capelló" research project are supported by the Generalitat de Catalunya, Ajuntament de Capellades and Tallers Gràfics Romanyà Valls S.A. We would also like to thank the organisers of the refitting symposium for the opportunity to participate.

BIBLIOGRAPHY

BARTON, R.N.E. & C.A. BERGMAN 1982 Hunters at Hengistbury: some evidence from experimental archaeology. *World Archaeology* 14: 237-248.

BINFORD, L.R. 1978 Dimensional analysis of behavior and site structure: learning from an Eskimo hunting stand. *American Antiquity* 43(3): 330-361.

BINFORD, L.R. 1989 Isolating the transition to cultural adaptations: an organizational approach. In *The Emergence of Modern Humans: Biocultural Adaptations in the Later Pleistocene*, edited by E. TRINKAUS. Cambridge: Cambridge University Press.

BINFORD, L.R. 1998 Hearth and home: the spatial analysis of ethnographically documented rock shelter occupations as a template for distinguishing between human and hominid use of sheltered space. In *XIII U.I.S.P.P. Congress Proceedings – Forli, 8-14 September 1996*. pp. 229-239. Forli: A.B.A.C.O. Edizioni, Forli.

BISCHOFF, J., R. JULIÀ & R. MORA 1988 Uranium-series dating of the Mousterian occupation at the Abric Romani, Spain. *Nature* 332: 68-70.

BOËDA, E. & J. PELEGRIN 1985a Approche expérimentale des amas de Marsagny. *Archéologie Expérimentale* 1: 19-36.

BOËDA, E., & J. PELEGRIN 1985b Réflexion méthodologique à partir de l'étude de quelques remontages. *Archéologie Expérimentale* 1: 37-64.

BRAVO, P. 2001 *Estudio zooarqueológico y de remontajes del subnivel Ja del Abric Romaní (Capellades, Barcelona)*. Tesis de licenciatura inédita. Tarragona: Universitat Rovira i Virgili.

BURJACHS, F., & R. JULIÀ 1994 Abrupt Climatic Changes during the Last Glaciation Based on Pollen Analysis of the Abric Romani, Catalonia, Spain. *Quaternary Research* 42: 308-315.

CÁCERES, I., J. ROSELL & R. HUGUET 1998 Séquence d'utilisation de la biomasse animale dans le gisement de l'Abric Romaní (Barcelone, Espagne). *Quaternaire* 9: 379-383.

CAHEN, D., & L.H. KEELEY 1980 Not less than two, not more than three. *World Prehistory* 2: 166-180.

CARBONELL, E. (ed.) 1992 Abric Romaní, nivell H: un model d'estratègia ocupacional al Plistocé Superior mediterrani. *Estrat* 5: 157-308.

CARBONELL, E., A. CEBRIÀ, E. ALLUÉ, I. CÁCERES, Z. CASTRO, R. DÍAZ, M. ESTEBAN, A. OLLÉ, I. PASTÓ, X.P. RODRÍGUEZ, J. ROSELL, R. SALA, J. VALLVERDÚ, M. VAQUERO & J.M. VERGÉS 1996 Behavioural and organizational complexity in the Middle Palaeolithic from the Abric Romaní. In *The last neandertals, the first anatomically modern humans: a tale about the human diversity*, edited by E. CARBONELL & M. VAQUERO. Tarragona: Universitat Rovira i Virgili, p. 385-434

CARBONELL, E., S. GIRALT & M. VAQUERO 1994 Abric Romani (Capellades, Barcelone, Espagne): une important séquence anthropisée du Pleistocéne Supérieur. *Bulletin de la Société Préhistorique Française* 91: 47-55.

CLOSE, A.E. 2000 Reconstructing Movement in Prehistory. *Journal of Archaeological Method and Theory* 7(1): 49-77.

CONARD, N. J., & D.S. ADLER 1997 Lithic Reduction and Hominid Behavior in the Middle Paleolithic of the Rhineland. *Journal of Anthropological Research* 53: 147-175.

DE LOECKER, D. 1994 On the Refitting Analysis of Site K: A Middle Paleolithic Findspot at Maastricht-Belvédère (The Netherlands). Ethnographisch-Archäologische Zeitschrift 35: 107-117.

DELOZE, V., P. DEPAEPE, J.-M. GOUEDO, V. KRIER & J.L. LOCHT 1994, *Le Paléolithique moyen dans le nord du Sénonais (Yonne). Contexte géomorphologique, industries lithiques et chronostratigraphie*. Documents d'Archéologie française 47. Paris: MSH.

DIBBLE, H.L. 1995 Raw Material Availability, Intensity of Utilization, and Middle Paleolithic Assemblage Variability. In *The Middle Paleolithic Site of Combe-Capelle Bas (France)*, edited by H.L. DIBBLE & M. LENOIR. Philadelphia: The University Museum. University of Pennsylvania, pp. 289-315.

ENLOE, J.G., F. DAVID. & T. HARE 1994 Patterns of Faunal Processing at Section 27 of Pincevent: The Use of Spatial Analysis and Ethnoarchaeological Data in the Interpretation of Archaeological Site Structure. *Journal of Anthropological Archaeology* 13: 105-124.

FARIZY, C. 1994 Spatial Patterning of Middle Paleolithic Sites. *Journal of Anthropological Archaeology* 13: 153-60.

GENESTE, J.-M. 1988 Les industries de la Grotte Vaufrey: technologie du debitage, economie et circulation de la matière première lithique. In *La Grotte Vaufrey à Cenac et Saint-Julien (Dordogne). Paleoenvironnements, chronologie et activités humaines*, edited by J.-PH. RIGAUD. Paris: Mémoires de la Société Préhistorique Française, XIX, pp. 441-517.

JULIEN, M., F. AUDOUZE, D. BAFFIER, P. BODU, P. COUDRET, F. DAVID, G. GAUCHER, C. KARLIN, M. LARRIERE, P. MASSON, M. OLIVE, M. ORLIAC, N. PIGEOT, J.L. RIEU, B. SCHMIDER, Y. TABORIN. 1988 Organisation de l'espace et fonction des habitats magdaleniens du Bassin Parisien. In De la Loire à l'Oder. Les civilisations du Paléolithique final dans le nord-ouest européen, edited by M. OTTE. Oxford: BAR International Series 444, pp. 85-123.

KUHN, S.L. 1995 *Mousterian Lithic Technology. An Ecological Perspective*. Princeton: Princeton University Press.

LARSON, M.L., & E.E. INGBAR 1992 Perspectives on refitting: critique and a complementary approach. In Piecing Together the Past: Applications of Refitting Studies in Archaeology, edited by J.L. HOFMAN & J.G.

ENLOE. Oxford: BAR International Series 578, pp. 21-35.

LOCHT, J.-L. 2001 Modalités d'implantation et fonctionnement interne des sites. L'apport de trois gisements de plein air de la phase recente du Paléolithique moyen dans le nord de la France (Bettencourt-Saint-Ouen, Villiers-Adam et Beauvais). In *Settlement Dynamics of the Middle Paleolithic and Middle Stone Age*, edited by N.J. CONARD. Tübingen: Kerns Verlag, pp. 361-393.

MARTÍNEZ MOLINA, K. & J.M. RANDO 2000 Organización espacial y de la producción lítica en el desarrollo de las actividades durante las ocupaciones del Paleolítico Medio. Nivel Ja del Abric Romaní (Capellades, Barcelona). In *Actas do 3º Congresso de Arqueologia Peninsular.*, vol. II. Porto: ADECAP, pp. 215-229.

MEIGNEN, L. 1988 Un exemple de comportement technologique differentiel selon les matières premières: Marillac, couches 9 et 10". In *L'Homme de Néandertal, vol. 4. La technique.* Liège: E.R.A.U.L., pp. 71-79.

MELLARS, P.A. 1996 *The Neanderthal Legacy. An Archaeological Perspective from Western Europe.* Princeton: Princeton University Press.

NEWCOMER, M.H. & G. SIEVEKING 1989 Experimental flake scatter-patterns: a new interpretative technique. *Journal of Field Archaeology* 7: 345-352.

O'CONNELL, J.F. 1987 Alyawara site structure and its archaeological implications. *American Antiquity* 52(1): 74-108.

OLIVE, M. 1988 *Une habitation magdalénienne d'Étiolles. L'unité P15.* Mémoires de la Société Préhistorique Française, 20. Paris

PASTÓ, I., E. ALLUÉ & J. VALLVERDÚ. 2000 Mousterian Hearths at Abric Romaní, Catalonia (Spain). In *Neanderthals on the Edge*, edited by C. B. STRINGER, R. N. E. BARTON, & J. C. FINLAYSON. Oxford: Oxbow Books, pp. 59-67.

PETTITT, P.B. 1997 High resolution Neanderthals? Interpreting Middle Palaeolithic intrasite spatial data. *World Archaeology* 29(2): 208-224.

ROEBROEKS, W. 1988 From find scatters to early hominid behaviour: a study of Middle Palaeolithic riverside settlements at Maastricht-Belvédère (The Netherlands). *Analecta Praehistorica Leidensia*, 21.

ROEBROEKS, W., & P. HENNEKENS 1990 Transport of Lithics in the Middle Paleolithic: Conjoining Evidence from Maastricht-Belvédère (NL). In *The Big Puzzle.*

International Symposium on Refitting Stone Artifacts, edited by E. CZIESLA, S. EICKHOFF, N. ARTS, & D. WINTER. Bonn: Holos, pp. 283-295.

SCHMIDER, B. & E. de CROISSET 1990 The contribution of lithic refitting for spatial analysis of campsite H17 and D14 at Marsagny. In *The Big Puzzle. International Symposium on Refitting Stone Artifacts*, edited by E. CZIESLA, S. EICKHOFF, N. ARTS, & D. WINTER. Bonn: Holos, pp. 431-445.

STEVENSON, M.G. 1991 Beyond the Formation of Hearth-Associated Artifact Assemblages. In *The Interpretation of Archaeological Spatial Patterning*, edited by E.M. KROLL & T.D. PRICE. New York & London: Plenum Press, pp. 269-299.

VAQUERO, M. 1999 Intrasite spatial organization of lithic production in the Middle Palaeolithic: the evidence of the Abric Romaní (Capellades, Spain). *Antiquity* 73: 493-504.

VAQUERO, M. 1999 Variabilidad de las estrategias de talla y cambio tecnológico en el Paleolítico Medio del Abric Romaní (Capellades, Barcelona). *Trabajos de Prehistoria* 56: 37-58.

VAQUERO, M., G. CHACÓN, C. FERNÁNDEZ, K. MARTÍNEZ, & J.M. RANDO 2001 Intrasite Spatial Patterning and Transport in the Abric Romaní Middle Paleolithic Site (Capellades, Barcelona, Spain). In *Settlement Dynamics of the Middle Paleolithic and Middle Stone Age*, edited by N.J. CONARD. Tübingen: Kerns Verlag, pp. 573-595.

VAQUERO. M., D. GARÍA-ANTÓN, C. MALLOL, & N. MORANT 1998 L'organisation spatiale de la production lithique dans un gisement du Paléolithique moyen: le niveau Ja de l'Abric Romaní (Capellades, Barcelona, Espagne). In *XIII U.I.S.P.P. Congress Proceedings - Forli, 8-14 September 1996.* Forli: ABACO Editions, pp. 777-782.

VAQUERO, M. & I. PASTÓ 2001 The Definition of Spatial Units in Middle Palaeolithic Sites: The Hearth-Related Assemblages. *Journal of Archaeological Science* 28(11): 1209-1220.

YELLEN, J.E. 1977 *Archaeological Approaches to the Present.* Academic Press: New York.

Corresponding author address:

Manuel VAQUERO
Institut d'Estudis Avançats. Universitat Rovira i Virgili.
Pl. Imperial Tarraco, 1;
43005 Tarragona, Spain.

mavr@iea.ur

REFITTING OF LITHIC REDUCTION SEQUENCES, FORMAL CLASSIFICATION SYSTEMS, AND MIDDLE PALAEOLITHIC INDIVIDUALS AT WORK

Philip VAN PEER[1]

Abstract

This paper explores the contribution of reduction sequence refitting to the definition of the Levallois reduction strategy and to the isolation of behaviourally appropriate units of analysis for Middle Palaeolithic artefact assemblages. After a consideration of the nature of typological classification, it is argued that refitting data support a simple definition of the Levallois concept. In the actual application of the latter in Middle Palaeolithic assemblages from the late Nubian Complex in the Nile Valley, procedural signatures of different individual knappers can apparently be recognized. Together with other evidence, this leads to the inference that task specialisation was a feature of the social organisation of these late Middle Palaeolithic groups. At the epistemological level, it is concluded that the role of the individual as a source of patterned variation in the archaeological record should be reconsidered.

Résumé

Cette article explore l'apport des remontages de séquences de réduction concernant la définition du concept Levallois et l'identification d'unités d'analyse adéquates sur le plan comportemental, pour les ensembles paléolithiques moyen. Après une considération de la nature de la classification typologique, une définition simple du concept Levallois est proposée. Dans son application dans le Complexe nubien tardif dans la Vallée du Nil, les signatures des artisans individuels semblent représentées. Avec d'autres données, ceci donne lieu à l' interprétation que la spécialisation était un principe important de l'organisation sociale de ces groupes du Paléolithique moyen tardif. Sur le plan épistémologique, il est conclu que le rôle de l'individu comme une source de variabilité structurée devrait être reconsidéré.

INTRODUCTION

The value of refitting stone artefacts as an analytic tool in prehistoric research has been established beyond any doubt (Cziesla *et al.* 1990; Hofman and Enloe 1992). When artefacts are fitted onto one another a sequence of prehistoric actions or events are observed. Reconstruced sequences provide a means to restitute a historic temporal dimension to the static archaeological record. We can actually see individuals at work during a rather sustained period of time. At the same time, refit sequences objectively unite isolated artefacts into larger units which make sense from a behavioural point of view. A reduction sequence may indeed be expected to have been carried out in a limited amount of time and by one or a few individuals. The composition of lithic assemblages as the basis for generalisations about human behaviour at a particular point in time and space, is usually a matter of rather formal choice. An assemblage or single site assemblage (Clarke 1968 : 363), then, refers to a spatially delimited collection of artefacts recovered from the same stratigraphic position (Clark and Kleindienst 2001 : 37). The presence of particular geometric structures or features as for instance hearths in the spatial context, as well as the recognition of apparent living surfaces within rapidly accumulated sediments or at stratigraphic interfaces, may all be taken to indicate its behavioural integrity. However, in actual fact there is no way of knowing if all the individual artefacts forming the context were deposited during the same uninterrupted presence of a number of prehistoric individuals (Roebroeks *et al.* 1992). Only reconstructed sequences are true proxies to increase the scale of generalisation beyond the individual artefact, i.e. the irreducible unit of spatial analysis (Isaac 1981 : 137). At the epistemological level, the contribution of refitting lies in the fact that interpretations can be based on objective analyses at a behaviourally appropriate scale. Refitting may also enhance the value of other, e.g. stratigraphic, evidence in high resolution behavioural interpretations. At Pincevent, for instance, micro-stratigraphic stages in the accumulation of archaeological debris were thus identified (Cahen 1987).

In this paper, I want to illustrate how these methodological assets can lead to surprising interpretations of behaviour at a Middle Palaeolithic site. These lead to a reconsideration of the role of the individual in prehistoric material culture production and, hence, of the unit of analysis to use (Cahen and Keeley 1980; Hill and Gunn, 1977; Hodder 1986). First, however, I will try to demonstrate that refitting is also an invaluable tool to establish useful levels of generalisation for the lithic archaeological record of the Middle Palaeolithic. Indeed, behavioural interpretations are, on the one hand, based on (assumed) integral sets of human actions and, on the other, on formal classifications of the material outcomes of these sets. Lithic assemblages are described and analyzed in terms of a number of classicifaction categories to which individual artefacts are assigned. Levallois is an obviously important concept of classification for the Middle Palaeolithic. Recent

Philip Van Peer

technological studies have resulted in quite divergent views on the definition of this analytic concept (see Chazan, 1997; Dibble and Bar-Yosef 1995). As the latter is evidenced in all the reconstructed sequences that will be used here, it seems important to devote some attention to it.

The sites

The reconstructed Levallois reduction sequences used here are from two sites in the Upper Egyptian Nile Valley. Makhadma-6 is a small scatter where about five chert nodules were reduced. Its lithic assemblage belongs to the Nubian Complex (Van Peer 2000). The site of Taramsa-1 (Vermeersch *et al*. 1990, 1998; Van Peer 2001). is a chert exploitation site where numerous exploitation features are present ranging from the early Middle Palaeolithic to the initial Upper Palaeolithic. The exploitation activities involved the digging of trenches in order to reach an *in situ* gravel deposit composed of well-rounded chert pebbles, which are perfectly suited for debitage. All the subsequent stages of the operational chain were performed in the immediate vicinity of the extraction spot. Dense concentrations of lithics are found within the fill of the ditches. They may be comprised within prehistoric dump deposits, resulting from the disposition of gravel matrix waste or they occur on top of the latter, covered by aeolian sands. In view of the rapid and alternating accumulation of different deposits within those extraction features, it is by no means easy to identify behaviourally integer lithic concentrations and their precise stratigraphical association. Further, the special nature of the stratigraphic units at this site implies that stratigraphically superimposed lithic concentrations may yet be behaviourally contemporaneous.

Such is the case in sector 91/04 of the site. Here, a number of spatially distinct concentrations of lithic material from different stratigraphic units, were shown to be likely the result from one extraction event, by means of inter-concentration refits (Van Peer 2001). According to classic techno-typological criteria, the assemblage can be classified as Taramsan (Vermeersch *et al.* 1990, 1998). This term designates a Middle Palaeolithic industry in which the Levallois reduction strategy is dominant. The Levallois concept, however, is present in a slightly modified form resulting in the production of elongated Levallois blanks or blades. This modified Levallois concept of which the principles have been stated elsewhere (Van Peer 1992) bears clear technical ressemblances to the Nubian Levallois method and, on that basis, the Taramsan can be integrated in the Nubian Complex (Van Peer 1998). While it is a newly defined entity, it seems that previously described assemblages from the Lower Nile Valley, such as for instance from site 113A (Guichard and Guichard 1965) belong to it.

The data

From the various subsectors in sector 91/04, a number of artefacts were refitted into the original chert pebbles, and as such show their complete reduction sequences.

Description of sequence progression

For each completely reconstructed reduction sequence, the precise order of flaking was determined and visually represented on a plan projection of the original nodule outline. The latter was divided into six sectors[2], the upper right sector being 1 and proceeding in clockwise direction to 6 in the upper left sector. This enabled the notation of the area on the core's perimeter from which each flake had been struck.

On the basis of these data, *shift values* can be calculated (Table 1). A shift value is a measure of the distance and direction travelled on the core perimeter from one removal to the next. To obtain this value the sector notation for a particular removal is subtracted from that of the next removal. For instance, a sequence starting in the upper right sector and proceeding radially to the middle right sector, would receive a value of -1. Negative values, thus, indicate a clockwise sequence.

Table 1
Calculation of the progression line for the first Levallois surface of reduction sequence 28/14 from Taramsa sector 91/04.

Sequence Order ID	Sector	Shift value	Trans-formed	Cumulative progression	Data for line graph
1	5	0	0	0	0
2	5	0	0	1	1
3	5	1	1	2	2
4	4	1	1	4	4
5	3	2	2	5	5
6	1	-5	1	4	4
7	6	5	-1	6	6
8	1	-4	2	8	8
9	5	2	2	10	10
10	3	2	2	10	
11	1	0	0	10	
12	1	0	0	10	
13	1	0	0	10	
14	1	0	0	11	11
15	1	-5	1	11	
16	6	0	0	11	
17	6	0	0	12	12
18	6	1	1	12	
19	5	0	0	13	13
20	5	1	1	14	14
21	4	1	1	14	
22	3	0	0		
23	3				14

This calculation procedure, however, leads to problems of consistency when the left sectors are involved. For instance, a simple sequence progression from the upper left (6) to the upper right sector (1) would give a value of 5 and the counterclock progression between these two sectors would give –5. Such values, therefore, were substituted with their small equivalents, i.e. –5 equals 1 and 5 equals –1. Likewise 4 and –4 were reset to –2 and 2, respectively. In other words, the travelled distance between two removals is always set to the smallest possible. A value of –3, finally, indicating a shift over precisely half of the core perimeter, was turned into 3. In this case, it is pointless to distinguish between a counterclockwise and a clockwise progression. A value of –1 or 1 is called an adjacent sector shift ; -2,2 or 3 are long shifts.

Using these transformation rules for the shift values, a progression line can be calculated by simply cumulating the subsequent shift values. Progression lines are calculated per Levallois surface, i.e. a preparation sequence that is terminated with the removal of one or more large blanks from the preferential striking platform. Subsequent removals in the same core sector are not taken into account in the line graph representation, although the next line node will take its position on the

X-axis of the graph according to its absolute position in the reduction sequence. For the length of the line to represent exactly the number of removals in a preparation sequence, the final cumulative shift value is assigned to the last removal in the sequence once again. A progression line presents a quick and general idea of the speed, direction, and rythm of a reduction sequence (Figure 1).

Description of pattern generation

All Levallois definitions involve the notion of morphological predetermination of particular products, which is achieved by imposing a particular pattern of ridges on the exploitation surface (Van Peer 1992). A number of specific patterns of preparation or 'Levallois methods' have been typologically identified suggesting that the imposition of a ridge pattern might be governed by specific blank morphologies to be obtained. Patterns of preparation have been quantitatively assessed by comparing the number of preparation scars in different sectors of flake or core surfaces (Boutié 1981; Crew 1975 ; Meignen & Bar-Yosef, 1988 ; Van Peer 1992). The sequence data on reconstructed Levallois sequences, however, can also describe dynamic pattern generations, i.e. how a particular pattern of preparation is formed in

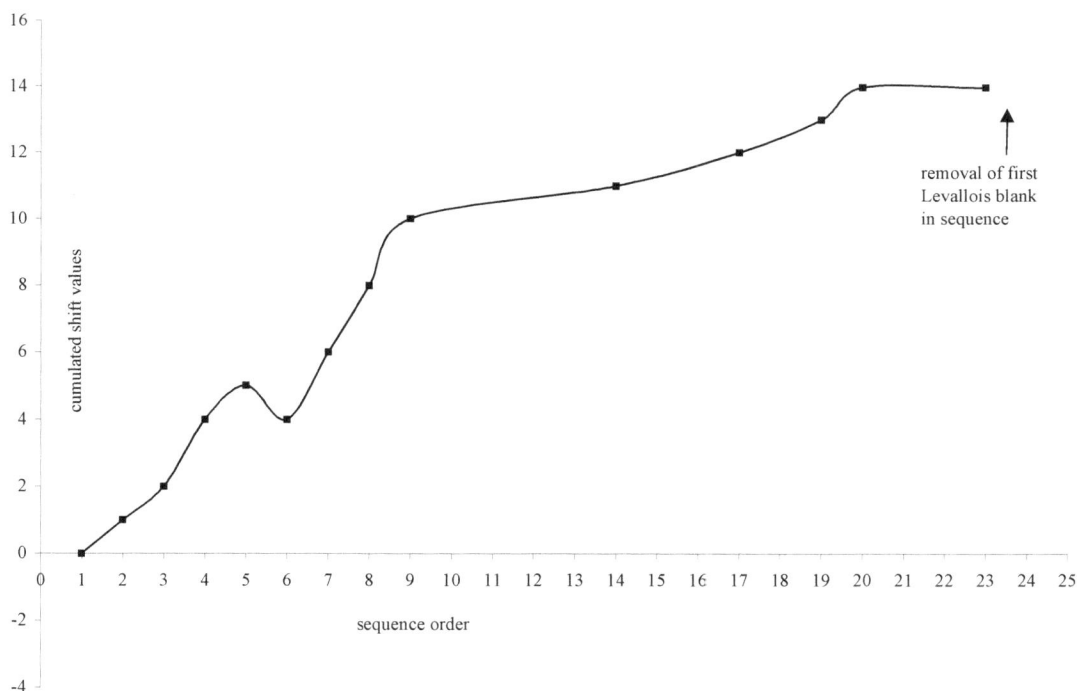

Figure 1. *Progression line for the first Levallois surface in reduction sequence 28/14 from Taramsa sector 91/04. The sequence proceeds in essentially clockwise direction. In the first stages, the progression is continuous and rapid as indicated by 2 and 3 shift values. In its later stage, it slows down and shifts are now between adjacent sectors.*

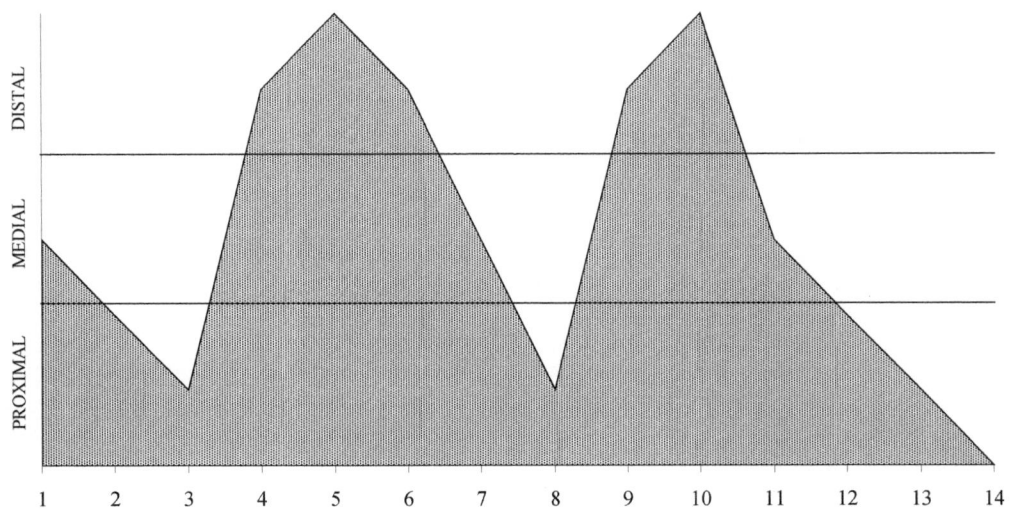

Figure 2. *Line plot of the pattern generation sequence for the first Levallois surface of reduction 28/14.*

the course of a preparation sequence. Figure 2, for instance, shows that the pattern of preparation of the first Levallois surface of reduction 28/14 is basically bidirectional. Medial sectors are prepared at the start and the end of the sequence while there are two phases of intensive distal sector preparation with consecutive shifts between the two distal sectors. In this graph, sector changes are plotted consecutively omitting phases of within-sector preparation. This is done to enhance the comparability of pattern generation plots for different Levallois surfaces.

Description of momentum

Information on the rhytm or momentum of a preparation sequence can be obtained from yet another type of generalisation about raw sequence data. Rather than the distance travelled on the core's perimeter from one removal to the next, the phasing of the sector switches is considered. Phases of intensive within-sector preparation are distinguished from phases of moderate and rapid progression. Rapid progression occurs when single, consecutive removals are struck in different sectors. Moderate progression involves the flaking of two removals in the same sector before a shift to another sector occurs. Within-sector preparation, finally, is identified if at least three consecutive removals occur in the same sector. Table 2 shows the momentum categories for the sequence presented in Table 1.

Momentum categories are visually represented as bar charts (Figure 3). This information can also be inferred from the progression lines, but here it is shown more elegantly as it is not blurred by a sequence of positive and negative directions. The detail of the momentum can now be quickly assessed. In the case of reduction sequence

Table 2

Raw data of reduction sequence 28/14 for construction of momentum chart. Momentum categories: 1: more than 2 consecutive removals in the same core sector; 2: 2 consecutive removals in the same core sector; 3: shift to another core sector after only one removal in a particular sector.

Sequence Order ID	Sector	Frequency	Momentum category
1	5	3	1
2	5		
3	5		
4	4	1	3
5	3	1	3
6	1	1	3
7	6	1	3
8	1	1	3
9	5	1	3
10	3	1	3
11	1	5	1
12	1		
13	1		
14	1		
15	1		
16	6	3	1
17	6		
18	6		
19	5	2	2
20	5		
21	4	1	3
22	3	2	2
23	3		

28/14, the opposition between rapid sector shifts in the first stage of the preparation sequence and frequent in-sector preparation later on, is very clear.

What is Levallois?

Levallois has been defined as a volumetric concept applied in the reduction of a block of raw material that opposes two convex volumes with their intersection situated in one plane (Boëda 1994). The perimeter of the latter serves as a striking platform for the exploitation of the upper Levallois surface. On the basis of experimental

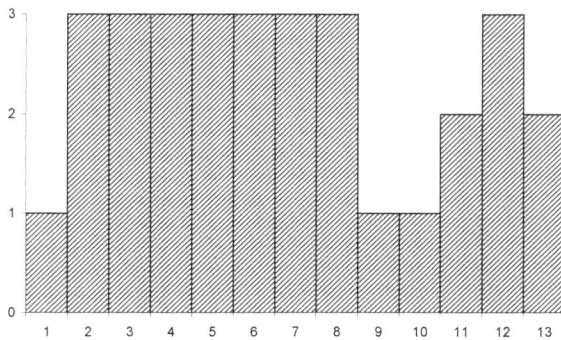

Figure 3. *Chart of momentum sequence for reduction 28/14 based on data in table 2.*

work, the possible variability in the exploitation of a Levallois surface was explored. This led to the definition of different methods of exploitation. On the one hand, there is a *lineal* method leading to the production of only one preferential Levallois flake from a Levallois surface and, on the other hand, there is the *recurrent* method whereby a suite of Levallois flakes are produced from one and the same surface. Though these are not preferential flakes, they are of predetermined shape and, therefore, Levallois flakes. At the same time, they are also predetermining as they are of influence on the morphology of the next Levallois flake struck from that same surface. According to the pattern of striking directions of recurrent Levallois flakes, a unipolar (all Levallois flakes from the same striking platform on the core's perimeter), bipolar (Levallois flakes from two opposed platforms) and centripetal (Levallois flakes from all over the core's perimeter) recurrent methods are distinguished.

Clearly, these definitions have inflated the morphological constraints within which individual flakes can be identified as Levallois. The divergent views on which systematics to use for the classification of Levallois, are in part the result of different methodologies. The broad definition (Copeland 1983) of methods and blank types relies on a procedure known as the *lecture des schémas diacritiques* (Boëda 1994, Dauvois 1976). This is considered an equivalent alternative to refitting in

technological studies, allowing a description of reduction dynamics. It is, however, my conviction that refitting remains a far superior tool. If prehistoric lithic reduction systems are defined as concepts of volumetric organisation and maintenance regulating such dynamic procedures, refitting should be called upon to define such concepts and their typical artefactual components. Only later certain morphological constants, characteristic of a particular concept, may perhaps be derived. These will help the technological classification of individual artefacts, when refitting cannot be used.

The purpose and nature of classification

It seems useful to remind ourselves of the purpose and meaning of categories of classification, whether they refer to abstract concepts or to factual entities (Clarke 1968; Dunnell 1971). Systems of classification, in principle, are formal frameworks for generalized descriptions of individual facts. In this regard, it seems to matter little how broad the Levallois flake category is, as long as its criteria of identification are well defined. As its relevance is limited to description, the design of a system of classification seems a matter of unconstrained, formal choice. This is obviously not true ; its construction must operate within certain constraints for classification categories are, and should be, inherently meaningful. A consideration of some properties of classification categories makes clear at which levels the attribution of meaning is involved.

Description

The categories of a system of classification must transcribe, in a standardized way, an order that seems apparent in the archaeological record, using empirical criteria. As the latter are most often related to morphology, classification categories disclose patterned morphological variation. Systems of classification are explicit and formal acknowledgements of observed directional trends that seem to be a property of the archaeological record. They are subordinate to empirical realities.

Identification

In the process of classification, facts are not only described but also identified. They are provided with categorical names, the latter making up an etic structure that is imposed on the archaeological record. According to our own etic frame of reference, morphological categories acquire other connotations. We may think of technological classification, for instance, as a structure describing stages in the development of an operational

sequence of lithic production. Yet, while a Levallois flake may be defined 'technologically' as the intended product of a particular operational chain of lithic production, it is identified on the basis of certain morphological aspects. Abstract concepts, e.g. the Levallois concept or any other concept of lithic production, may be defined as underlying principles of that etic structure. Once defined, these concepts and the morphological categories that they include, become meaningful realities in our minds. There is no other way to reason about the archaeological record but through the filter of this etic structure (Hodder 1986 : 132). We may not know if those principles and categories have existed in the past, but we almost irresistably act as if they had. If this is so, classification inevitably involves an etic distortion of an emic reality (Harris 1979 : 32) and, therefore, simple classification systems using parsimony must be preferred. They can be used under the assumption that they represent an emic structure with at least a little confidence.

Logical consistency

If a system of morphological classification is bound to acquire 'real' behavioural connotations, it is imperative that the classification categories are not in contradiction with physical or technical principles that are involved in the overall etic construction.

For example, the existence of a recurrent centripetal method of Levallois exploitation (Boëda 1994) is logically inconsistent with the physical principles underlying the morphological predetermination of Levallois flakes. The latter quality follows from the fact that such flakes exploit the systematic pattern of ridges on a convex upper core surface. In order to do so, Levallois flakes need to be invasive, i.e. they must consume a maximal portion of the available core surface. Invasive debitage of *preferential* flakes can only be achieved when the plane of debitage is parallel to the plane of intersection of the core and when the upper core surface is sufficiently convex. A centripetal exploitation of a series of preferential Levallois flakes, therefore, is technically impossible as important parts of the core convexity are removed by previous blanks in the series.

The definition of the recurrent centripetal method seems to resolve this problem in holding that a series of non-invasive or *non-preferential* flakes (Boëda 1994) is aimed at. In doing so, however, it impedes the essential Levallois features of parallel plane debitage (cfr. *infra*) and, consequently, of morphological predetermination which necessarily requires invasiveness. The recurrent centripetal Levallois method, therefore, is incompatible with some essential principles implied in the overall set of Levallois definitions (Boëda 1994, Van Peer 1992). This raises serious questions as to its behavioural reality.

Emic meaning

Meaning is most obviously involved in classification when categories are, implicitly or explicitly taken to represent those that existed in the past. Here, they are no longer simply descriptive nor relevant to an etic frame of reference only, but categories are direct representations of past concepts (Dunnell 1971 : 132). Emic meaning is unlikely to be mirrored in our categories, at least not to an important degree. If, as indicated above, these categories are mostly the result of formal choice, what would be the probability that they refer to an emically relevant structure of classification ?

The definition of Levallois

Given these remarks about classification, what would be the most parsimonious system of classification for Levallois? The use of completely reconstructed sequences is most advantageous here as they provide some real behavioural evidence, independent from purely morphological considerations. The reconstructed reduction sequences from Makhadma-6 and Taramsa sector 91/04, in which the Levallois concept can be recognized, show without exception that the largest flakes are always struck from the same striking platform on the core's perimeter. Usually, their axis of flaking coïncides with the axis of longitudinal symmetry for the core and, hence, the flake itself is symmetrical as well. Often, however, more large flakes are produced from the same surface subsequent to the first central one, as for instance in Makhadma-6 reduction 173/1 (Figure 4). They exploit the marginal zones of the surface which may result in less symmetrical morphologies. Due to the limited amount of volume available for exploitation, a surface is quickly exhausted and further use of the core will require the installation of a new Levallois surface. Depending on the size and shape of the original raw material volume, Levallois surfaces may be renewed several times. These observations suggest that the exploitation of a Levallois core is an iterative, recurrent and unidirectional process.

Next to, and as a consequence of their large size relative to core size, Levallois flakes usually show numerous dorsal scars in an apparently regular disposition. From a morphological point of view, they correspond entirely to the classic definitions of Levallois flakes (e.g. Bordes 1961). These large, symmetrical blanks appear to constitute the final stages of a particular reduction phase and, therefore, they can be considered as technological end products. This can be inferred from the standardized pattern in which Levallois reductions appear to proceed. Preparation sequences of a Levallois surface are often interrupted after the production of a large blank from the preferential striking platform. The latter receives intensive secondary preparation just before the production of the preferential blank wich usually results in facetted butts, often of *chapeau de gendarme* type. The preparation of a subsequent surface will return to the same point on the core periphery as the first preparation sequence and proceed, from there, in almost exactly the

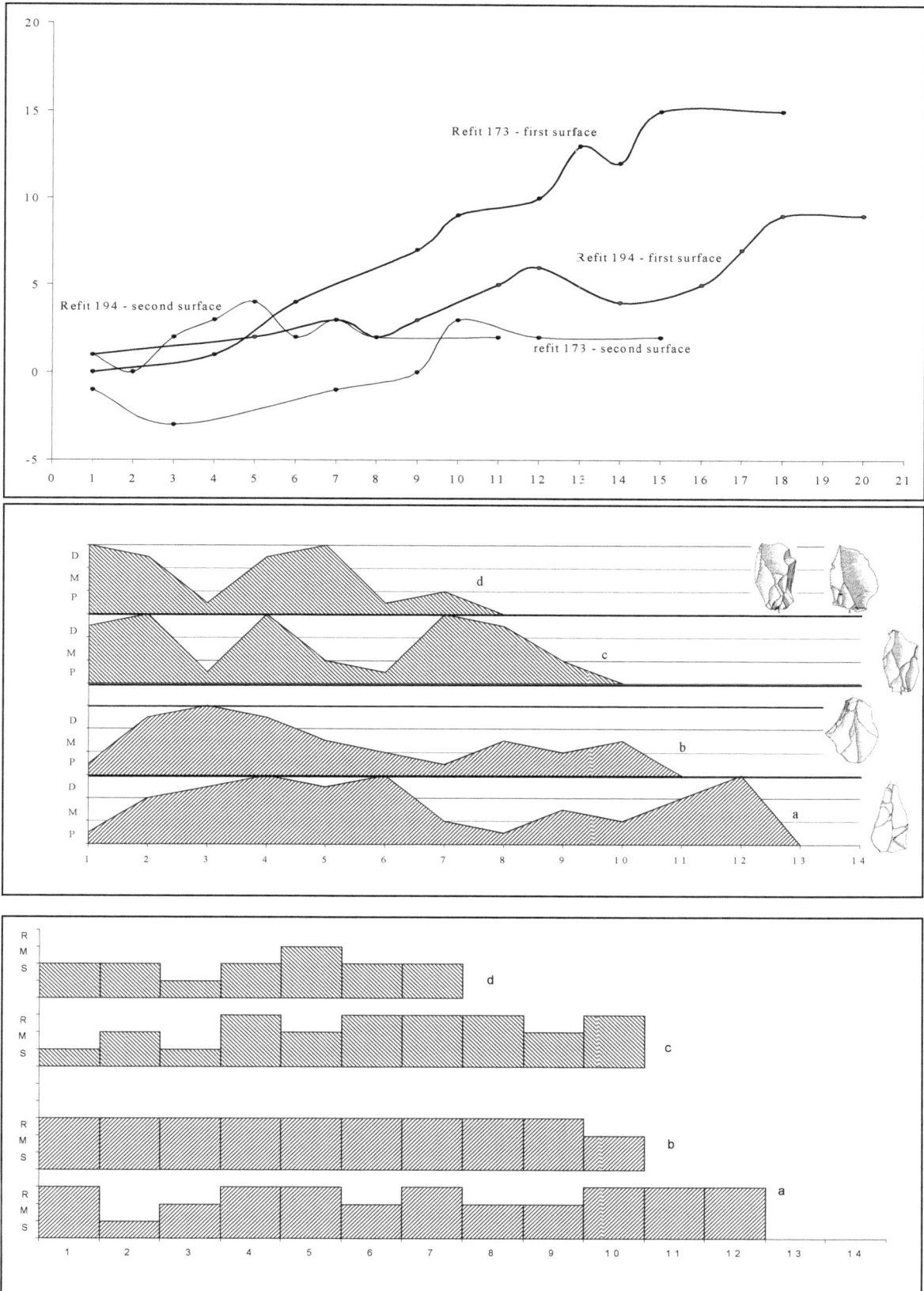

Figure 4. *Reduction dynamics charts for Makhadma-6. a: progression lines; b: pattern of preparation generations with Levallois blanks as conclusive stage (A: sequence 194/first; B: sequence 194/second; C: sequence 173/first; D: sequence 173/second); c: momentum sequence (legend as in b).*

same sequence. This is clearly evidenced in the two Makhamda-6 reductions (Fig. 4b). Any other subsequent Levallois surface will be prepared according to that same pattern. Often, the core exploitation is terminated after the production of a last large, central blank. I have argued elsewhere (Van Peer 1992) that this recurrent feature in itself is a good indication of the desired nature of such blanks. In Lower Nile Valley Middle Palaeolithic assemblages, more than half of the Levallois cores show the negative of a large central flake as the last removal. This high proportion contradicts the idea that Levallois is a particular system of continuous blank production (Dibble 1989 ; Noble and Davidson 1996 : 200).

Conversely, the reduction of almost half of the Levallois cores is not terminated with a large blank. This may be taken to indicate that (1) recurrent methods of exploitation using different striking platforms on the core's perimeter, exist and (2) that maximized size is not an inherent feature of Levallois end products (Boëda 1994). This, however, is logically incompatible with the technological definition of the Levallois concept. The latter includes the feature of exploitation of a Levallois surface in a plane, parallel to the plane of intersection of the core and intersecting the Levallois surface convexities. This kind of exploitation can only be achieved for large flakes. Flakes that consume less than half of the Levallois surface are necessarily detached in a tangential plane. A recurrent centripetal method of exploitation, aiming at a series of non-preferential flakes, cannot exist within the Levallois concept. Refitted sequences never show a blank with the morphological features of a Levallois blank, being struck from lateral striking platforms. In no sequence is there any evidence of a special preparation of lateral striking platforms, similar to that of the preferential striking platform. A few sequences do show a complete re-orientation of the core after its initial exploitation stages. Only in such cases, Levallois blanks can be observed to have axes of flaking at 90 degrees to a former one, but this has nothing to do with a recurrent centripetal method of exploitation.

A recurrent bipolar method, on the other hand, could exist in principle. The Taramsa 91/04 sequences do show some evidence of this. It is, however, clear that this bidirectional exploitation involves some major modifications of the volumetric conception of an initial raw material volume. In particular the relative proportions of striking platform and exploitation volumes are changed : the latter become much more important in terms of volume. This is technically achieved by initiating lateral preparation flakes under large angles to the plane of intersection of the core. Exploitation volumes, in other words, become much more domed than in classic Levallois cores. This volumetric conception further entails debitage of blanks in tangential planes which, as referred to above, is also a violation of the Levallois concept. The morphological consequences of

these changes, especially when applied to rather elongated raw material volumes as is the case in Taramsa 91/04, are blades. Reconstructed reductions, elaborated according to such principles, may show the exploitation of two opposed striking platforms. It is, however, clear that these principles are situated well beyond the limits of the Levallois concept. A new name, the Taramsa reduction strategy, seemingly showing some affinity with the Boker Tachtit reduction type (Marks and Volkman 1983), seems appropriate. Moreover, clear morphological differences usually exist between the end products struck from both striking platforms. Those from the true preferential 'Levallois' striking platform usually retain Levallois flake features (e.g. numerous dorsal scars and a reduced index of elongation) while only blanks from the opposed platform are true blades. This confirms that true Levallois reduction is intricately connected with one preferential striking platform exploitation. In their final stages of exploitation, Taramsa strategy cores cannot be distinguished from Levallois cores. This is not surprising as the initial domed exploitation volume has now been completely reduced. It takes the refitted sequence to be able to resolve this morphological equifinality and to observe the different principles that have governed the reduction sequence.

In conclusion, the reconstructed reduction sequences from Lower Nile Valley Middle Palaeolithic sites can be used to argue that Levallois is most parsimoniously defined in a rather strict way. It is a system of exploitation aiming at the production of the largest possible blanks from a core. Due to their large volume consumption and the elaborate preparation procedure involved, such blanks are few in number and they are always produced from the same preferential striking platform on the core. As their phases of production terminate particular reduction stages, there is reason to conceive of these large blanks as the anticipated and desired end products of the Levallois reduction system. Whether these were also the emic end products is unknown and irrelevant. As a matter of fact, I have come to believe that there is little emic relevance to Levallois as a system of core reduction. It would seem better, for the Middle Palaeolithic, to think of one overall system of flake production employing an essentially twodimensional volumetric conception where a plane rather than a volume is exploited. The 'Levallois grade' will emerge in specific conditions, as at workshops where raw material is abundant. This, however, does not prevent Levallois from remaining a valid concept for classification and description. The purpose of definitions is to bring a certain order to unordered facts and in such a way that every analist will arrive at the same order for similar facts. In order to achieve this, a strict definition of Levallois, strongly supported by refitting evidence, is the most useful.

IDENTIFICATION OF INDIVIDUAL KNAPPERS

The argument of parsimony underlying the acceptance of a simple and minimal definition of Levallois, does not at all imply that looking for patterned variability is pointless. It does suggest that variability may be more usefully researched along different lines of evidence than those being based on formal etic frameworks.

It was already mentioned that Levallois reductions appear very systematic from a dynamic point of view. I tried to turn this initial intuitive appreciation into an objective analysis by quantifying the dynamic process of reduction, as described earlier and using as little typological features as possible. Taramsa, Levallois and other reduction sequences were thus taken into account as the units of observation, although the latter are very rare in Taramsa sector 91/04. The only morphological (i.e. typological) observations were the identification of end products, which were used to delineate particular stages in the reduction sequences.

Intra-reduction patterning

By means of the data on reduction sequence characteristics, it is possible to objectively compare different reductions sequences. First, two reduction sequences with two Levallois surfaces each, are looked at from the point of view of intra-reduction variability. This will further illustrate the standardized nature of preparation sequences, leading to morphological similarty among the various end products within the same reduction. The two reduction sequences come from the site of Makhadma-6.

Within themselves, the two sequences appear very similar (Fig 4). The progression lines for the two Levallois surfaces are dominated by counter-clockwise shifts resulting in positively sloping lines. The two Levallois surfaces of sequence 173, however, evidence a more important share of long sector shifts, while those in sequence 194 are usually between adjacent sectors. As far as the dynamic generation of the pattern of preparation is concerned, the two surfaces are similar in both cases, though the first surface is logically more complex. Both the distal and proximal sectors are by far the most intensively prepared. In sequence 194, the first stages in the surface preparations exclusively concern the distal sectors. The two lateral sectors are only treated in the final phase of the preparation sequences. Sequence 173 shows an rapid alternation between the distal and proximal sectors. The starting point for the two surface preparations is the same in both cases : those of sequence 194 start in the lower right part ; those for 173 in the distal area. Rather important intra-reduction differences are attested in the momentum of the reduction progression, for sequence 194 in particular. Its first surface is characterized by a progression whereby phases

of rapid sector change are followed by in-sector preparation. The second surface, on the contrary, is almost exclusively made up of fast consecutive sector switches.

On the whole, the two Levallois reductions from Makhadma-6 evidence intra-reduction standardization to quite an important degree and, hence, an apparent intention to produce morphologically similar end products as conclusive exploitation stages of the respective Levallois surfaces (Fig. 4b). It is furthermore clear that the two reductions are quite similar to each other as well, notwithstanding the fact that in a traditional typological sense, two different methods are involved. In reduction 194, a Nubian pattern of preparation is applied to the consecutive Levallois surfaces, generating pointed morphologies. Sequence 173 is elaborated according to a bidirectional pattern of preparation resulting in parallel-sided rectangular flakes. This example shows that morphological differences that are grasped in present classification systems, real as their influence on reduction dynamics are, may be overridden by a more fundamental pattern of technological variability. The spatial context at the site, the small size of this *in situ* scatter in particular, would seem to suggest that we are faced here with the production of one prehistoric individual (Cahen and Keeley, 1980). The apparent similarities in terms of dynamics between two reductions, then, might be interpreted as an expression of this individual's 'style' of lithic reduction. However, more comparative research is necessary to validate this interpretation. In particular, a clear-cut pattern of discrete goups among a number of reduction sequences would have to be found.

An example of inter-reduction patterning

Data

If reduction sequence dynamics show individual knappers' ways of doing (Pigeot, 1990), Taramsa sector 91/04 subsector 28 is an excellent situation to look for patterning along these lines. It is a dense scatter of artefacts where at least 28 complete reductions were carried out during, likely, one contemporaneous event. Different individuals may have been at work here. However, do the dynamic reduction data show any discrete group patterns that could be interpreted as these individuals?

I will consider the first Levallois surfaces of seven reduction sequences (28/3, 28/9, 28/12, 28/14, 28/15, 28/18, 28/27). Among the progression lines two groups can be distinguished (Figure 5a, 5b). One comprises sequences 9, 14 and 27 which are characterized by a moderately sloping positive line with one depression. Thus, the reduction are carried out in a counter-clockwise pattern with mostly shifts between adjacent sectors. In the other reductions the trend of the progression lines is

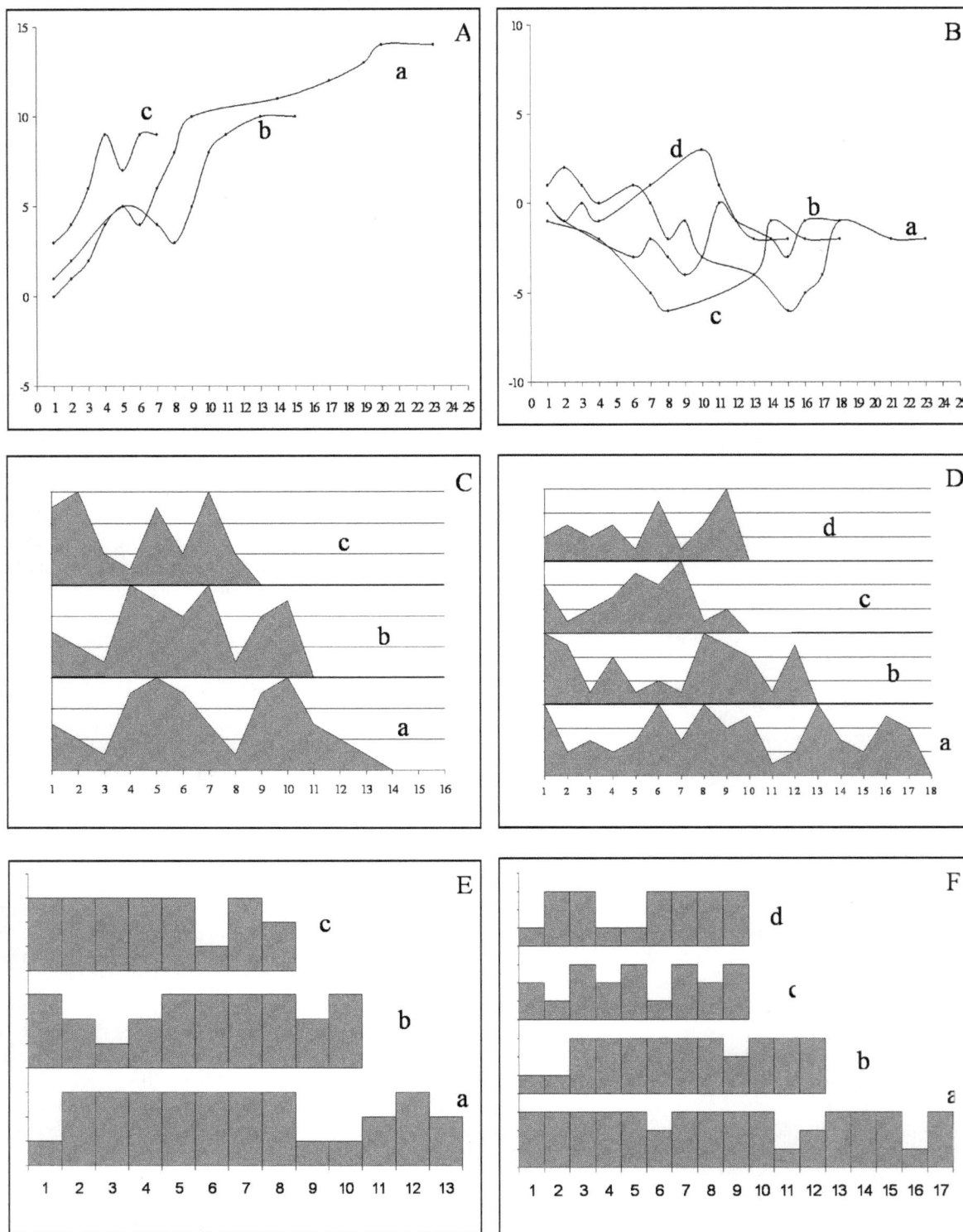

Figure 5: Reduction dynamics charts on two groups of reduction sequences from Taramsa sector 91/04, subconcentration 28. A: group alfa progression lines (a: 28/14; b: 28/27; c: 28/9); B: goup beta progession lines (a: 28/15; b: 28/3; c: 28/18; d: 28/12); C: group alfa: pattern of preparation generations (legend as in A); D: group beta: pattern of preparation generations (legend as in B); E:group alfa: momentum sequence (legend as in A); F: group beta: momentum sequence (legend as in B). For Y-axis labels C-F: see fig. 4.

negative though a few positive bulges are always present, especially for reduction 28/12. They are clockwise procedures and, as the steeper parts of the lines show, the share of long shifts is rather important.

Among the patterns of preparation, reductions 27 and 14 are again very similar. The preparation sequences start in the left medial sector and shift to the left proximal sector. Then follows a sequence of distal sector preparation which is continued after a proximal intermezzo. In general, both reductions are characterized by an important emphasis on the elaboration of the distal sector while the lateral sector receives very marginal treatment. Reduction 28/9 is somewhat different in shape, but it shares with the former its important distal sector preparation which is elaborated in different phases. Medial sector preparation is generally more explicit in the other reductions, which display a more angular outline of the pattern generation lines. This indicates more frequent shifts among sectors in different core areas or a more 'disorganized' pattern of progression, a feature also suggested by the shape of the progression lines. Reduction 28/18 is somewhat exceptional in this respect and might eventually be classified among the reductions of the former group.

From the momentum charts, it is clear that reductions 28/9, 28/14 and 28/27 are characterized by the presence of one long phase of rapid shifts where each consecutive removal is placed in another core sector. An alternation of sustained phases of rapid shift with moments of repeated in-sector preparation is attested among the reductions of the other group.

DISCUSSION

While the precise group assignment of a number of individual reductions according to any individual feature can be argued about, the distinction of two overall reduction groups as presented here seems to be quite straightforward. These data suggest that discrete patterned variability in reduction dynamics can be expected. It is important to stress that this analysis is only concerned with reduction progression data and that no direct morphological attributes come into play. Furthermore, the analysis was done without any recourse to the reduction sequences themselves[3]. When this is done after the classification procedure, the morphological similarities between the different sequences of each group are very striking. It would seem that for each reduction style, specific raw material morphologies were chosen and that the final core shapes are quite similar as well. The latter should not be too surprising as the uniformity and recurrent nature of the pattern of preparation generation were noticed in the analysis.

The correspondence between these two lines of data, which should be explored further, might suggest that

reduction styles are only generated by morpho-functional considerations regarding the end products that will be produced. In that sense, they would simply represent methods as defined earlier. However, I find it hard to see how eventual morphological templates would determine the kind of technical variability measured in the reduction dynamics data. In my opinion, the causal relationship is precisely the reverse. It is due to a particular, personal, way of doing that idiosyncratic product morphologies are arrived at. In terms of the traditionally identified preparation methods, for instance, there is no differentiation at all among the products from sector 91/04. The method applied is a classical preparation method, with more or less explicit radial patterning, in order to arrive generally at elongated and distally converging blanks. Within this latter category, however, significant and unpatterned variation is attested.

Further analysis of the Taramsa sector 91/04 sequences is in progress, but there seem indications that more or less four discrete pattern groups are represented in sub-sector 28. Within the general context of sector 91/04, which represents one phase of chert extraction activities, zones of different functionality within a raw material processing *chaîne opératoire*, are clearly represented here (Van Peer 2001). Sub-sector 28 has been interpreted as an area of full reduction. It was furthermore regarded as a spot where knapping specialists might have been at work, while other functions, for example, the extraction of the nodules themselves, were assumed by differently skilled members of the group. Task specialisation, in other words, is seen as a characteristic feature of the social structure of these late Nubian Complex groups in the Lower Nile Valley (Roux, 1990).

The present findings are in line with this earlier interpretation. Personal ways of doing, generated by experience, would not be unexpected among task specialists. This would be the case particularly when that task is both conceptually and technically complex, a feature which by its very presence almost necessarily presupposes specialisation.

CONCLUSION

While the reconstruction of lithic reduction sequences has become a standard procedure in lithic studies the value of which needs no further demonstration, it has been my intention here to show that refitting results have much unexplored analytic potential. They are an obvious tool for technological studies and should be used to arrive at sensible classification systems of lithic reduction systems. As far as Levallois is concerned, the dynamic evidence from reconstructed sequences suggests that a simple definition is required. The Levallois system can be thought of as a grade within a general concept of lithic reduction, aiming at the production of large-sized symmetrical end products. This aim is realized in practice through reductions of which the level of complexity generally seems to increase through time. Reductions as attested in late Nubian Complex sector 91/04 of Taramsa, often involve the elaboration of several subsequent exploitation surfaces according to uniform sequences of preparation. Furthermore, a rigid order is apparent in the alternation between Levallois surface preparation and the installation of a prepared striking platform in view of the production of a large blank. The latter preparation is initiated each time an exploitation surface has received its final organisation and immediately before the production of end products from that particular surface.

Further, it was argued that this complex system of production may have been the domain of task specialists showing evidence of personal styles. The particular patterns in the quantitative reduction data would seem to reflect particular ways and rhytms in which cores are held and turned in the hand while being worked. This is an issue that can be further explored with experimental work but whatever the actual technical processes involved, the patterning is clear and discrete. It corroborates an interpretation of the late Nubian Complex as a complex phenomenon in terms of social organisation, relying on the principle of division of labour and specialisation. While this may be speculation, at least for now, it shows that an objective analysis of refitting patterns may lead to inferences on questions that would intuitively seem far beyond the realm of the production of basic subsistence technology. It should also urge us to reconsider the role of the individual as a possible source of patterned variability in the archaeological record.

[1] The financial support of the Research Council of Leuven University, permitting the development of some ideas underlying this paper, is acknowledged.
[2] Reduction sequences were oriented with the preferential striking platforms at the bottom
[3] As I have refitted most of the sequences myself, I knew the sequences involved. However, the quantitative reduction data were recorded at the time of the refitting and a period of a few years elapsed before the present analysis.

BIBLIOGRAPHY

BOEDA, E. 1994. *Le concept Levallois: variabilité des méthodes*. Monographes du CRA, 9. Paris: éditions CNRS.

BORDES, F. 1961. *Typologie du Paléolithique ancien et moyen*. Bordeaux: Publication de l'Institut de Préhistoire de l'Université de Bordeaux.

BOUTIE, P. 1981. *L'industrie moustérienne de la grotte du Kébara, Mont Carmel – Israël*. Paris: Muséum national d'histoire naturelle, Musé de l'Homme, mémoire 10.

CAHEN, D. 1987. Refitting stone artefacts: why bother? In *The human uses of flint and chert*, edited by G. DE SIEVEKING and M.H. NEWCOMER. Cambridge: Cambridge University Press, pp. 1-10.

CAHEN, D. & L.H. KEELEY 1980. Not less than two, not more than three. *World Archaeology* 12: 166-180.

CLARKE, D.L. 1968. *Analytical Archaeology*. London: Methuen & Co.

CHAZAN, M. 1997. Redefining Levallois. *Journal of Human Evolution* 33: 719-735.

CLARK, J.D. & M. KLEINDIENST 2001. The Stone Age cultural sequence: terminology, typology and raw material. *In Kalambo Falls prehistoric site, volume III. The earlier cultures: Middle and Earlier Stone Age*, edited by J.D. CLARK. Cambridge University Press, Cambridge

COPELAND, L. 1983. Levallois/non-Levallois determinations in the Levant: problems and questions for 1983. *Paléorient* 9, pp. 15-27.

CREW, H.L. 1975. An evaluation of the relationship between the Mousterian complexes of the Eastern Mediterranean: a technological perspective. In *Problems in Prehistory: North Africa and the Levant*, edited by F. WENDORF & A.E. MARKS. Dallas: Southern Methodist University Press, pp. 427-438.

CZIESLA, E., S. EICKHOFF, N. ARTS & D. WINTER (eds.) 1990. *The Big Puzzle. International Symposium on Refitting Stone Artefacts*. Holos, Bonn.

DAUVOIS, M. 1976. *Précis de dessin dynamique et structural des industries lithiques préhistoriques*. Pierre Fanlac, Périgueux.

DIBBLE, H. L. 1989. The Implications of Stone Tool Types for the Presence of Language during the Lower and Middle Palaeolithic. In *The Human Revolution. Behavioural and Biological Perspectives in the Origins of Modern Humans*, editeb by P. MELLARS & C. STRINGER. Edinburgh: Edinburgh University Press.

DIBBLE, H. & O. BAR-YOSEF (eds.) 1995. *The Definition and Interpretation of Levallois Technology*. Monographs in World Archaeology, Prehistory Press, Madison.

DUNNELL, R. C. 1971. *Systematics in Prehistory*. The Free Press, New York.

GUICHARD, J. & G. GUICHARD 1965. The Early and Middle Paleolithic of Nubia. In *Contributions to the Prehistory of Nubia*, edited by F. WENDORF. Fort Burgwin Research Center and Southern Methodist University Press, Dallas, pp. 57-166.

HARRIS, M. 1979. *Cultural materialism. The struggle for a science of culture*. Random House, New York.

HILL, N.J. & J. GUNN 1977. The individual in prehistory. Studies of variability in style in prehistoric technologies. Academic Press, New York

HODDER, I. 1986. *Reading the past. Current approaches to interpretation in archaeology*. Cambridge University Press, Cambridge.

HOFMAN, J.L. & J.G. ENLOE (editors) 1992. *Piecing Together the Past. Applications of Refitting Studies in Archaeology*. British Archaeological Reports, International Series, 578. Oxford: BAR Publishing.

ISAAC, G. 1981. Stone Age visiting cards: approaches to the study of early land use patterns. In *Pattern of the Past. Studies in honour of David Clarke*. Edited by I. HODDER, G. ISAAC & N. HAMMOND. Cambridge University Press, Cambridge, pp. 131-156.

MARKS, A.E. & P. VOLKMAN 1983. Changing core reduction strategies: a technological shift from the Middle to the Upper Palaeolithic in the southern Levant. In *The Mousterian legacy: human biocultural change in the Upper Pleistocene*, edited by E. TRINKAUS. British Archaeological Reports, International Series, 164, pp. 13-34.

MEIGNEN, L. & O. BAR-YOSEF 1988. Variabilité technologique au Proche-Orient: l'exemple de Kébara. *Etudes et Recherches archéologiques de l'Université de Liège*, 31, pp. 81-96.

NOBLE, W. & I. DAVIDSON 1996. *Human evolution, language and mind. A psychological and archaeological inquiry*. Cambridge University Press, Cambridge.

PIGEOT, N. 1990. Technical and Social Actors: Flintknapping Specialists at Magdalenian Etiolles. *Archaeological Review from Cambridge*, 9: 126-141.

ROEBROEKS, W. , D. DE LOECKER, P. HENNEKENS & M. VAN IEPEREN 1992. "A veil of stones": on the interpretation of an early Middle Palaeolithic low density scatter at Maastricht-Belvédère (The Netherlands). *Analecta Praehistorica Leidensia*, 25: 1-16.

ROUX, V. 1990. The Psychosocial Analysis of Technical Actvities: a Contribution to the Study of Craft Specialisation. *Archaeological Review from Cambridge*, 9: 142-153.

VAN PEER, P. 1992. *The Levallois Reduction Strategy*. Monographs in World Archaeology 13. Prehistory Press, Madison.

VAN PEER P. 1998. The River Nile Corridor and Out of Africa: an Examination of the Archaeological Record. *Current Anthropology* 39: S115-S140.

VAN PEER, P. 2000. Makhadma-6 : A Nubian Complex site. In *Palaeolithic living sites in Upper and Middle Egypt*, Egyptian Prehistory Monographs 2. Edited by P.M. VERMEERSCH. Leuven University Press, Leuven, pp. 91-101.

VAN PEER, P. 2001. The Nubian Complex settlement system in Northeast Africa. In *Settlement Dynamics of the Middle Paleolithic and Middle Stone Age*. Edited by N.J. CONARD. Kerns, Tübingen, pp.45-64.

VERMEERSCH, P.M., E. PAULISSEN & P. VAN PEER 1990. Palaeolithic Chert Exploitation in the Limestone Stretch of the Egyptian Nile Valley. *The African Archaeological Review* 8: 77-102.

VERMEERSCH P.M., E. PAULISSEN, S. STOKES, C. CHARLIER, P. VAN PEER, C. STRINGER. & W. LINDSAY 1998. A Middle Palaeolithic burial of a modern human at Taramsa Hill, Egypt. *Antiquity* 72: 475-484.

Address of the author:

Katholieke Universiteit Leuven
Laboratorium voor Prehistorie
Redingenstraat 16
3000 Leuven, Belgium

philip.vanpeer@geo.kuleuven.ac.be

AUSTRALIAN POINT AND CORE REDUCTION VIEWED THROUGH REFITTING

Peter HISCOCK

Abstract

Refitting of knapping floors in northern Australia is used to analyse the production technology employed during the mid- to late-Holocene. Examination of refits at quarries is the basis of a study not only of the general sequence of reduction but also the solutions that knappers apply to solve problems they encounter. A series of refitted knapping floors at increasing distances from quarries reveal the progressive modification of bifacial points and cores as material is transported through the landscape. This case study is employed as an illustration of the value of refitting studies as a means of explicating regional technological and economic patterns. It is argued that future refitting analyses will more powerfully exploit the potential of the technique when quantitative measurements are used to evaluate not only technological trajectories during the reduction process but also the variability that occurs within and between sequences.

Résumé

Cet article fait appel au remontage d'artéfacts de sols de débitage en Australie du Nord pour analyser la technologie lithique de l'Holocène moyen et final. L'examen de sets de remontage provenant de sites d'exploitation sont à la base d'une étude, non seulement de la séquence usuelle de réduction, mais également de solutions que les tailleurs ont appliqué pour résoudre les problèmes rencontrés. Une série de sols de taille remontés, de plus en plus éloignés des sites d'exploitation, révèle une modification progressive despointes bifaciales et desnucléus lors de leur transport à travers le paysage. Cette étude est exemplaire pour illustrer la valeur d'études de remontage comme moyen pour comprendre les modèles technologiques et économiques régionaux. A l'avenir, les analyses de remontage, à notre avis, pourront mieux exploiter les possibilités de cette technique si on applique également des mensurations précises pour évaluer, non seulement les trajectoires technologiques pendant le processus de réduction, mais aussi la variabilité que l'on observe dans et entre les séquences.

INTRODUCTION

Refitting assists archaeologists to develop models of lithic artefact manufacture which describe the entire reduction process rather than merely the end products, that measure variability in knapping rather than only

normative images of technology, and which depict the relationships between localities in terms of the regional socio-economic strategies that prevailed in the past. Such models act as powerful interpretative devices and are increasingly being generated by archaeological research. Outstanding examples of refitting being used to construct details of prehistoric technology exist; like Barton's (1992) discussion of the extent, strategy and variation in core reduction at Hengistbury Head. However it is rare for all of these elements to be present in a single model. More commonly excellent refitting studies rely on the researcher's unquantified textual descriptions, perhaps aided by photographs or realistic drawings of artefacts, to advance the interpretation of the manufacturing process (e.g. Ahler 1992; Arnold 1990; Gilead and Fabian 1990; Lohr 1990; Morrow 1996; Rensink 1990; Schafer 1990; Weiner 1990; Wyckoff 1992). Refitting is not in and of itself an analysis of the technological patterns that exist in a reduction sequence. Refitting orders artefacts into their sequence of production, thereby facilitating measurements of the trends in reduction sequences. By developing models of quantitative analysis for refitted sequences the potential of conjoining can be more powerfully exploited. For instance, quantitative research can assist in portraying and understanding variation within a technology, thereby moving beyond normative depictions to an image of the complexity and diversity of technological activities. This in turn may enhance our ability to understand assemblage differences within the economic variation that occurs within any region. In this way refitting plays a central role in an ongoing exploration of analytical frameworks that can describe the complexity of knapping by studying characteristics such as error rates, variations of reduction strategies, strategy switching, responses to raw material properties, and so on. This paper provides an example of the value of refitting analyses in the explication of technological variation that occurred in a small region. The example is drawn from Australia and involves an examination of core reduction and point production. A normative view of antipodean implements had at one stage created an image of very simple and uniform technologies (see White 1977), whereas the quantitative study of refitted artefacts has now revealed a varied and complex technological system represented in these Australian assemblages.

POINT AND CORE REDUCTION IN NORTHERN AUSTRALIA

Across northern and central Australia archaeological sites contain unifacial and bifacial points, and large, elongated flakes often called 'leilira', some of which have lateral retouch. The relationship of these artefact forms to each other, and to the processes of initial core reduction, is poorly understood and the subject of current investigation. It is now clear that in many regions unifacial and bifacial points represent morphological and

investigations of the northern leilira and point assemblages (although Clarkson is currently undertaking such an analysis). In the following pages I outline a conjoining study of Holocene aged sites from the semi-arid plain immediately south of the Gulf of Carpentaria (see Figure 2). These sites yielded a series of refitted

Figure 1 *Examples of bifacial points from northern Australia showing progressive reduction from unifacial and unimarginal retouch (left) to bifacial and bimarginal (right).*

reduction continuums (Hiscock 1994), and that the elongated leilira flakes have many histories: some were traded and used without retouch, some were transformed into points, while some were retouched in other ways (Jones and White 1988:52). Part of this variation may reflect recycling and changes in the role of trading systems (Allen 1994), but much of this variation probably reflects behavioural differences arising from dissimilar local and regional circumstances. Studies of flake production, and of retouching patterns, would illuminate the causes of these archaeological differences, but although Jones and White (1988:62-76) have provided ethnographic descriptions of production, detailed archaeological studies of core reduction and point manufacture in these industries have been minimal (although see the important studies of Clarkson and David 1995; Cundy 1990; Thorley et al. 1994). Studies of reduction processes have a long history in Australia (see Hiscock 1998), but have often been based on technological classifications (e.g. Wright 1972), attribute analyses (e.g. Clarkson and David 1995; Lamb 1996), or seriation of artefact size and shape (e.g. Hiscock and Attenbrow 2003; Hiscock and Veth 1991). Refitting has only intermittently been employed as an aid to interpreting assemblages (e.g. Noetling 1908; Hiscock 1993), but has not previously been carried out in

knapping floors at increasing distances from quarries, revealing the progressive modification of bifacial points and cores as material is transported through the landscape. Transportation of artefacts across this lateritic plain is readily identified because the only source of flakeable rock for many kilometres is a low ridge of greywacke, bisected by Page Creek, on which a number of quarries are evident.

PAGE CREEK QUARRIES

The example that will be used to illustrate the advantages of refitting in investigations of point and core production focuses on the extraction of greywacke from a source on the flood plains surrounding the Gulf of Carpentaria in tropical semi-arid northern Australia (Figure 2). In the area south of Lawn Hill Homestead an extensive, flat flood plain slopes gently to the north and has local relief up to 100 m in the form of hills and mesas. A steep rocky ridge protrudes from the flood plain, and runs roughly west to east for a distance of 3 kilometres. Covered by a thin mantle of siltstone and greywacke cobbles and blocks, the ridge has artefact scatters indicating quarrying where cobbles of suitable quality and form were located. Two quarry localities were recorded on this

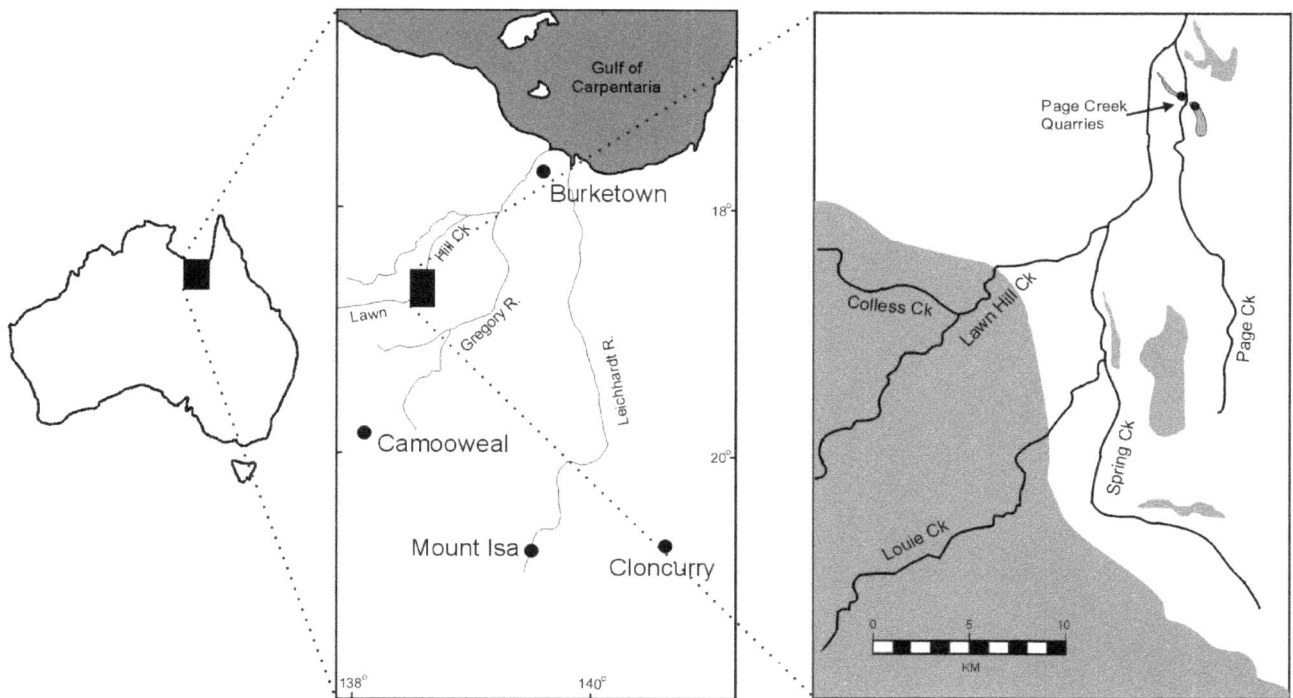

Figure 2. *Map showing the location of the Page Creek quarries in northern Australia.*

ridge. Page Creek Quarry 1 has a scatter of artefacts covering an area of 9350 m², with artefact densities varying from 0.25/m² to 39/m² and averaging 7/m². A short distance to the east Page Creek Quarry 2 is positioned on the crest and flank of the ridge, as indicated by a scatter of chipped artefacts at low densities, averaging 0.5/m².

The quarried material ranges from greywacke through silty greywacke to tuffaceous siltstone but is here all grouped under the term 'greywacke'. The greywacke is a dark, vivid green-grey or blue-grey with brown or yellow flecks, but the surface of many artefacts has been weathered to a light grey. Cortex is thick, often more than 1 cm, rough and dull, and is generally cream in colour. Thin-section examination reveals that the greywacke consists of angular and subrounded quartz grains, chalcedony grains, and particles of plagioclase in varying proportions. Grain size varies but is generally less than 0.2 mm (see Hiscock 1988 for details).

Physical characteristics of the greywacke at cropping out at Page Creek can be expressed in terms of compressive and tensile strength, and modulus of elasticity. Table 1 provides these characteristics for the greywacke and for the only other frequently used lithic material in the region, a banded chert. In contrast to chert the strength of greywacke is markedly lower, and values for the Modulus of Elasticity are always lower for greywacke than for chert, indicating that greywacke is markedly less stiff than chert. Thus, while less force was required to initiate fractures in greywacke than in chert, the lower elasticity and stiffness of the material made fracture in greywacke less controllable. As a result of the relative inelasticity, platform shattering and step terminations occur frequently on greywacke. The properties of greywacke suit it to the production of large, thick flakes,

Table 1

Physical properties of chert and greywacke from Lawn Hill (data from Hiscock 1988)

	Greywacke (N=23)	Chert (N=29)
Tensile strength*	44.5 ± 8.4	76.6 ± 25.6
Compressive strength*	347.5 ± 116.9	1044.8 ± 167.4
Modulus of Elasticity**	47,401.3 ± 6,892.7	58,087.6 ± 1,706.0

* = Newtons per mm²   ** = Newtons per mm

107

Peter Hiscock

and the potential use-life of greywacke artefacts is comparatively short, encouraging repeated resharpening. The greywacke occurs as rounded and subrounded cobbles and boulders and as angular slabs. At Page Creek the cobble size is relatively uniform, averaging 5,337 cm³ in volume. Specimens examined in thin-section were homogeneous in terms of grain size, but in many cobbles there are also distinct weathered cracks running parallel to the long axis. Greywacke fractures well but flakes struck across these cracks are likely to be truncated.

The antiquity of quarrying and knapping at the Page Creek sites is uncertain. Rockshelter sites less than 30 kilometres to the south contain greywacke artefacts in levels older than 20,000 BP, but the exact source of this material has not been established (Hiscock 1988). Variation in the flaked surface of artefacts, ranging form thickly patinated grey to unpatinated dark rock, suggests that quarrying took place over an extended period perhaps covering the late Pleistocene as well as the Holocene.

REDUCTION AT PAGE CREEK QUARRIES

At Page Creek the cobbles of greywacke were large and rounded, and prehistoric knappers often removed large numbers of flakes in each reduction sequence. The amount of reduction on each cobble can be roughly estimated from the flake:core ratio of 30:1; although interpretation of this ratio is always complicated by the possibility that cores and/or flakes have been added or removed from the assemblage. Refitting provides a far more reliable basis for estimating the 'length of reduction' (ie. number of flakes) for each cobble. Interpretations of the extent and sequence of reduction at the Page Creek quarries are therefore based on refitting flakes and cores. Five distinct knapping floors were identified in the two quarries on the Page Creek ridge, each represented by a spatially isolated concentration of artefacts. All artefacts in these knapping floors were collected and subjected to a refitting analysis. The result was the reconstruction of conjoined sequences that represent the flaking of nine different cobbles.

Refitted sequences could be described in detail. Even missing flakes, indicated by gaps in the refitted cobble, could be counted and have a number of characteristics measured, including an estimate of weight based on the volume of missing material. This enabled estimates of the original weight of the cobble, and of the amount of stone removed from the cores. Prior to the initiation of knapping these cobbles varied dramatically in size, from 1.5 kg to 8 kg. Extent of reduction also varied between cobbles. Measured as the weight of rock removed reduction varied from 734 grams to 7.5 kg. In terms of the number of flakes removed cobbles varied from 11 to 47. Much of the variability in the extent of reduction

relates to the two major problems these knappers faced:
1. The establishment of a suitable platform, and
2. Maintenance of the core face in an appropriate state when the removal of large flakes from this greywacke had a high likelihood of generating step terminations that would leave a large mass at the base of the core.

Reduction of all nine refitted cobbles, and all other cores observed on the quarries, followed the same general strategy. Flakes were struck, by hard hammer direct percussion, down the long axis of the cobble, from a single platform. Production of a platform was usually accomplished by striking one or two large flakes. Very little choice was available for the position of initial blows because most of the cobble surface was covered with cortex more that 1cm thick. Cobble selected for reduction had one surface with relatively thin (1-3mm) cortex that appeared to be hard and smooth compared with cortex covering the rest of the cobble. Prehistoric knappers applied their first blows to those surfaces, typically removing large flakes across the short axis of the cobble to yield conchoidal surfaces that could serve as a platform. The number of flakes subsequently struck from the platform was clearly related to the flatness of the surface created by the initial large flakes. If the flakes setting up a platform terminated abruptly or produced radically undulating surfaces, the capacity to reduce the core was often greatly limited.

Cross-sections through reconstructed cobbles reveal the strategy of flake removal, and the problems of core shape that threatened to prevent further reduction (Figure 3). The undulation in the platform surface shown in Figure 3c created a barrier to extended reduction and the core was abandoned after only eleven flakes were removed. In contrast the gently curving platform surface depicted in Figure 3a imposed no major problem for reduction, and forty-six flakes were struck from the cobble.

Once a platform was established the main threat to continued reduction was the production of abrupt terminations on the core face. To remove such terminations, and thereby prolong reduction, knappers employed five specific variations in the location of their blows. In order of the frequency of application these procedures were:
1. Striking the platform to the side of step terminated scars.
2. Striking further from the core edge.
3. Removing platform overhang.
4. Production of outrepasse terminations.
5. Initiation of a second platform positioned to remove the base of the core.

Since all five procedures are displayed in a single refitted sequence we can infer that they were probably known to and used by all knappers who worked at the quarry, but

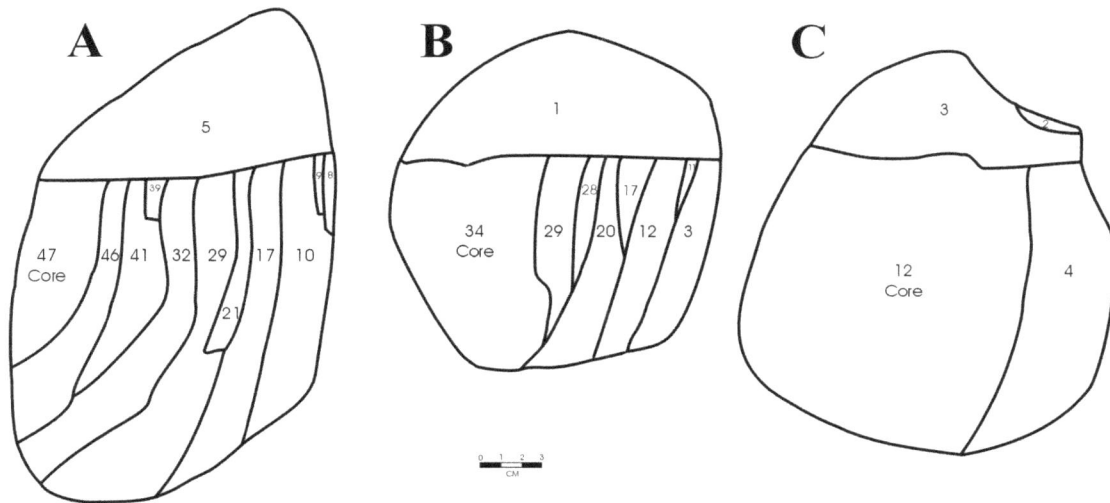

Figure 3. Cross-sections through three cobbles from Page Creek Quarry 1.

each procedure was employed only in suitable circumstances. This inference leads to an obvious but intriguing conclusion, that the archaeological manifestation of a stoneworking technology reflects the circumstances confronting the knapper. In any stoneworking technology, the knappers possess a repertoire of strategies and techniques they can employ to rectify emerging difficulties with the artefact being worked. Any problem can be prevented or solved by the application of only a limited portion of this repertoire, and so the emergence of a given problem in the reduction of one nodule is likely to elicit from the knapper behaviour that might not otherwise occur. Moreover, in some technologies a knapper may have more than one viable response to particular problems. Choosing one response rather than another may affect the size and shape of the resulting core and create circumstances in which different problems emerge which in turn will require their own particular solutions. The result can be reduction sequences that diverge as the cumulative effects of these choices alter core morphology. The implication for an understanding of stone working is that a variety of technological procedures may be applied by knappers within one 'technology' and it is possible for there to be a number of different archaeological manifestations of that technology. The success or failure of these problem-solving procedures, and the way that their application causes sequences to diverge, can be measured in two ways, each dependent on conjoining.

MEASURING THE ONSET OF PROBLEMS

Creation of abrupt terminations on the core face potentially reduces the capacity to continue reduction. A description of the timing and magnitude of these alterations to the core face has the capacity to assist our understanding of the knappers struggle to control core shape. Refitting provides the opportunity to measure the changing rate and severity of abrupt terminations through the sequence of reduction. Figure 4 illustrates for one cobble the abundance of abrupt terminations at different points in the reduction process. Two patterns are apparent. Firstly, after the platform was created and cortex stripped from the core face, thereby creating a pattern of scars, a series of blows regularly produced feather terminations (see Figure 4a). These flakes were comparatively thick, with expanding lateral margins, but had feather terminations because they ran the entire length of the core. As the mass of the core decreased, and thin flakes were often removed from a flat core face, there was a gradual but consistent, seemingly inexorable, increase in the proportion of flakes with abrupt terminations. The directionality of this trend, sustained over a sequence of thirty flake removals, suggests that the knapper would have been aware of the gradual emergence of unsuitable features on the core face, but was unable to prevent the continuing production of these terminations. The continued reduction suggests that either feather terminations were not an essential requirement of flakes being produced (see below) and/or the knappers were prepared to continue investing energy despite the ongoing difficulties. A second pattern existed within this trend of increasing abrupt terminations (see Figure 4b). During the final stages of core reduction step terminations were very frequently produced. The onset of this high frequency production of step terminations was extremely sudden, and marked the transition of core size and morphology to a state in which production of feather terminated flakes was extremely difficult. One consequence of this trend was that the frequent step terminations at the end of the reduction sequence

A

B

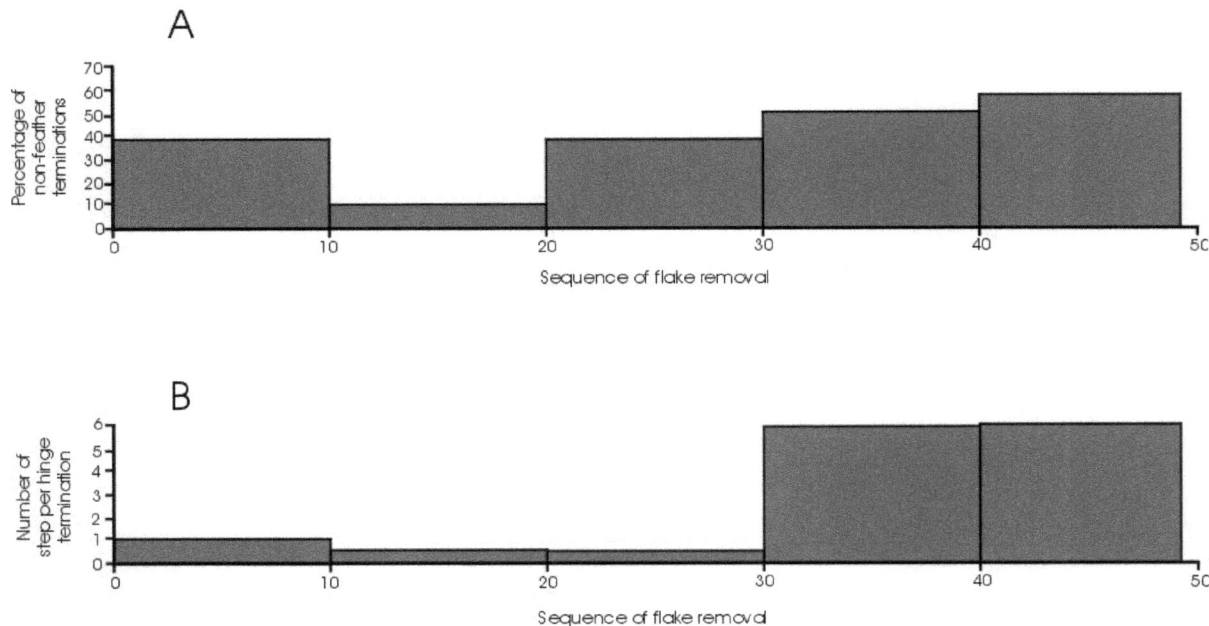

Figure 4. *Histograms revealing the variation in flake termination frequencies during the reduction of one cobble, measured by a) the frequency of non-feather terminations, and b) the ratio of step:hinge terminations*

produced cores with protruding mass near the bottom of the core. This was a common pattern emerging in the reduction of cores continued at Page Creek.

TRACING THE REDUCTION PROCESS

The knapper's success in maintaining the core face free from abrupt terminations can be evaluated by measuring the stability of core shape through the reduction process. A simple index of core shape, constructed as area of the platform surface divided by cross-sectional area of the base of the core, was used to evaluate the degree to which abrupt terminations have caused the core base to protrude. Values less than one represent a protruding core base, while values much greater than one indicate a contracting core shape with acute platform angles. Smaller values imply increasingly greater problems for continuation of flaking from the existing platform.

Examination of the core shape index for thirty cores recorded at Page Creek Quarry 1 reveals a distinct relationship between the weight of cores when discarded and their shape (see Figure 5). This relationship can be expressed in a number of ways. One way is to note the inverse pattern of observations. For core shapes values higher than 1, core weights are one kilogram or less; whereas for core shapes less than 1 many cores were discarded when they were still substantially heavier than one kilogram. A Lowess curve fitted to 80% of observations illustrates the tendency to higher weights at discard with lower core shape indices (see Figure 5).

Another way to understand size/shape relationships on these cores is to examine the thresholds that appear to mark points at which specimens are likely to be abandoned. Two thresholds are suggested. One is simply core weight: if cores have been reduced to 450-600 grams they are discarded at that size irrespective of core shape. This value is called the 'core weight threshold' (see Figure 5). The other factor obviously linked to core abandonment is the extent to which the base of the base of the core protrudes beyond the platform. Designated the 'core shape threshold' in Figure 5, this value

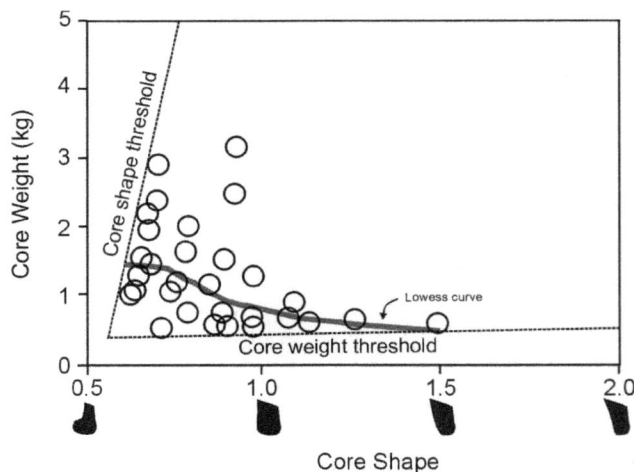

Figure 5. *A scatterplot of weights and shapes for cores recorded at Page Creek, showing inferred discard thresholds*

110

(approximately described by the equation *core weight = -14.4 + 26.19 * shape index*) characterises the relationship between core size and shape which represents the limits of reduction for the prehistoric knappers at Page Creek. Together these two inferred thresholds probably mark the boundaries of viable reduction using the techniques and strategies described above. Note the way that many of the recorded cores lay along the inferred thresholds, indicating that these are zones of morphology and size in which discard is much more likely.

Figure 5, plotting thirty abandoned cores, reveals the pattern of discard but does little to explore the process by which cores reach those final states. Questions concerning the uniformity of core reduction at and immediately prior to the moment of discard can be answered by examining these data, but to comprehend the variation of reduction throughout the knapping process further information is necessary. This additional information can be found in the nine refitted cobbles, where conjoining allows core shape and weight to be calculated for not only the start and end of the manufacturing process, but also *for all points during*

each reduction sequence. By measuring the reconstructed cores at different stages in their manufacturing history it is possible to examine the changing relationships between mass and shape as reduction continues. Figure 6 plots the changes in the weight and shape index of these nine cores throughout their reduction. By charting the entire history of core reduction in this way several patterns are revealed.

The general trend that can be observed is that as reduction proceeded the shape of the core increasingly altered towards relatively smaller platforms, and large bases. This trend reveals that on most cobbles the knapper was unable to maintain core shape. Where core shape attained values less than 0.9-1, the specimen was typically abandoned at the core shape threshold when it was still well above the minimum size to which cores with other shapes could be reduced.

However while following a single strategy the reduction of these cobbles was varied. For example, the direction of change in core shape differs between cobbles, most showing a decline in the shape index during the manufacturing sequence, but some display a slight

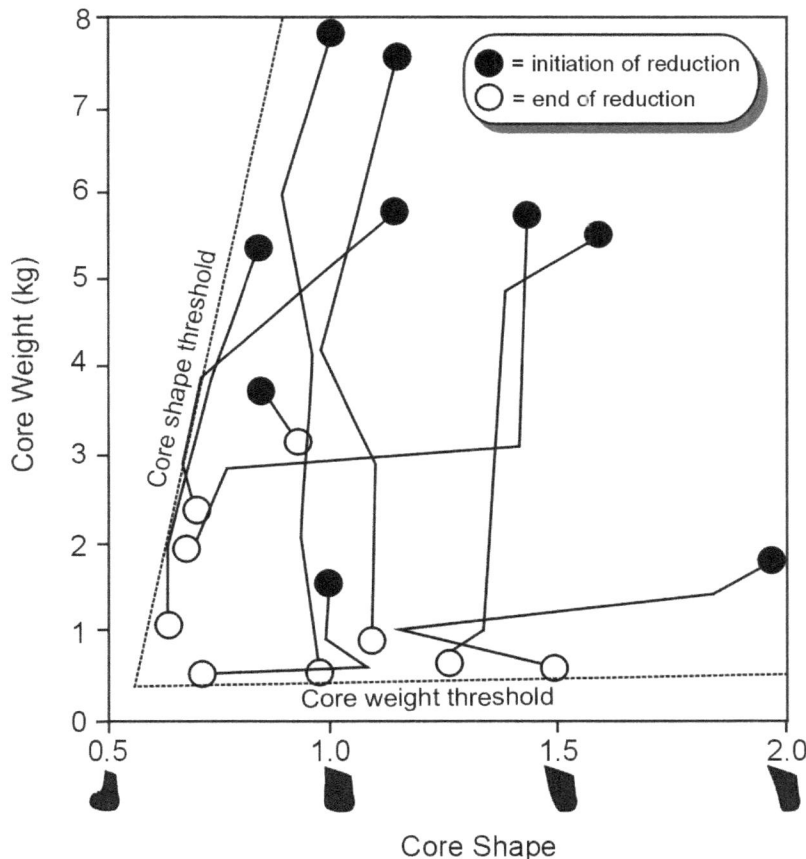

Figure 6. *A scatterplot of weights and shapes for refitted cobbles, showing weight and shape of each core at different points during its reduction. Solid circles represent the core at the start of reduction, hollow circles represent the discarded core, and connecting lines trace the changes in shape and size during reduction*

increase in the index with reduction. Even within the reduction history of a single cobble there are changes in the direction of change in core morphology. Two of the refitted cobbles show a dramatic reversal in core shape late in the sequence of flake removal. Other cobbles show minimal alterations in core shape despite the reduction of substantial amounts of material. These differences represent the contrast between reduction sequences that reveal dynamic instability in core morphology and sequences that reveal the knapper removed flakes while keeping the core morphology in a stable state.

One pattern that is apparent is that prior to discard of the core its morphology and size often changes parallel to one of the discard thresholds during the removal of a number of flakes. This reflects the emergence of abundant problematic features, such as multiple step terminations, late in the reduction sequence, and suggests that during the terminal stage of flaking many knappers struggle to maintain or correct core morphology before eventually abandoning the object.

direction and ultimately the outcome of the flaking, perhaps eliciting knapping actions that would not otherwise have been employed. The existence of these situationally determined (or evoked) shifts in knapping behaviour and artefact morphology may confound inferences about all phases of the manufacturing process based on a simple analysis of end products. This conclusion emphasizes the importance of studying process rather than static discard products; and, since this example illustrates the capacity of refitting to reveal sequential changes in the reduction process, it can be argued that conjoin analyses deserve a central role in describing stoneworking technology.

MISSING FLAKES AND POINT PRODUCTION

Refitting is the only technique that provides detailed information about artefacts manufactured at a knapping floor but not recovered. At the Page Creek knapping floors many flakes were missing. Conjoining revealed 45.9% of flakes that had been struck had been removed from the location of production. Relatively large and elongated flakes, without cortex, low angled symmetrical

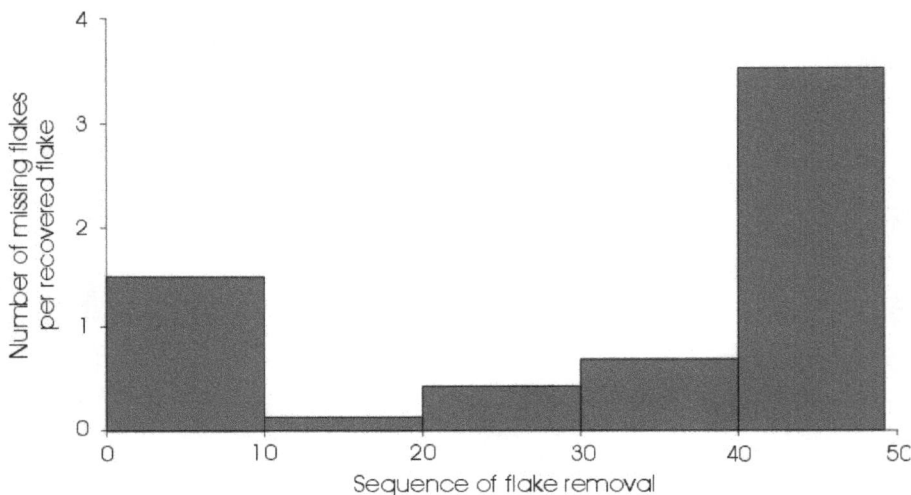

Figure 7. *Histogram showing changing frequencies of missing flakes in one refitted sequence from Page Creek*

More significantly, the variation between cobbles in the direction of alteration to core morphology during reduction reveals that at Page Creek there was no necessary relationship between the initial and terminal core morphology. Cores were discarded at similar sizes and shapes even though they began the reduction process in radically different states; and conversely cobbles of similar sizes and shapes produced distinctly different cores. The inability to predict outcomes in any simple way is an outcome of the contingency of the complex process of knapping. Particular events in flake removal, such as the production of an undulating platform at the beginning of core reduction, or an outrepasse or step termination in the final stages of reduction, may alter the

cross-sections and feather terminations were selected and carried away from the quarries. Flakes of this kind were produced more frequently later in the sequence, and it follows that missing flakes are typically much more frequent in the middle to late stages of reduction. Figure 7 illustrates changing frequencies of removed flakes in a single refitted sequence, revealing a typical pattern of greatly increased rates of flake selection late in the sequence when curvature and ridges on the core surface facilitated production of elongated flakes.

Measurements of these missing flakes were taken from the cavities created by refitting the surrounding flakes. These measurements indicate that only flakes of a very specific size and shape were being removed for use and/or retouching elsewhere. In particular the selected (ie. missing) flakes displayed a strong linear relationship (r^2 of 0.9224) between length and elongation. The regularity of flakes selected for transportation elsewhere suggests a coherent set of characteristics were required, and that all missing flakes were selected for the same scheme. A comparison of these missing quarry flakes with unifacial and bifacial points made on greywacke and found in the same region indicates that the missing flakes were suitable for manufacture into retouched points. This is shown in Figure 8 by a plot of the missing flakes and of 27 complete greywacke points found within a 10km radius of the quarry. Points also display a positive relationship between size and elongation, but are off-set from the data points of missing flakes because retouching of the lateral margins has increased the elongation for a specimen of a given length. It is likely that the retouched points were manufactured on blanks that were similar to the flakes removed from the Page Creek quarries. Consequently it is hypothesized that missing flakes are removed for conversion into unifacial and bifacial points.

This inference is reinforced by information about the nature of point reduction. Hiscock (1994) has demonstrated that in the Lawn Hill region, as in other areas of northern Australia, there is a technological continuum from unifacial to bifacial points, as the former are gradually transformed into the latter by re-sharpening and re-shaping. This reduction of flakes to form points

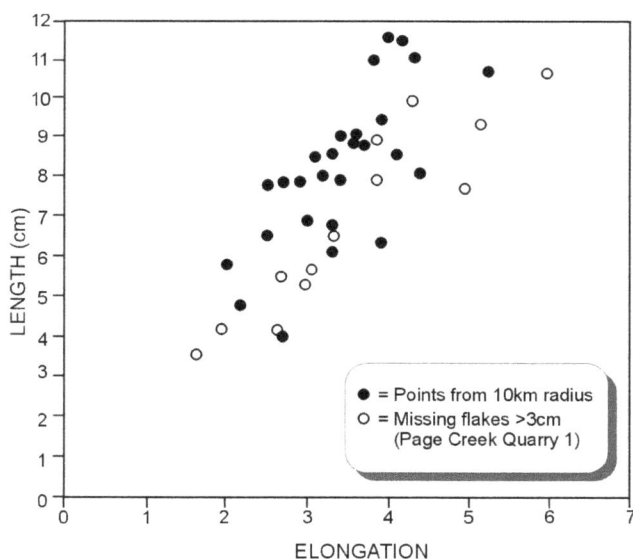

Figure 8. *Scattergram comparing dimensions of missing flakes and bifacial points in the vicinity of Page Creek*

was an activity not carried out on the quarries. Retouching of the points continued as they were transported around the landscape, broken, re-shaped and re-hafted. When flakes were removed from the

greywacke quarries they were usually retouched by removing flakes from along one lateral margin on the dorsal surface. At a later time the second margin might have been flaked in a similar fashion. And eventually one or both of these margins might have been made bifacial by the removal of flakes from the ventral surface. This gradual process of reduction displays a spatial variation, as points are transported and increased reduction increased the proportion of points with bifacial retouch. Figure 9 shows the rise in the abundance of bifacial points with increasing distance from the Page Creek quarries; a pattern that could be expected if flakes produced at those quarries were removed for conversion into retouched points.

CORE TRANSPORTATION AND REDUCTION

Flakes that could be made into points were not the only artefacts removed from the greywacke quarries. Small cores were also carried away for reduction at other localities. Refitted sequences have been obtained from two sites within a short distance of the Page Creek sources. Mount Jennifer 1 is 2.2 km from Page Creek and consisted of thirty greywacke artefacts scattered over a

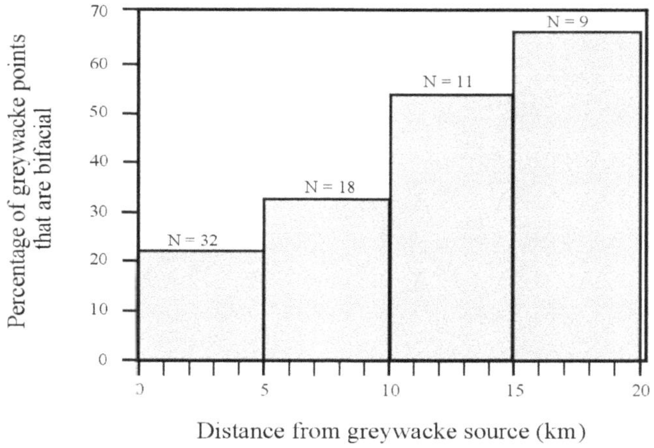

Figure 9. *Histogram showing the increase in bifacial points with distance from the Page Creek quarries.*

5m^2 area. This debris was subjected to a refitting analysis, with eighteen of the specimens being conjoined. In conjunction with observations of raw material variation the refits demonstrated that the assemblage derived from four different cores although only one was discarded at Mount Jennifer 1. The longest conjoin set consisted of seven flakes revealing a sequence of ten flakes removed from a core. The second site was Mount Jennifer 2, a scatter of eleven greywacke flakes spread over a 4m^2 area, located 4.5 km from Page Creek. These flakes derive from three cores, although none were discarded. Six of the flakes were refitted into one conjoin set, revealing three missing flakes in a sequence of nine flake removals. Taken together the refitted artefacts from the seven cores represented by flakes at these two sites reveal details about core reduction on the plains away from the greywacke source.

Knapping strategies applied to these cores were different from those employed in the quarries of Page Creek. Away from the quarry knappers rotated the cores, preparing a number of different platforms and changing platforms regularly as a device to help maintain core shape. The result was that shape indices for cores found away from the quarries ranged between 1 and 3, indicating that these cores typically had platforms larger than core bases. Figure 10 uses a single refit sequence, from Mount Jennifer 1, to illustrate the cyclical patterns of the knapper's actions and the resulting flakes that are

sequence illustrated in Figure 10 the number of flakes struck from a platform prior to rotation ranges between one and four.

This variation in the number of flakes removed from each platform depends, at least in part, from the success of core rotation as a means of maintaining appropriate core morphology. The refitted sequences, including those reported in Figure 10, reveal the condition of the core immediately prior to the switch to a new platform, and these core conditions can be used to infer the factors that trigger core rotation. Cores were rotated to a new platform when the flakes being removed dropped below 3.8 cm in length, or 1.1-1.3 in elongation

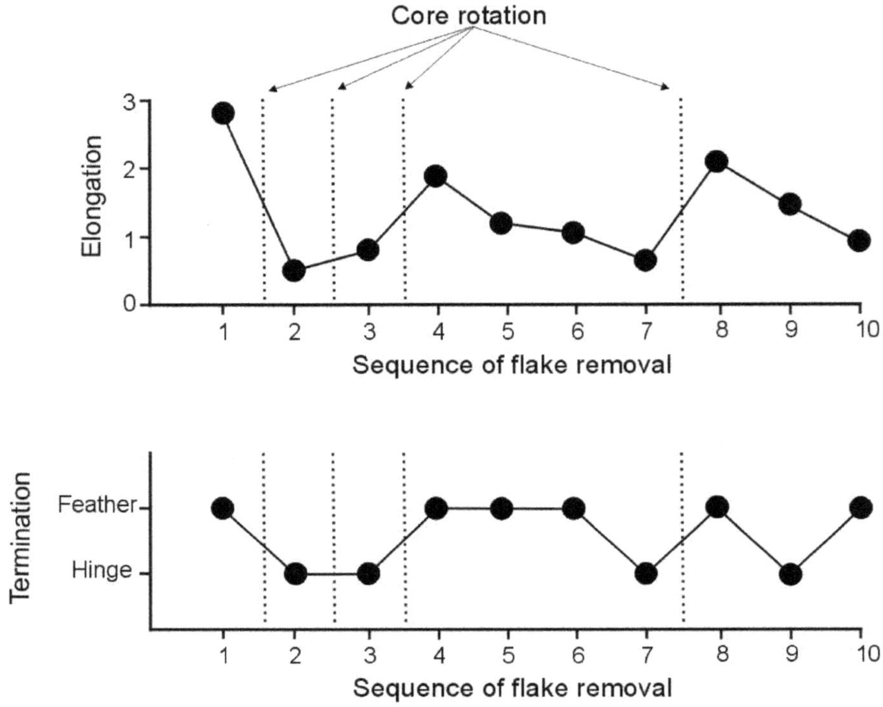

Figure 10. *Sequential changes in flakes removed from a refitted sequence away from Page Creek.*

associated with this strategy of core rotation. Flakes struck off a new platform were relatively large but decreased in size as reduction from that platform continues. Trends towards smaller, squatter and more irregular flakes during flake removal from each platform resulted from the increase in hinge terminations and flatter core faces. Abrupt truncation of the fracture caused shorter flakes and flatter cross-sections resulted in the fracture plane spreading out and causing squat flakes rather than being directed along the percussion axis to cause elongated flakes. These trends are eventually terminated when the knapper relocated blows to an alternative platform. The sequence of blows to the new platform typically displayed similar trends. The number of flakes struck from each platform, and hence the periodicity of these cycles, was variable. In the refitted

index, or the platform angle dropped below 80°. These characteristics stimulated core rotation, even if only one flake had been struck from a platform. The cyclical patterns of flake size morphology induced by regular core rotation reflect the recurrent emergence of problems and the application of temporary solutions. The problems that recurred were related to the development of inappropriate core shapes in a condition of low inertia. Because the inertia of the core was low relative to the size of flakes being removed from it, the likelihood of desirable flakes being removed was easily altered by subtle changes in core shape or size. The continual removal of relatively large flakes with prominent bulbs almost inevitably resulted in the presence of pronounced overhang and decreased platform angles. This led to short flakes and flakes with hinge terminations, which left prominences on the lower part of the core face. Without pronounced ridges to strike down, the prominences left by short and truncated flakes were impossible to remove by continued use of the same platform. This was the problem encountered by the knapper, and without a solution it would most likely have necessitated abandoning the core. It is not possible to determine what characteristics allowed the knapper to perceive the approaching threshold but the trends, such as the dramatic decrease in flake size, must have been apparent. Core rotation was the solution employed by the knapper. By changing platforms it was possible not only to continue reduction, but also to remove the problematic features on the old face of the core and alter the characteristics of the old platform. The advantage of this procedure was that when a problem recurred other platforms and associated core faces were often available to allow reduction to continue. Eventually, of course, this strategy of reduction would meet difficulties for which the knapper had no solution.

The degree to which this procedure facilitated reduction is shown by the average weight of 38 grams for cores discarded away from the quarry, less than one-tenth the weight of the smallest core produced by knappers at the quarry. Using this observation and adding information obtained from refitting it is possible to calculate the amount and structure of core reduction that took place away from the Page Creek quarries. This calculation can be developed as follows:

• At the Page Creek quarries the estimate of the weight of cores, when they were first carried away, was developed from measurements of cores weighing less than 1,000 grams that had appropriate morphologies for further reduction. These cores had not developed low platform indices but were too small to produce the long flakes suitable for point manufacture. Such cores ranged between 474 and 954 grams, with an average of 632 grams. This average figure is employed as an estimate of the typical cores carried off the quarries.

• Since the average weight of cores discarded away from the quarry is only 38 grams, I calculate an average of 594 grams of material was removed from cores being transported around the landscape.

• The average weight of flakes away from quarry, at sites like Mount Jennifer 1 and 2, is 13 grams. Simple calculations indicate that 46 flakes of this weight could have been produced from the 594 grams removed from cores in off-quarry contexts.

• Refitting of artefacts at Mount Jennifer 1 and 2 indicates that on average 6.6 flakes were removed from each core at a single location (with a range of 2 to 10 flakes per core per locality). This figure can be used to suggest that the 46 flakes struck from the average core were removed in knapping on about on 5-8 occasions, with an average seven different occasions.

• Finally, the refitting at sites way from the quarry indicates that each time the knapper worked the core, about two or three flakes were not discarded on the spot but were carried away, presumably for use. This implies that about 30% of flakes made at these off-quarry knapping floors were removed for use elsewhere.

Even acknowledging that such a calculation is built on numerous average values, and therefore fails to express the variation that must have occurred in prehistoric behaviour patterns, it provides a useful heuristic for describing the general scale and structure of core reduction. In particular, this kind of rough calculation supports the suggestion that cores were carried around the landscape as a convenient source of flakes.

CONCLUSION

Refitting of knapping floors in one region of northern Australia has been used to help analyse the production technology employed during the mid-late Holocene. The focus of this example is on the production of flaked artefacts at a number of quarries on one raw material source, and the distribution and further reduction of artefacts in the local landscape. At outcrops of the rock, knappers repeatedly used a particular reduction strategy to produce artefacts that they carried to other parts of the landscape. The application of this approach was flexible in the sense that circumstances elicited different elements of the strategy. Large, elongated flakes of a particular shape were carried away and at least some were retouched to form unifacial and bifacial points. Cores were also carried away from the quarry, and flakes were struck off whenever they were required. Striking flakes from these small cores was accomplished by employing a strategy different to that at the quarry. Large single platform cores are dominant at the quarry, but away from the quarry the small cores were constantly rotated as they were worked. Rotating cores in this way removed undesirable features from the core and facilitated continued reduction, thereby rationing the material. The success of this strategy is indicated by the apparent ability of the knappers to employ small greywacke cores as a portable source of flakes as they moved about the landscape. These strands of information combine to provide a picture of the technology employed by prehistoric humans knapping greywacke in this locality, and at the same time illustrate the value of refitting for these kinds of technological analyses.

These inferences highlight benefits that have long been acknowledged in refitting studies. Refitting provides a capacity to reconstruct and measure the sizes and shapes not only the discarded core but also of those cores at earlier stages in their reduction history and even the initial cobble. This potential is particularly pronounced in lengthy reduction sequences, in which early stages of reduction have been removed by later ones. One reason that this ability to measure artefact form at all stages is important is that extended reduction may, at least in some cases, standardise the size or shape of the object being worked, thereby hiding variability that may have existed early in the reduction process. Complete reconstruction of knapped blocks through refitting is the means by which such possibilities can be tested.

This also reflects one of the ways refitting can assist the study of technological variability rather than simply the construction of normative depictions of stoneworking. The ability that refitting adds, to study all stages of reduction by providing a sequential order for the activities evidenced, encourages more elaborate depictions of the reduction process. Examples of these opportunities have been provided in this paper. The notion that initial reduction of cores can enlighten us about the repertoire and preferential selection of actions in a technological system, as knapping problem elicit responses from the knapper, signals an approach which is sensitive to differences in stoneworking at different scales (differences in the work of one knapper in changing situations, differences between knappers, and differences between groups of knappers, and so on). The variability that can be revealed by studying the contrasts between refitted sequences is often hidden in other analytical approaches. For instance, depictions of reduction processes obtained by seriation of different artefacts typically begin with the presumption that only a single system of reduction exists and that variation within that system is minimal. Refitting not only avoids the need to assume minimal variation but also encourages non-normative explorations of the archaeological record by facilitating an examination of human activities involved in the production of all components of the preserved assemblage, without presupposing that information resides only in 'end-products'. In this way refitting studies greatly contribute to descriptions of the overall production system.

The pursuit of information about variation obtained through this examination of ancient Australian technology reveals issues of general interest. For example, the variation between cobbles in the direction of alteration to core morphology during reduction reveals that at Page Creek there was no necessary relationship between the initial and terminal core morphology. Cores were discarded at similar sizes and shapes even though they began the reduction process in radically different states; and conversely cobbles of similar sizes and shapes produced distinctly different cores. This conclusion echoes the recent findings of De Bie and Caspar (2000:116) who argued that in many instances the characteristics of abandoned cores did not necessarily

reveal manufacturing processes that had been applied to them at early stages in their reduction. They too conclude that only refitting provides a means of describing the entire reduction process.

That verdict is also demanded, as many archaeologists have noted, when refitting identifies characteristics of absent forms. No other observation can document those artefacts removed from an assemblage. In the case study presented here the shape and size of missing flakes, the timing of their production, and the similarity of their form with bifacial points were established only by reference to the refitting analysis. In the same way, the information obtained from refitting in this study facilitated inferences about the length of reduction sequences (that is the number of flakes struck), the variation between refitted sequences, and the causes for that variation. Refitting analyses provide this information with a precision and detail that is absent from non-refitting approaches such as the calculation of flake:core ratios.

None of the inferences outlined here, or the conclusion to which they point, are likely to be as accurately inferred without refitting. For this reason refitting forms a key methodology that can be employed in analyses of prehistoric stoneworking. What this paper advocates is the desirability of developing approaches that integrate refitting with other analytical techniques (such as attribute analyses), and which facilitate the quantitative depiction of trends that are revealed by refitting. By employing refitting studies within a composite analytical framework the power of refitting can be exploited in studies of variability in past production systems and their articulation within regional systems of manufacturing and artefact use. The quantitative examinations of regional patterns in Holocene reduction technology in Australia presented here hint at the opportunities that exist for extracting information from refitted lithic artefacts.

BIBLIOGRAPHY

AHLER, S. 1992 Use-phase classification and manufacturing technology in Plains village arrowpoints. In *Piecing together the past: applications of refitting studies in archaeology,* edited by J.L. HOFMAN & J.G. ENLOE. BAR International Series 578, pp. 36-62

ALLEN, H. 1994 The distribution of large blades (leilira): evidence for recent changes in Aboriginal ceremonial and exchange networks. In *Archaeology and linguistics: understanding ancient Australia,* edited by P. MCCONVELL & N. EVANS Oxford University Press, Oxford.

ARNOLD, V. 1990 Refitting of waste material from dagger production of site Tegelbarg (Quern-Neukirchen, Schleswig-Holstein). In *The big puzzle. International symposium on refitting stone artefacts,* edited by E. CZIESLA, S. EICKHOFF, N. ARTS, & D. WINTER. Holos, Bonn, pp. 211-216

BARTON, R.N.E. 1992 Refitting and reduction sequences. In *Hengistbury Head Dorset. Volume 2: the Late Upper Palaeolithic and Early Mesolithic,* edited by R.N.E. BARTON. Oxford Institute of Archaeology, pp. 138-159.

CLARKSON, C. & B. DAVID 1995 The antiquity of blades and points revisited. Investigating the emergence of systematic blade production south-west of Arnhem Land, northern Australia. *The Artefact* 18: 22-44.

CUNDY, B.J. 1990 An Analysis of the Ingaladdi Assemblage: A Critique of the Understanding of Lithic Technology. Unpublished PhD thesis, Australian National University.

CUNDY, B.J. 1985 The secondary use and reduction of cylindro-conical stone artifacts from the Northern Territory. *The Beagle* 2: 115-127.

DE BIE, M. & J-P. CASPAR 2000 *Rekem. A Federmesser camp on the Meuse River Bank.* Leuven University Press, Leuven.

GILEAD, I. & P. FABIAN 1990 Conjoinable artefacts from the Middle Palaeolithic open air site Fara II, northern Negev, Israel: a preliminary report. In *The big puzzle. International symposium on refitting stone artefacts,* edited by E. CZIESLA, S. EICKHOFF, N. ARTS, & D. WINTER. Holos, Bonn, pp. 101-112.

HISCOCK, P. 1988 Prehistoric settlement patterns and artefact manufacture at Lawn Hill, Northwest Queensland. Unpublished PhD thesis, University of Queensland.

HISCOCK, P. 1993 Bondaian technology in the Hunter Valley, New South Wales. *Archaeology in Oceania* 28: 64-75.

HISCOCK, P. 1994 The end of points. In *Archaeology in the North,* edited by M. SULLIVAN, S. BROCKWELL & A. WEBB. North Australia Research Unit, Australian National University, pp. 72-83.

HISCOCK, P. 1998 Revitalising artefact analysis. In *Archaeology of Aboriginal Australia,* edited by T. MURRAY. Unwin and Allen, Sydney, pp. 257-265.

HISCOCK, P. & V. ATTENBROW 2003 Early Australian implement variation: a reduction model. *Journal of Archaeological Science* 30: 239-249.

HISCOCK, P., & P. VETH 1991 Change in the Australian Desert Culture: a reanalysis of tulas from Puntutjarpa. *World Archaeology* 22: 332-345.

JONES, R. & N. WHITE 1988 Point blank: stone tool manufacture at the Ngilipitji Quarry, Arnhem Land, 1981. In *Archaeology with ethnography: an Australian perspective,* edited by B. MEEHAN & R. JONES. Highland Press, pp. 51-87.

LAMB, L. 1996 A methodology for the analysis of backed artefact production on the South Molle Island Quarry, Whitsunday Islands. In *Australian Archaeology 95,* edited by S. ULM, I. LILLEY & A. ROSS. St. Lucia: Anthropology Museum, University of Queensland. *Tempus* 6, pp. 151-159.

LOHR, H. 1990 Serial production of chipped stone tools since Upper Palaeolithic times. In *The big puzzle. International symposium on refitting stone artefacts,* edited by E. CZIESLA, S. EICKHOFF, N. ARTS, & D. WINTER. Holos, Bonn, pp. 129-142.

MORROW, T.M. 1996 Lithic refitting and archaeological site formation processes. In *Stone tools. Theoretical insights into human prehistory,* edited by G.H. ODELL Plenum Press, pp. 345-373.

NOETLING, F. 1908 Notes on a chipped boulder found near Kempton, *Papers and Proceedings of the Royal Society of Tasmania* 1-9.

RENSINK, E. 1990 The Magdalenian site Mesch-Steenberg (Province of Limburg, the Netherlands): manufacture of blades and maintenance of tools at an observation stand? In *The big puzzle. International symposium on refitting stone artefacts,* edited by E. CZIESLA, S. EICKHOFF, N. ARTS, & D. WINTER. Holos, Bonn, pp. 164-175.

SCHAFER, J. 1990 Conjoining artefacts and consideration of raw-material: their application at the Middle Palaeolithic site of the Scheinskopf-Karmelenberg. In *The big puzzle. International symposium on refitting stone artefacts,* edited by E. CZIESLA, S. EICKHOFF, N. ARTS, & D. WINTER. Holos, Bonn, pp. 83-100.

THORLEY, P., L. WARREN & P. VETH 1994 Wardaman point technology. An examination of sites recorded during CRM investigations in the Victoria River region. In *Archaeology in the North,* edited by M. SULLIVAN, S. BROCKWELL & A. WEBB. North Australia Research Unit, Australian National University, pp. 57-71.

WEINER, J. 1990 Intra-site analysis by refitting lithic artefacts from a flint-workshop on the Neolithic flint-mine "Lousberg" in Aachen (Northrhine Westfalia, FRG). In *The big puzzle. International symposium on refitting stone artefacts*, edited by E. CZIESLA, S. EICKHOFF, N. ARTS, & D. WINTER. Holos, Bonn, pp. 177-196.

WHITE, J.P. 1977 Crude, colourless and unenterprising: Prehistorians and their views on the stone age of Sunda and Sahul. In *Sunda and Sahul. Prehistoric studies in Southeast Asia, Melanesia and Australia*, edited by J. ALLEN, J. GOLSON, and R. JONES. Academic Press, pp. 13-30.

WRIGHT, R.V.S. 1972 The flints. In *Archaeology of the Gallus Site, Koonalda Cave*, edited by R.V.S. WRIGHT. Canberra:.Australian Institute of Aboriginal Studies. *A.I.A.S. M*onograph 26, pp. 48-60.

WYCKOFF, D.G. 1992 Refitting and protohistoric knapping behavior: the Lowrance example. In *Piecing together the past: applications of refitting studies in archaeology*, edited by J.L. HOFMAN & J.G.ENLOE. BAR International Series 578, pp.83-127.

Address of the author:

Peter HISCOCK
School of Archaeology and Anthropology,
Australian National University,
Canberra, A.C.T., 0200,
Australia

peter.hiscock@anu.edu.au

www.ingramcontent.com/pod-product-compliance
Lightning Source LLC
Chambersburg PA
CBHW061004030426
42334CB00033B/3359